Praise for *I Can't Believe I Lived the Whole Thing ...*

"Cohen writes in a punchy, funny and consistently surprising style. An entertaining account of a career in the highest echelons of advertising."

—Kirkus Reviews

"Buy it, you'll like it. After you've read it, you'll say, 'I can't believe I read the whole thing—in two days!' That's how delightful a read this book really is."

—Tom Cordner, Professor, Art Center College of Design

"Laugh and learn. Howie's case histories are in the form of entertaining real-life stories. They provide a much-needed reminder about the exponential power of a creative idea for driving business growth."

—Bill Duggan, Group EVP, ANA
(Association of National Advertisers)

"The funniest book about advertising in the past fifty years. From the first page, I was transported to a time when advertising was the most fun you could have with your clothes on."

—Jerry Della Femina, Creative Hall of Fame

"Howie Cohen is probably best known as the advertising executive—advertising genius, really—who created two of the most ubiquitous catch phrases ever, 'Try it, you'll like it' and 'I can't believe I ate the whole thing.'" His stories about the old days when Madison Avenue unleashed a never-before-seen brand of advertising—propelled by humor and an arched eyebrow—are well worth read

BlueInk Review

D1602727

I CAN'T BELIEVE ~~I ATE~~ *Lived* THE WHOLE THING

I CAN'T BELIEVE I ATE *Lived* THE WHOLE THING

A MEMOIR FROM THE GOLDEN AGE OF ADVERTISING

HOWIE COHEN

I Can't Believe I Lived the Whole Thing
A Memoir from the Golden Age of Advertising

Author Howie Cohen
Published by Red Rascal Press
Van Nuys, CA

ISBN: 978-0692081228

MEMOIR / Personal Memoirs

QUANTITY PURCHASES: Schools, companies, professional
groups, clubs, and other organizations may qualify for special
terms when ordering quantities of this title. For information, email
howiecohencreative@gmail.com.

RED RASCAL
P R E S S

To Carol, for your love, wit, and wisdom.
This wouldn't be a book without you.
This wouldn't be a life without you.

CONTENTS

Introduction

Return with me now to those thrilling days of yesteryear when advertising was funny, sexy, crazy, and cool. By the mid-sixties, the Creative Revolution was sweeping across Madison Avenue and a sea change was taking place. WASPS were out. Jewish copywriters and Italian art directors were in. These brash, young, creative upstarts were bringing a fresh new voice to advertising, born on the streets of Brooklyn and The Bronx.

I was a nice little Jewish boy from Pelham Parkway in The Bronx who dreamed of becoming a big-time copywriter in the glamorous world of advertising. I struggled to break in. I slipped; I stumbled; I sucked wind. But then I got lucky. I was hired by Doyle Dane Bernbach, followed by Wells, Rich, Greene—two of the most creative ad agencies on the planet—where I soaked up inspiration from creative giants all around me.

My crowning glory was two Clio Hall of Fame TV commercials for Alka Seltzer that had the whole world saying, "I can't believe I ate the whole thing!" and "Try it, you'll like it." Above all else was my marriage to a beautiful woman named Carol Trifari, who showed me there's more to life than just advertising.

Yes, this is also a love story.

During a career that spanned five decades, I experienced it all: glad-handers and backstabbers, mad movie moguls and Machiavellian plots, hard drugs and soft pet food, a dumb shoe, an exploding clown, and getting naked with 500 of my closest friends.

It's all here—the good, the bad, and the idiotic. Everything in this book is true. I'm a creative guy, but even I couldn't make this stuff up.

This is the whole thing.

If You Have to Fail, Fail Up

We were dead meat. We just couldn't accept it yet. The year was 1978, and our hot creative ad agency had gone as cold as the ice cubes in my twelve-year-old scotch. I instructed my wife, Carol, to hide the razor blades and flush all the sleeping pills down the toilet. I think she knew I was kidding, but nothing seemed funny in those grim days.

How did it all go so wrong? Just a few short years earlier my art director and partner, Bob Pasqualina, and I were standing on advertising's biggest awards stage, Clio statues held high, spotlight shining down, crowd cheering, champagne flowing, beautiful women at our sides (and four more in the limo), our names in *The New York Times* and *New York Magazine*, investors with bags of cash imploring us to start our own ad agency—and I had just turned twenty-eight.

So what happened? We screwed it up; that's what happened.

Bob and I knew how to make great ads, but we sucked at running a business. For that, we depended on our third partner: the business guy, a.k.a. "The Suit."

First came Burt Lowe. When he didn't work out, we found Suit Number Two in the form of Tim Timberman, a big guy with an even bigger personality and dazzling white teeth. On paper, he was the perfect choice. Six feet four, handsome, impeccably dressed in a starched white shirt and a pinstripe suit, whip smart, and with a resume to die for. But as soon as we partnered up, we got a rude awakening. Suddenly, he started showing up for work wearing cowboy boots, thick garrison belts with big silver buckles, and shiny western shirts. At a time when we needed a tough businessman, we got a rhinestone cowboy. To make matters worse, our sweet little bookkeeper, Peggy, was writing sweet little forged checks and robbing our agency blind. *Oy vey!*

Now here I was, sitting behind my glass-and-chrome desk, contemplating my future and my navel. (My navel looked better.) Just then, the phone rang. It was Charlie Moss on the other end of the line. He was my former boss and the creative director of Wells, Rich, Greene, the legendary creative agency we had left to start our own agency. "What's going on?" Charlie asked. "I hear you guys have problems."

Shit, the word was already on the street. Still, it was great to hear his voice. I started thinking back to all the good times we'd had working for Charlie and the great Mary Wells, the first name on the agency door. She ultimately became Mary Wells Lawrence when she married her knight in shining armor, Harding Lawrence, president and chairman of Braniff Airlines.

Mary Wells Lawrence was the first woman to take on the good old boys of Madison Avenue and beat them at their own game. It

Mary Wells Lawrence and Charlie Moss
leading the creative charge

was Mary who put Braniff Airlines on the map, painting their planes fashion-forward colors and adorning their stewardesses in sexy Pucci outfits. It was Mary who inspired irreverent ad campaigns like bending cigarettes for Benson & Hedges to point out "the disadvantages" of the extra length. And it was Mary who led the charge to bring a dying city back to life with the rousing emotional campaign, "I love New York."

Mary meant a lot to our industry and to all of us who worked for her. She was one person, but she had many personas, depending on who she needed to be at the time. She was everything from our fearless leader to our intimidating boss to our caring momma to (okay, I'll admit it) the sexy blonde who appeared in our dreams. She knew all of this and used it to maximum effect.

It's no accident that Mary always referred to Bob and me as "the boys." It was an endearing term that also served to position her above us. Rather than resent it, I believe it made us feel more secure. Momma would always take care of us.

Both Bob and I loved our time at Wells. So why had we left? Because we were morons, that's why. Okay, maybe that's too harsh. We left to follow a dream, chart our own course, and pursue our own destiny. (So much for destiny.)

Charlie's voice crackled back on the phone. "Look, it's none of my business, but if your agency is in trouble, I want you to know about some big opportunities here ... I mean big! Can we talk?"

"Sorry, Charlie ... no." My ego wouldn't let me go there. Our agency was on life support, but we weren't dead yet.

The next day, Charlie called again. "Okay, here's the deal. I'm talking about California." *Wait! Did he just say California?* "Wells is booming in L.A., and you guys could run the creative show. We've got big accounts out there ... Columbia Pictures, Max Factor, Jack in the Box ..."

Charlie started pouring it on thick. "Mary thinks you guys would be perfect for this, and she's willing to pay a lot of money. Howie, I'm talking a healthy six figures ... each ... for you and Bob." *Wait! Did he just say six figures?* This was 1978, and that was a shitload of money. Charlie pushed, "What do you say? Can I set up a meeting with Mary?"

"Yes, yes, count me in!" is what I wanted to say. "No," is what came out of my mouth. My pride was strangling my common sense. Charlie called back that same afternoon and picked up where he'd left off. "Big salaries plus big expense accounts," he added. "And if you miss New York, we'll fly you and your families back first class

anytime you want. And you're going to need a house out there."
Wait! Did he just say a house? "We can help with a down payment.
You'll have a backyard, a pool, and a Jacuzzi. Howie, you and Bob
could live like kings. Don't be an idiot!"

He had me at "idiot." This was just too good to pass up, even for
a stubborn fool like me. "Okay, Charlie, okay," I said. "I'll talk to
Bob again, and we'll get back to you tomorrow."

"Make it today," he said. "I don't want to put pressure on you (oh
yes, he did!), but we need to move fast … the window is closing."

As conflicted as I was about this big career and life change,
that's how un-conflicted Carol was. At least she was delicate about
it. "Are you crazy!" she said. "We could move to L.A. and buy our
first home and get our kids out of this crowded, dirty city! Howie,
this is our chance for a brand-new start."

Damn, why did she always have to be so smart? My resistance
was just about gone, but I had one last card to play. I said, "How
could I live in Los Angeles? I'm a New Yorker through and through.
We have the ballet, the opera, Broadway … and where else can you
get a bagel at three in the morning?"

Now Carol lowered the boom. "Are you kidding me?" she said.
"When was the last time you went to the ballet?"

"Um, never."

"And what about the opera?"

"Well, I did see *La Boheme* … once ... in 1964."

"Exactly. And when have you ever had a bagel at three in the
morning? Howie, you're in bed every night by nine!"

She was right, of course. All of my rational reasons were just
lame excuses to avoid facing the failure of my agency. It was time
for a fresh start, and Bob Pasqualina and his wife, Janet, had come to

the same conclusion. Los Angeles was a go. I called Charlie, and he arranged for Bob and me to meet with Mary the very next morning.

At 11:00 a.m. sharp, we showed up in Mary's office. There were flowers everywhere, and their fresh fragrance seemed to signal the promise of a new day. When Mary saw us for the first time in five years, she sprung out of her chair and greeted us with open arms and a warm, welcoming hug. She was all sunshine and enthusiasm.

"Boys," she said. "I'm just so excited. L.A. is the next big thing. It's going to be even bigger than New York. And they need you. They *really* need you." (When Mary sold, she really sold.)

"Mary," I said. "Do you really think L.A. is going to be bigger than New York?"

"Absolutely," she said with gusto. "Don't you know? L.A. is movies, star power, the gateway to the Pacific Rim … it's where everything is happening now." Wow, this was getting exciting!

We spent the next two hours discussing the future, along with details of a generous three-year contract for both Bob and me. When we blasted out of the General Motors building, we were totally stoked. Our ears were ringing and our adrenaline was pumping as we set off on a vigorous walk through Central Park.

At the Wollman Skating Rink, Bob and I turned to each other and shared a big man-hug. All the angst and pain of the past few years was over. Our bright futures were signed, sealed, and about to be delivered. Bob and I were ready to pack up our pens, pads, pets, cars, and kids, along with our slightly bruised egos, and head west to be co-creative directors of Wells, Rich, Greene/L.A. We were coming home to Mary.

ONE

Starting Out

Take Me to the Revolution

I first arrived at Wells, Rich, Greene in 1967. It was an amazing time to be in the advertising business. Everything was changing—fast—and it was all to the advantage of creative people, especially those with ethnic backgrounds. Prior to that, few agencies would have hired a guy like me. "Cohen, that's a Jewish name, isn't it?"

The ad business had been ruled by WASPs from Ivy League schools who pledged the same fraternities, played golf at the same country clubs, and ate the same ham sandwiches with mayonnaise on white bread. But thanks to the pioneering success of Doyle Dane Bernbach, the original creative agency founded by a Jewish creative genius named Bill Bernbach, the advertising world had changed.

Doyle Dane Bernbach, where I was lucky enough to start my

career, had taken the ad business by storm with campaign after clever campaign, often using self-deprecating humor. Examples: Volkswagen "Think Small," Avis "We're number two. We try harder," not to mention, "You don't have to be Jewish to love Levy's (rye bread)."

These disarming campaigns had traditional ad men in their grey flannel suits scratching their heads. "What! Advertising that doesn't shout or brag or talk down to people? How do you expect to sell anything?" Very nicely, thank you. The new advertising was refreshingly honest, and it connected with consumers in a very human and emotional way.

One of my favorite billboards at the time was for a ski resort located within a comfortable driving distance from New York City. In the old world of uninspired communications, a respectable headline might have read, "Great skiing is closer than you think!" In the brave new ethnic world of clever advertising, the headline read:

ALL THE SHUSSING
WITHOUT ALL THE SCHLEPPING

The creative revolution was definitely heating up. Young twenty-something Jewish copywriters and Italian art directors were suddenly in high demand. These "street kids" instinctively knew how to go beyond the consumers' heads to touch their hearts. Most importantly, this new creative advertising was moving goods and building brands. Now every agency in town was scrambling to hire their share of cute Italians and clever Jews.

As a result, salaries were skyrocketing. The average American worker was earning around $9,200 a year, but young hotshots in the ad business were making three, four, and five times that much. When *The Wall Street Journal* got wind of this, they decided to do a story on it.

In a 1967 article titled "The Rich Kids," they interviewed many young creative talents, including Jerry Della Femina (an Italian who was a great writer— go figure). He would go on to write the very funny advertising book of that era, *From Those Wonderful Folks Who Gave You Pearl Harbor.*

Although I had only been in the business for a couple of years, Wells, Rich, Greene was paying me a lot of money. Somehow, the reporter got my name and interviewed me over the phone. This resulted in a very cute accidental quote: "Howie Cohen is reported to be 23 years old and making $25,000 a year. 'Not so,' says Mr. Cohen, 'I'm 25.'" Little did I know that this article would eventually play a part in spoiling my perfect bachelorhood, but I'm getting ahead of myself.

When Mary Wells Lawrence read the article, she sent one of her surrogates down to my floor to confirm that I actually worked at the agency. Although I had been at Wells for more than three months, I'd never met the great lady. That may sound strange, but not when you understand how crazy and exciting the agency was at the time. New accounts were pouring in every month, and the place was a madhouse of activity.

To service all this business, the best creative talent in New York was being gobbled up by the Clio-ful. A small army of high-salaried writers and art directors were piling up in the halls like spare furniture. We were almost out of space in our old building on Madison Avenue, and it was cramped, crazy, and exhilarating.

I was on my way up but was still just a *pisher* in a world of creative stars. As a result, I was relegated to doing "fill-in" kinds of work—the stuff the big guys just didn't want to be bothered with: a small space newspaper ad here, a quickie trade ad there. This was a frustrating time for me because I wasn't getting enough work. And I was feeling guilty about it. *Why are they paying me all this money if they aren't going to use me?*

At the time, I was just beginning to date my future wife, a pretty lady named Carol Trifari, and she would invite me over for dinner. It would just be Carol, her adorable five-year-old daughter (Cristina), and me. Having grown up in an Italian family, Carol always made pasta, except when she wanted to impress her guests (me!) and experimented with weird stuff like spicy Czechoslovakian meatballs. I couldn't help thinking to myself, *If she loves me, why is she trying to kill me?*

In any case, as the three of us sat at the table eating dinner, little Cristina and I had a standard routine born out of my frustration at work.

Howie: "How many ads did I do today?"
Cristina: "None."
Howie: "What am I doing with my life?"
Cristina: "Nothing."
Howie: "Where am I going?"
Cristina: "NOWHERE!"

We got a good laugh out of it, but the reality wasn't so funny. I was invisible to the agency, and I hadn't even met Mary Wells

Lawrence yet. What could I do? I just sucked it up every day and hoped something would come along. Then one day, opportunity knocked. The agency needed a ten-second TV spot for Personna razor blades.

Since it was only a ten-second TV spot and there was no budget for it, the big guys on the account turned their noses up at it. To me, though, it was ... *TV, baby!* They teamed me up with an art director, and our job was to write a clever commercial and produce it, using existing footage from the expensive sixty-second spots that were running on national TV.

The theme of the national campaign was that Personna blades were "electro-coated" for a sharper edge and a smoother shave. The visual centerpiece of the ads was a Personna razor blade being zapped all around (think Frankenstein's laboratory).

Here's the simple little spot that we came up with:

OPEN ON A PERSONNA BLADE FILLING
THE SCREEN AS IT GETS ZAPPED BY BOLTS OF
ELECTRICITY
  VO ANNCR: The electro-coated blade from
Personna. (ZZZAPPPPPP!) The naked eye can't tell the
difference ...
  CUT TO CU OF MAN AS HE SMILES AND RUNS
HIS HAND OVER HIS CLEAN-SHAVEN FACE
  VO ANNCR: But the naked face can.

Short, simple, sweet. We showed our spot to the account guy, and he loved it. Then, on the very next day, he hit me with a big surprise. Since I had done such a good job writing the spot, I would get to present it to Mary Wells Lawrence herself. *Whoa!* My first meeting with Mary was going to be a creative presentation!

Mary Wells Lawrence, the First Hello

I was *ferklempt*. (That's Jewish for nervous, flustered, sick to my stomach ... I could go on.) In anticipation of this acid-producing event, I spent four hours practicing my ten-second commercial. Then came the moment of truth. The little kid from The Bronx was about to present his work to the great Mary Wells Lawrence. (Sound of testicles hitting floor goes here.) I was ushered into Mary's office by the account guy.

As we entered, Mary was absorbed with another creative team, and they were hanging on her every word. She seemed to be making some sort of creative suggestion that apparently made light bulbs go off in their heads. They nodded enthusiastically, grabbed their stuff, turned, and walked past me as they exited the office. That's when Mary looked up and saw me for the first time.

"Mary," the account guy said. "I want you to meet Howie Cohen, one of our new young copywriters."

"Hello, Howie," she said.

"Hello, Mary, it's an honor to make your acquaintance." *What? Did I just say that? What a* schmuck*!*

"Howie is going to present the ten-second spot for Personna."

I reached my hand into a huge, oversized black bag and pulled out a small, undersized storyboard. I cleared my throat and cleared it again. I couldn't figure out why the storyboard was shaking, until

I realized it was attached to my hand. I pointed to the pictures. And when I began to speak, my voice actually squeaked like a teenager's. I bravely forged ahead for the whole ten seconds. And when I delivered the last line, "... but the naked face can," Mary lit up and said, "Nifty."

That's all she said, one word. "Nifty." To me, however, it was like fireworks had erupted over Madison Avenue. Mary liked my work. She smiled, shook my hand, and turned to greet another group as they were entering the room.

When I left Mary's office, I actually skipped down the hall as one profound thought stuck in my head. *Mary Wells Lawrence knows who Howie Cohen is!*

Love Thy Coworkers (Just Don't Get Caught)

Mary's brilliance wasn't just in inspiring great ad campaigns. It was in coming up with big business ideas and inventing timely new brands. One of them was for our client Menley & James. It was a sexy new line of lipsticks that came in a long, slender, erect tube. (How do you spell phallic?) Mary dubbed the brand Love Cosmetics.

The products took off when Mary convinced the client to hire a former photographer's assistant to be the face of their brand. She was none other than Ali McGraw before she became a movie star for her roles in *Goodbye Columbus* and *Love Story*. The word got around that Love Cosmetics was paying Ms. McGraw $100,000 a year—an astronomical amount at that time—but Mary persuaded the company it was worth it, and she was right.

Love Cosmetics personified the raw sexuality that was going on in society in general—and at Wells, Rich, Greene, in particular. By the end of the decade, one of the ads for Love Cosmetics featured the not-so-subtle headline:

THIS IS LOVE IN ·69

Apparently, in the right context, sex does sell.

If Wells, Rich, Greene was a hotbed of creative talent, it was also a volcano of raging hormones. Many of us were just starting out in life and were driven by a desire to do great work, enjoy our unfair share of sex, and live a glorious New York lifestyle. We loved working at Wells, and we loved each other. I mean … *we loved each other.*

Everywhere you looked, there were beautiful people roaming the halls of our glamorous Billy-Baldwin-styled offices in the General Motors building twenty-four floors above Central Park. Sexy young ladies wore miniskirts so skimpy, when they bent down you could see all the way to Cleveland. If dating were a poker game, everybody was "all in." Recreational drugs and alcohol helped fuel the newfound feelings of passion. The birth control pill had been out for just five or six years, and this swung the doors (and everything else) wide open to sexual freedom. Lots of young single people were getting into some healthy sexual experimentation. And, not to be outdone, some of the married guys were letting their hair—and their wives—down too.

Growing up on the streets of Brooklyn and The Bronx, many of our talented creative ad stars never imagined the lifestyles they would be living. So they had taken the more familiar path and married their high school sweethearts. Now they were immersed in the intoxicating world of supermodels, super parties, and super sex. As a result, there were bitter breakups and divorces.

For a while, I worked with an art director named Kenny, the son of a Brooklyn cab driver. Over the course of a year, I saw him change from a nice *mensch-y* guy into a self-impressed ladies' man who started to believe his own bullshit. He divorced his high school sweetheart and left her and his two adorable kids for a Skinny Minny Ford model. "I can't believe it, Howie, she's gorgeous—and she loves me!" A year later, she left Kenny for a fashion photographer with a big studio, a large bank account, and much better drugs. There were lots of guys like Kenny, and they came from every side of the business.

As a friend of mine at Wells said at the time, "Howie, everybody's doing everybody." Account executives were dating producers, copywriters were romancing secretaries, art directors were falling for media people, and then it was, "Everybody change partners and start all over again."

Some would say it was all about sex, but a Mary Wells Lawrence agency was built on love. When you entered the agency, there was a big colorful poster by Robert Indiana in the waiting room with four big letters on it—L-O-V-E—as if to say, "Hey, this is what we're all about—feel it, love it, live it." And there were always fresh flowers everywhere—big bouquets to fill your olfactory passages with intoxicating aromas and spread a sense of beauty and optimism.

Mary had a credo: "Love your clients or someone else will." One of the ways she showed her love was by giving internships to clients' daughters. This prompted some smartass copywriter at the agency to give them the unflattering moniker, DORCs—Daughters of Rich Clients. In truth, these young women were exceptionally smart and quite attractive.

One of them was Kitty Hawks—a striking, long-legged brunette who was the daughter of the legendary director Howard Hawks. Christy Wilson was another standout. She was the vivacious, raven-haired offspring of Bill Wilson, owner of the Buffalo Bills football team.

And then there was Paula, a sexy young blonde from Texas who worked at the agency for one summer. When she walked down the hall swinging her hips in her tight little miniskirt, all the guys' tongues would hang out. But she was strictly off-limits because she was dating the son of Harding Lawrence, Mary's husband. If you crossed that line, it was a one-way ticket to Palookaville.

These so-called DORCs brought an extra level of glamour to the agency, and I'm sure they went on to have successful careers and exciting lives. I'm not sure I can say the same for the a-hole who gave them their nickname.

That same year, one of our clients, American Motors, was putting the pedal to the metal on their game changer of a car, the AMX. It was a sleek muscle car that was designed to get young hearts pumping. The agency put a hot young copywriter on this, whom I will call Tony. He could write, write, write, but he couldn't edit, edit, edit. And what the agency didn't know was that Tony was madly in love with another agency writer, whom I will call Kathy, who apparently shared his ardor. Nothing wrong with that, except that on the day the copy for the ad was supposed to show up, Tony didn't. It seems that he and Kathy decided to run off to the desert to commune with nature—and each other.

Charlie Moss, our indomitable creative leader, was waiting with great anticipation to see the concept for the AMX from this talented writer. What he got instead was a "Dear Charlie" letter saying, "Bye-bye. Love calls. Here's the copy. Good luck." The letter was accompanied by page after page of copy—written in longhand.

Given the importance of this ad to the success of this new car, and the success of our relationship with American Motors, the pressure was on. Lesser creative directors might have wilted. Not Charlie. Out of this mess of rambling copy, Charlie actually found little gems, and he sat down to craft it all into an ad. By the next day, he had molded it into a great piece of copy and discovered an award-winning headline buried as a copy point. It said:

THE AMX WILL BE SOLD AS DEMOCRATICALLY AS POSSIBLE

It was perfect, communicating that this thrilling new muscle machine was in short supply, which ultimately led to big demand. Thanks to Charlie, the agency had its ad.

Tony and Kathy remained MIA until about three weeks later, when the exhausted couple returned home, looking tired and disheveled, with big bags under their eyes. They immediately got back to work as if nothing had happened, and the amazing thing was that nobody got fired. Like I said, this was love in '69.

It was a wild time of working hard and playing hard. One of my friends at the agency was a talented copywriter named Timothy. He was a Brit—tall, dark, and dapper. Timothy always dressed in sleek dark suits, so he looked far more elegant than the rest of us who were growing our first beards and wearing outfits inspired by Sgt. Pepper. Timothy had a thick British accent, which was a real turn-on for the ladies, and he played it to the hilt.

It seems he always had dates lined up with some of the most beautiful women, and he was determined not to settle down. So imagine my surprise when we were having lunch one day and, after the third martini, he began to let his hair down.

"You know, Howie, I've been dating Linda," he said.

"Yes, everybody knows," I answered.

"But did you know that we've been seeing each other for three months?"

"Really? Wow, what happened to your three-date rule?"

"This is different. Howie, I think I'm in love with her ... which is why I'm so upset."

In love ... upset ... I was confused. Was it the martinis?

He went on. "I thought Linda was different from the others, you know? I mean, she's really smart, she's great in bed, and she's actually funny."

"Funny is good," I said. "Sex is easy, but a girl who's funny is hard to find. So what's the problem?"

"Well, just when I was about to bare my soul to Linda, I found out she was also dating that guy Walter."

"Walter?" I asked. "The fat, sweaty guy in the mailroom?"

"Exactly. So what does that say about Linda ... and what does that say about our relationship?"

I was beginning to see his point. Walter was pretty sweaty.

"I don't know what to do about it," he went on. "I'm good at sex, but not so much at this love thing."

"Why don't you have a long talk with her?" I suggested. "Open your heart, and tell her how you really feel. Maybe she's just screwing around because she thinks you're not serious ... like your relationship won't go anywhere, so she has to keep her options open."

That seemed rational to Timothy, but rational wasn't his strong suit. "I've got a better idea. I'm going to ask out Maria. Linda has always been intimidated by Maria, probably because she has big breasts. It's a sore point with Linda because she has small ones." He thought for a moment and felt a need to add, "But they're perky, and they stand up, and—"

I cut him off. "Okay, Timothy, I get it. I just don't understand the point of all this."

"The point is she'll get really jealous, and it will piss her off. I'll have her in the palm of my hand, and she'll never want to date anyone else ... especially a loser like Walter."

"Timothy, that sounds like a really bad idea. I think you're just going to drive her away."

But he was confident he had the right strategy—piss her off to win her back.

Thinking back on those times, it's amazing to me how such brilliant and talented people like Timothy could have also been so immature and childish about relationships. Then again, maybe it was just a sixties thing.

Meanwhile, the promiscuity at Wells, Rich, Greene was becoming common knowledge, and the word had reached the highest levels. One day, a guy named Hank, who had a reputation for being an agency spy and a snitch with direct lines to Mary Wells Lawrence, popped into my office. I was sitting with an art director, working on a trade ad, when Hank closed the door and pulled up a seat. We dropped what we were doing.

"Gentlemen," Hank said. *Did he say gentlemen?* This was obviously serious. "I'm going from office to office. It's going to take me all day and maybe all of tomorrow too, but this is very serious. I've been asked to relay this message to everyone in the agency. It's a personal message from Mary herself, and I quote: 'Do not dip your quill in the company ink!'"

It could not have been clearer or more powerful. Screw around with agency people, and you're screwed! All of a sudden, everyone became more discreet. I know the sexual activity didn't stop, but it definitely went underground. We no longer knew who was doing whom or where or when or how often.

As for Timothy, he must have had the right strategy after all. That year, he and Linda flew to Vegas and got married. I'm told she wore a tight white dress and her breasts were very perky.

Making Silk Purses

During this time, I was working with an art director named Julio DiIorio, a super guy with a great talent. But like me, he wasn't an agency star, so we didn't get the plum assignments. And since Wells was still in the old, cramped office building on Madison Avenue, we were relegated to sharing a small out-of-the-way office on another floor where nobody came. I think everyone thought we had died. Every once in a while, though, we would get a little assignment, and we were determined to make the most of it. We would turn these sows' ears into silk purses.

One "biggie" assignment was to announce that Rainier Beer had added one extra ounce to their bottled beer. Big whoop, alert the media, this was a real game changer for beer lovers. *Not!*

However, Julio and I came up with a creative solution that made that one ounce of beer feel important. We recommended that the client do a big full-page newspaper ad to accommodate our big idea. Julio filled the entire page with an elegant tapered beer glass that touched the bottom and top of the page. But instead of the usual cliché photo of frothy beer spilling over the sides, he showed only one little golden ounce of beer at the bottom of the glass. The headline read,

HAVE ONE MORE ON US

The ad was an attention-grabber. To magnify the relevance of one little extra ounce, I wrote copy that went something like this: "One more ounce may not sound like a lot, but do the math. If you drink twelve beers a week, that's an extra twelve ounces or one extra bottle of beer a week ... multiply that by fifty-two weeks and you've got fifty-two extra bottles or four whole cases ... which is a lot of great beer ... which is a lot of great times ... which is incredible." All of a sudden, one silly ounce of beer seemed like a meaningful thing. That ad won awards—it was our first silk purse.

Another groundbreaking assignment was to do a print ad for Personna blades offering a twenty-five-cents-off coupon, not the most thrilling challenge, but we were into making silk purses, re-member? Our idea was to do an aggressive ad going right at the competition, Gillette, which basically owned the shaving category. In another full-page newspaper ad, I wrote a headline that could not be ignored. I was inspired by a famous line from history, created by

that great Italian ad man, Julius Caesar. "Friends, Romans, country-
men, lend me your ears."

GILLETTE USERS, LEND US YOUR FACE!

It talked about a better shave from a better blade, and it went
over big. The twenty-five-cent-coupon at the bottom had people rip-
ping the ads out and rushing to the store, giving Persona a nice sales
bump.

The work Julio and I were doing was good, but it wasn't the big
stuff and there wasn't enough of it. So in our downtime, which was
most of the time, we found ways to relieve the boredom by indulg-
ing in long, decadent lunches and sometimes playing practical jokes
on unsuspecting friends.

Tommy and the Lemon Soup

One such victim was a young guy at the agency named Tommy,
who'd grown up in an extremely orthodox Jewish family. He was a
twenty-five-year-old virgin—yes, a virgin in New York City—working in the exciting, sexy, creative world of advertising—at Wells,
Rich, Greene, no less! Tommy felt stifled by his strict religious up-
bringing, and he was ready to expand his horizons.

Julio and I decided to take Tommy under our wing. If he wanted
to experience the life he had never known, we would be the ones
to show him the way. Yet Tommy's biggest fantasy, believe it or
not, had nothing to do with sex, drugs, or rock 'n' roll. What he
longed for most in life was to taste his first lobster. Apparently, the

Jewish orthodoxy forbade going near these delectable crustaceans. So when Tommy was sure he was ready to take the big plunge, Julio and I treated him to lunch at the classic Palm Restaurant on Second Avenue, where the average lobster was as big as a Labrador retriever.

Because it was Tommy's first experience, we were being helpful, recommending different dishes and explaining how to eat them. I suggested, "Let's start with the clams oreganata, followed by a big chilled salad with blue cheese dressing."

"Yeah," Julio agreed. "Then we can dive into our four-pound lobsters and big baked potatoes with sour cream and chives." *Mmm,* I was salivating just thinking about it, and so was Tommy.

When Tommy's lobster arrived at the table, his eyes lit up. We showed him how to crack the claws and use the tiny fork to pull out the tender meat and dip it into the melted butter for extra flavor—as if these lobsters needed it. From his very first bite, the taste of lobster rocked Tommy's world. All he could say was, "I've waited my whole life for this."

Julio and I felt proud that we had facilitated this important gastronomic passage. But, of course, we couldn't let the afternoon go by without pulling a little prank. After Tommy had finished his last morsel of lobster and was sucking on the claw, Julio said, "Man, that was delicious. I can't wait for the chilled lemon soup."

"Lemon soup?" Tommy asked. "I've never had that either."

To which I said, "Tommy, Tommy. You can't have lobster without chilled lemon soup. It's a tradition." At that point, the waiter arrived at the table with three finger bowls filled with water and lemon slices to wash our hands in.

"You're going to love this," Julio told Tommy.

"It looks good ... very fresh," Tommy responded. "But there's no spoon."

Julio explained, "You don't eat chilled lemon soup with a spoon. You sip it right out of the bowl."

With that, Tommy began to lift the bowl to his lips, and he was just about to drink it when Julio and I stopped him cold. "No, no, Tommy. It's a finger bowl ... you wash your hands in it! We were just joking."

Tommy immediately put the bowl down and gave us a look, as if to say, "You guys are so bad!" Then he smiled and stuck both his hands in the bowl and started to splash the water over his fingers.

That's when Julio and I shouted, "No, Tommy. It's soup!"

For most Jewish kids, having a bar mitzvah at age thirteen is how you tell the world, "Today I am a man." Tommy had to wait a few years longer. But on that day, Tommy clawed his way to manhood.

Blame It on Woodstock

You may have heard the expression, "If you remember Woodstock, you weren't there." Well, I was there, and I may not remember everything, but I can tell you one thing for sure. Woodstock changed my life. Two weeks after the concert, in September 1969, I met my wife, Carol, and began a romance that has lasted to this day. One month after the event, I grew the beard that is still on my face.

And within eighteen months, Bob Pasqualina and I broke through creatively at Wells, Rich, Greene with our career and life-altering Alka Seltzer commercials, "Try it, you'll like it" and "I can't believe I ate the whole thing" that would eventually make it into the Clio Hall of Fame.

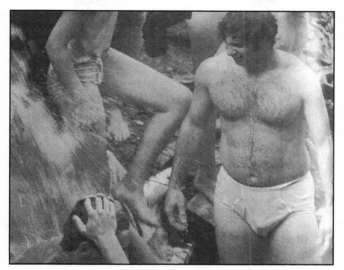

Woodstock Landed Me in *LIFE Magazine*

Was it a coincidence? Or was it the impact of being in the presence of immortals like Janis Joplin; Jimmy Hendrix; Joe Cocker; Crosby, Stills & Nash; Richie Havens; and many of the greatest rockers of all time? Was it the drugs? They were everywhere, and they were good. They made the brownies taste better, the jokes seem funnier, and the music sound fucking amazing. Or was it the experience of communing with 400,000 like-minded souls huddled under tarps and blankets in the mud and the rain? The answer is, "Yes, yes, and yes!" It was all of that and something more. It was "the pond."

On the morning of the second day at Woodstock, my good friend Gary Geyer and I were walking up a path toward the concert grounds when we passed a large pond. Out of the corners of our eyes, we noticed that guys and girls were stripping down to their skivvies, bras, and panties and washing themselves off in the water. Then they were taking it off—all off! This prompted Gary to suggest, "Maybe we should go down there." Gary always had the best ideas. We made our way down to the bank as hundreds more people began to join in, whipping off their clothes, jumping into the water, and splashing and laughing like children.

I felt an involuntary smile come over my face. Could we really muster up the courage to get naked with hundreds of people? Gary and I stripped down to our Fruit of the Looms, stood in the water, and watched for a while. And then we did it—we bared it all.

It was laugh-out-loud exhilarating. In that moment, I felt liberated, bold, freed up! Woodstock opened up my mind and lifted my heart, and I believe the experience contributed in a big way to the important changes that were about to happen in my life.

In August 1989, on the twentieth anniversary of Woodstock, *LIFE Magazine* devoted an entire issue to this historic event. It was filled with photographs and personal stories supplied by the people who were there—the real Woodstock-ers.

My story was one of them. Since Gary was a great art director and an equally great photographer, he had been snapping pictures of this whole event for posterity. Gary supplied our story to *LIFE Magazine* along with a photograph of me standing by a waterfall in my underwear. *LIFE Magazine* loved it and devoted a full page to it. (Was this a tribute to Gary's photographic talents? Or my extraordinary, masculine Jewish body?) To publicize this important issue, *LIFE Magazine* arranged for me and two other "credible witnesses" to appear on *Good Morning America*.

The three of us were sitting in the green room waiting to go on TV when I looked up at the monitor and saw a promo for our upcoming segment. There, up on the TV screen, was that same photograph of me in my skivvies, full frame. However, since this was network TV, they felt obligated to cover up my private area with one of those blurry circles. To be safe, they used a really big oversized circle. I never felt like such a manly man.

Gary's Dilemma

I'll always be grateful to Gary for convincing me to go to Woodstock. He and I had been friends ever since we first met at Doyle Dane Bernbach in 1965. It's worth taking a minute to talk about Gary here because he was a pioneer of sorts. I think of him as the poster boy for the pursuit of self-improvement and inner happiness that was going on at the time.

The world was changing, and our generation was trying to figure out what it all meant and how we fit into the greater scheme of things, asking cosmic questions like, "Who am I? What is the meaning of existence? What's it all about, Alfie?"

Among all my friends, Gary was the most willing to try just about anything to find peace, happiness, and greater meaning in life. So he tried everything! For example, when the Beatles found spirituality with the Maharishi and his transcendental meditation movement, Gary was first in line to get his very own personalized mantra: "Ommmm." It helped Gary to relax, focus, and feel at peace. And it was good.

Then, when the EST movement was revving up, Gary started going to meetings headed by their charismatic leader, Werner Erhard. EST focused on taking responsibility for oneself and seizing control of your own life. They had slogans like, "Create your future from your future, not your past." You know, good shit like that. Being part of EST gave Gary more confidence and a greater sense of self. And it was good.

Then Gary wanted to understand his motivations, so he started seeing a psychologist. There, in the safety of his shrink's office, he connected with his innermost feelings—and his mommy. And it was good.

Not to ignore his body, Gary also decided to join one of the new-age gyms that were popping up all over New York City. And it was there that he started building up his muscles and strengthening his core. And it was good.

Of course, like most of us, Gary also got into some experimentation with good weed, laughing hysterically and getting the munchies. It made him feel loose and free. And it was good.

So now, Gary was doing it all—meditating, ESTing, shrinking, exercising, and getting stoned—and it was all good. The only problem was, in trying to do it all, he was totally exhausted all of the time. In an effort to be helpful, I asked him, "Gary, why don't you just keep doing the stuff that's working for you and give up the stuff that's not?" His frantic answer was, "Howie, I can't! I have no idea which ones are working, and I'm afraid to fuck it all up!"

Poor Gary was stuck. Then one day, he was introduced to a pretty young girl named Linda. They dated, fell in love, and all of a sudden, only one thing took up all of Gary's time: his marriage.

Sadly, Gary passed away recently. I gave a tearful eulogy at his funeral, and there was an outpouring of love for him from friends and family. I miss Gary terribly. It gives me comfort, though, to know that he's somewhere up there checking out all the latest techniques in the pursuit of heavenly happiness. And it is good.

Julio and the Jets

The liberating feeling that Gary and I felt at Woodstock was still with me three months later, when everyone at Wells, Rich, Greene was offered a special perk. One of Mary Wells Lawrence's many rich friends was developing an amazing property in Acapulco called Tres Vidas En La Playa. They were just putting the finishing touches on this sprawling vacation resort, and before they opened to the general public, they wanted to get some real world feedback on how great the place was from "hip and trendy Americans in the know." I guess they thought that was us. So anyone at Wells who wanted to go there could do so for less than half the normal price. I jumped at the chance, and so did Julio and about thirty other party-loving, adventure-seeking Wells, Rich, Greene-ers.

We arrived at a heavenly place overlooking the Pacific Ocean with a golf course and rolling grassy hills dotted with Mexican casitas, each with its own sparkling pool. Julio and I shared a casita, but there was a lot of partying going on, so we got to hang out in everyone else's too.

One of the female producers at the agency, an attractive woman named Sherry, had heard of my adventures at Woodstock and said, "Hey, when we get to Acapulco, we should all swim naked together." *Yay, a kindred spirit.* It didn't even bother me that she was bringing along her boyfriend. The whole idea was for all of us to drop our inhibitions and our bathing suits and experience Acapulco, pure, raw, and naked.

Sadly, the nude event never happened. I was a little pissed off at Sherry because I thought she chickened out. But a few months later, over drinks, her boyfriend admitted to me that he was the one who put the *kibosh* on it.

"Sorry about that, Howie. I gotta take the blame for ruining the whole nude thing."

"It's okay, Bob. I probably wouldn't have felt comfortable if my girlfriend got naked in front of everyone either."

"No, that wasn't it," he said. "She's got a great body, and I would've been proud of her showing it off."

"Really?" I asked, quite surprised. "Then what was the reason?"

"Howie," he said. "The pool was very cold, and I was concerned about shrinkage!" Ah, a universal man issue that I could understand.

Oh well, that didn't stop us from having a fabulous time—until the fifth day when disaster struck and almost changed Julio's life forever. Each day, he liked to float in the water for a while and then walk around the perimeter of the pool with a drink in his hand. One afternoon, Julio discovered a "sweet spot" in our pool. He felt a powerful air jet at just the right level to provide a pleasant, sensual sensation in the area of his private parts. Each time he went to that spot, he smiled, enjoying the rapid vibrations of the water for a few moments, and then he moved on.

As he glided through the water on the fifth day, he spotted another jet on the other side of the pool. He sidled up to the portal, expecting to enjoy the same pleasant sensation, when all of a sudden I heard a mortal scream. "Aaargh!" It lasted only a few seconds, but it seemed like forever. Gasping for breath, Julio yanked his body away from the jet and rolled up onto the side of the pool, moaning and trying to catch his breath. I ran over to him to see what was wrong.

"What happened, Julio, are you alright?"

"It wasn't a jet," he exclaimed with panic in his voice. "It was suction! It nearly pulled my dick off. Thank god this time I was wearing my Speedo."

I didn't mean to laugh. But suddenly an image popped into my head of Julio's dick being whipped out of its socket and zooming through the underground pipes until it was spit out into the Pacific Ocean. *Pffft!*

We took Julio to the infirmary, and the official diagnosis was something along the lines of Penile-ectus Catastrophus. The Mexican doctor attended to it and prescribed some heavy-duty pain-killers that put a smile back on Julio's face.

For all of us Wells, Rich, Greene-ers, the trip was a wonderful experience ... until the very last day. We all got a bad case of Montezuma's Revenge, and on the flight back everyone was fighting to get to the bathroom—everyone except Julio. He sat relaxed in his seat—with powerful meds in his body, an ice pack on his lap, and a very pleasant smile on his face.

Julio and I worked together for another six months before he left the agency for greener (as in more money) pastures. I missed him. But for me, creatively, things were about to get even better.

TWO

Rising Up

Finding My Ginger Rogers

What is a perfect partner? He or she is the yin to your yang, the Rogers to your Astaire, the cherries to your Garcia. A perfect partner has complementary skills, so that your talents are stronger together than they would be if you were working solo. In the words of Bill Bernbach, who was the first to recognize the power of putting two talented creative people together as a team: $1 + 1 = 3$.

After Julio left, I was waiting for a new partner, any partner. Then one day, the perfect one walked in. Hank the Snitch knocked on my door and was standing there with a mustachioed Italian art director named Bob Pasqualina. "Howie, I want you to meet Bob. Bob, meet Howie. Mary thinks you guys would be great together."

The rest, as they say, is history. For the next fourteen years, we would create together, win awards together, open an agency together, and move our families 3,000 miles across the country to Los Angeles together.

Knowing how well our partnership worked and how long it lasted, you might think we were very much alike. Not so much. Bob was an Italian art director from Queens, and I was a Jewish copywriter from The Bronx. He was six years older than me and married with a young son. I was single, restless, and free. Bob's taste was very old world. He loved antique furniture, old country farmhouses, vintage clothes, and drove a classic old Porsche. My motto was, "I want it new, and I want it now!"

We also had different creative strengths. Bob was the eyes, and I was the ears. He was very sensitive to everything visual that happened around him, whereas I picked up on the sounds all around me. We could walk into a room together, spend five minutes, and after we walked out he could tell me the color and pattern of the wallpaper, that there were coffered ceilings and wainscoting on the walls, and that the chair was Chippendale.

I would counter with, "Great, but did you notice that the music they were playing was Pachelbel?" Our complementary skills would prove to be a big strength in our creative relationship.

Bob was brilliant, but he tended to have charming gaps in his communication skills. He sometimes spoke in circular phrases and had a problem remembering people's names. This made us even more perfect for each other because I actually understood him and could fill in the blanks—most of the time.

One day, he turned to me and said, "Howie ... who was that guy?"

I had gotten pretty good at reading Bob's mind, but this was too cosmic even for me. "What guy, Bob? Can you narrow the field for me?"

"You know," he said. "The guy from World War II."

"Bob, there were a lot of guys from World War II. What side was he on?"

"The German guy, Howie. I'm talking about the German guy."

"Bob, are you talking about Hermann Goering?"

"No."

"Was it Himmler?

"No, Howie. No!"

I continued down the list. "Hess? Joseph Goebbels?"

"No, no. I'm talking about the famous guy. You know, the one with the funny mustache."

Suddenly it hit me, but I couldn't really believe it.

"Bob," I said. "You can't possibly be talking about Adolph Hitler?"

"That's the guy!" he said.

Bob is a unique and beautiful person. That's why I loved working with him and why we were able to do so much great stuff together for so many years. But back in 1969, we were still relative nobodies at Wells, Rich, Greene, waiting for our first big shot.

See You in the Screening Room, Boys

As Bob and I started to gel as a team, we began to spend more time presenting to Charlie Moss and his partner, Stan Dragoti. I must admit, I was kind of in awe of them. If there were any two creative stars who Mary Wells Lawrence could count on when the chips were down, it was Charlie and Stan. They came through for the agency with big ideas in pressured situations.

THE END OF THE PLAIN PLANE

That was Charlie's simple but inspired line and a powerful introduction to Braniff Airlines, which helped put the airline—and Wells—on the map.

Charlie and Stan's hilarious American Motors TV spot called "Driving School" was meant to prove the durability of the Rebel. The car was strong enough to stand up to anything. That's why it was the number one car used by driving schools. The commercial showed a bunch of clueless student drivers trying to follow instructions from their terrified driving instructor as they careened in and out of city traffic.

In the last scene, the car is stopped and rain pours down on the windshield, but as the camera pulls back, we realize it's not rain but water from a fire hydrant the driver has plowed into. This led to the punch line of the spot, "Sh ... sh ... should I turn the windshield wipers on now?"

The entire advertising community was there at the Clios that year when Charlie and Stan accepted their statues, which helped to further cement the agency's reputation as the creative leader in New York—which meant creative leader of the free world.

Charlie Moss was born to be creative. He actually started out as a child actor in a small award-winning movie called *The Little Fugitive*. And he never lost his theatrical flair. In a world of somber ad execs who took themselves far too seriously, Charlie was more of a man-child who always lit up the room with a quip or a joke. Charlie was tall and boyishly handsome, with a big mop of curly black hair and a twinkly presence that was impossible to ignore.

Stan Dragoti was Charlie's handsome and magnetic other half, and as a team, those guys were a lethal combination. So you'd have to be crazy to question their opinion or challenge their authority, right? Yes, unless you're Howie Cohen and Bob Pasqualina.

On one particular occasion, Bob and I were assigned to do a thirty-second TV spot for a General Mills snack product called Rye Crisps. The first time I tasted the product, I loved it. And Rye Crisps reminded me of something from my childhood.

Every Saturday morning in The Bronx, my father would shove a few quarters in my hand and ask me to go around the corner to the Snowflake Bakery on White Plains Road and pick up a "sliced seeded rye." Let me tell you, that was one heavenly, fresh-baked bread with a crispy crust and a delicious rye taste. The best part of the bread, though, was the super crispy little end piece. It was so good that my father and I would actually fight over it. I would try to grab it when he wasn't looking, but his hand was always a little faster than mine. Every Sunday, he got to that crispy little piece first.

This story became the focus of our TV spot. Bob and I wrote a script about a thirty-year-old man reminiscing about the crispy piece of rye bread. In the spot, we hear his voice telling the story.

As we open, he is seated at his kitchen table tasting the new Rye Crisps for the first time. He's reminded of the taste from his childhood and the camera ripple dissolves to him as an eight-year-old boy in the 1950s, sitting at the dinner table. Through his own voiceover, he shares his memory of the little hand battle with his dad, as we see them both reach for the luscious, crispy end piece. His dad gently slaps his hand and grabs the piece for himself. Then we ripple dissolve back to present day, as he tells us that's exactly what Rye Crisps taste like. And the best part, he doesn't have to fight for it anymore. He can eat all he wants right out of the box.

We loved our little story, and when we presented it to Charlie and Stan, they liked it too. But then Charlie said, "Too bad it'll never work."

Quick background here. Throughout the 1960s, the agency primarily created sixty-second commercials. At this point in time, the industry and the agency were transitioning to "30s" to get double the media exposure for our clients. The challenge—you had to tell the story in half the time.

"What do you mean, Charlie?" I asked. "Why won't it work?"

"It's too complicated for thirty seconds, Howie. You've got the grown man in the present, the kid in the past, rye breads and rye crisps, and a long, convoluted story. It's a charming story, but forget it, boys. It won't work."

Stan chimed in, "I have to agree with Charlie. Sorry, guys."

Bob and I respected them a lot, but we weren't going to roll over on this one. "Let us just present it to the client and see what they think," I proposed.

To our surprise, they agreed. I guess they thought the client would be wise enough to kill it. Well, the client actually liked the spot and approved it. When we told Charlie and Stan "the good news," they slowly shook their heads. And then, in the sly, knowing way that only a Charlie Moss could do, he uttered the fateful words, "See you in the screening room, boys."

He said it with a bit of a twinkle, but it was an ominous message:

This thing won't work, and the truth will come out in the screening room. You just sold a spot that can't be done. Gulp. You're going to blow $50,000 on production. Gulp, gulp. We might even lose this client. And you'll see we were right when the moment of truth arrives ... in the screening room. Gulp, gulp, gulp.

As they left the room, Stan repeated Charlie's line, "See you in the screening room, boys."

Over the course of the next few weeks, as Bob and I were steeped in production, we would pass Charlie or Stan in the hall and they would ask, "So, how is your thirty-second epic coming?"

"Um, it should be okay," we answered each time.

"Ha!" Charlie goaded, detecting some weakness. Then, with that same look on his face, he said, "See you in the screening room, boys."

Five weeks later, after we had finished editing and polishing the spot, we were ready to show it to Charlie and Stan in the room they had made famous—the screening room. As the lights went down and the film started clickety-clacking through the projector, Bob and I held our breaths. But then, to our surprise, we could see Charlie and Stan opening their eyes and maybe their minds. I even detected smiles.

And when the lights went back on, Charlie said, "Geez, it works." And Stan added, "Nice spot! Got to hand it to you guys, you pulled it off." To which I said, "See you at the Clios, boys."

Selling Soda, Playing Cupid

Little victories like that were starting to get Bob and me noticed. Unfortunately, we still didn't have an account we could call our own. For all creative people, that was the goal: to rise to the point where you would lead your own account and have the title "creative supervisor," have control over the creative product and build your own creative group. Then earn a fancy title like VP creative supervisor. The benefits were many, including pride of authorship, creative control, a fancy title, and … money!

Bob and I weren't there just yet. Then one rainy, windy day in New York, Mary Wells Lawrence summoned us to her office, and the clouds parted. "Boys," she said. "You know Royal Crown is a very important client of ours. Well, we have a little problem with their Diet Rite Cola brand."

"Oh, sorry," I said. "What's the problem, Mary?"

"They hate the advertising!" she said with a tinge of anger. But Mary quickly did what she did best. She turned a big negative into an exciting positive. "But, boys, we have a great opportunity to fix this, and we will. Bob, Howie, I think the two of you could be perfect for this job."

My heart started to beat faster. *Could this be it?* She went on to give us more background. The agency had created a celebrity campaign for Diet Rite Cola, and one of the spots featured the legendary Lena Horne. She was dazzling in the commercial, but the client didn't like it. Let me be more specific. They fucking hated it! But why? The spot was shot beautifully, she looked gorgeous, and her voice was spectacular. Apparently, none of that mattered.

While no one mentioned the word "race," it wasn't hard to

connect the dots. The company was based in Columbus, Georgia, and these guys still had a fondness for Robert E. Lee and the Confederate flag. Now one of their biggest bottlers was refusing to run the campaign and threatening to make a TV spot himself.

Hold on! Mary got on the phone with this guy and said if he wanted his own TV spot, we would make it for him, separate and apart from the campaign. And, in her typical fashion, she promised it would be great and he would love it. He got excited and said he would be happy to pay for it. There was only one caveat. It had to be produced for a measly $10,000, which was *bupkis* for a thirty-second TV spot, even in 1969. As we turned to leave Mary's office, we thanked her for the opportunity. She smiled and said just two words. "Be brilliant!" Okay, no pressure.

This was our chance, and we dove into this assignment with all of our creative hearts. The strategy was simple and unremarkable. Diet Rite Cola tastes as good as regular cola with only half the calories. But we came up with an idea and a line that could make it stand out: we would do a TV spot that focused on people who didn't need to lose weight but drank Diet Rite Cola just because they liked the taste. Our theme (with a slightly sexy double meaning) was:

I DONT NEED IT, BUT I LIKE IT

Bob and I liked the line so much that we wanted to hear it repeated, so we came up with the idea to do humorous vignettes with people expressing it in their own wonderful ways. People who were in good shape: a small town beauty queen, a semi-pro football player, etc.

Our biggest challenge was finding a production company that

could pull this off for ten grand. Our producer found the answer in Charlotte, North Carolina, in the form of a little production company that specialized in shooting on videotape. In those days, everything was shot on film. Videotape was the brave new world of lesser production values with a more live look and feel. Many in our business thought this made a commercial look cheap. And it usually did. However, we felt the live look would give it a spontaneity that could work for us.

We were also thrilled to learn that for our little budget, this down south production company would provide a casting director, producer, director, cameraman, composer, and editor. What we didn't know is that all those roles would be filled by one guy—a local Cecil B. DeBullshit with an oversized self-image and undersized talent. His actual name was Beauregard.

We knew there was a problem the first day he showed up wearing a silk ascot and speaking in an English accent with a Southern drawl. Bob and I looked at each other with the same thought. *Oh shit, we're going to have to do everything ourselves.* Casting was a real challenge because Charlotte is not exactly your biggest talent market. In New York, we might have brought in forty candidates for each part. In Charlotte, we were lucky if we saw five.

But in advertising, as in life, sometimes you get lucky. For the part of the local beauty queen, a fetching young blonde came in and performed the script with wide-eyed innocence. "Dear Diet Rite Cola, I was Miss Corrugated Cardboard, 1969. I don't need it, but I like it!" She ended every sentence like it was a question, and her delivery was so imperfect, it was perfect.

Finding a football player who could actually speak was a lot tougher. Then Dwayne walked in. He was a big bear of a man who was missing one front tooth—a gentle giant with a soft, polite voice. Dwayne was probably ten years older than me, but he called me Mr. Cohen. He had tried out for a couple of pro football teams but never made it. After suffering two concussions, he pursued odd jobs—as a truck driver, a handyman, and a forklift operator on the graveyard shift. He was also divorced from his high school sweetheart and seemed a little sad, lost, and alone. There was something so naïve and sweet about him that Bob and I both agreed—it was risky, but Dwayne was our guy.

Over the course of several days, Bob and I rolled up our sleeves and put everything we had into this little production. Bob styled the sets, I picked the wardrobe, Bob positioned the camera, I held the big boom mike, Bob directed the talent (and even swept the floors), and I made sure we never ran out of donuts. Beauregard didn't seem to mind because we gave him an important role. After each take, he was allowed to yell "Cut!" He was excellent at that.

It was a stressful shoot, but in the end, we felt we had something good that looked and felt like no other soft drink advertising, big budget or small. And when we showed it to Mary—*score*—she loved it! And, just as importantly, the bottler loved it too. Bob and I had finally broken through, and we were on our way.

But the happiest part of this story belongs to Dwayne. The Diet Rite Cola spot ran heavily in North Carolina and, after seeing the commercial several times, a local librarian became smitten with him. She somehow got through to the production company, who gave her Dwayne's contact information.

They met over a bottle of Diet Rite and (this is the corny part, but it's true) it was love at first sight. A short time later, Dwayne and the librarian exchanged vows and became husband and wife. Proof, once again, that advertising makes the world a better place.

Howie and the Horse Boy

With the success of our little $10,000 Diet Rite Cola TV spot, all of the bottlers were clamoring for a new TV campaign based on our theme line, "I don't need it, but I like it." Bob and I were asked to pool it into a full-fledged campaign. We would get to present it to their top guys in Georgia, and if they liked what they saw, it would run nationally. *Wow!*

Bob and I huddled for three weeks writing new scripts. This campaign was so important to the agency that Mary decided to fly down with us to "show the flag." *Gulp!* We had never presented to a client in front of Mary before. It was enough pressure that we were presenting to descendants of slave owners, but to have Mary in the room was even more intimidating.

On the plane ride down, she had some sage advice for me. "Howie," she said. "You're just so charming with your New York *shtick*, don't ever lose that. But for these guys in Georgia, you might want to ease off the ethnic thing." In other words, she was telling me not to be too Jewish. Good advice. Except that once a Jew, always a Jew.

We arrived at their headquarters and started setting up in the executive conference room. The top management of Royal Crown Cola began filing in. They were all dressed casually and seemed like a nice bunch of Southern gents, but we also knew they were tough.

They had to be to compete with the likes of Coke and Pepsi. They couldn't outspend the competition, so they needed to outsmart them with better, more intrusive advertising. That's why we were there. This was a high stakes meeting.

Mary did a wonderful job of introducing us and warming up the room. The Diet Rite guys were honored that she even showed up. And they seemed relaxed and smiled as I began to take them through the first storyboard and explained the scenes. Each vignette centered around another interesting and fit person who didn't need Diet Rite Cola but loved it for the taste. I began to describe the first story this way ...

"So, there's this southern belle, very slim and pretty, who lives in a classic southern antebellum mansion (I was playing to the crowd). And as the scene opens, we find her standing in front of a row of whitewashed stables. Her eyes light up as she sees her magnificent black stallion being led out of the paddock by a horse boy and then—"

"Whoa! Whoa!" Diet Rite's VP of marketing interrupted with a booming voice, stopping me dead in my tracks. "Howie!" he barked. "What the hell is a horse boy?"

Everything came to a halt, and the room went silent. I saw the whole crowd staring at me, including Mary, and my mouth went dry. Then he said, "Son, around here, we call that guy a 'groom!'"

Everyone waited for my reply. In that moment, I felt like I was in a Woody Allen movie, and I was this little, conspicuous Jew in a crowd of confederates ready to secede from my union. In an inspired moment born of desperation, I spoke up using my best Yiddish accent. "Lissen, I'm a Jewish kid from da Bronx. Vot do I know from grooms?"

The room erupted in laughter. I mean these guys laughed their southern asses off. And when Mary stood up and applauded, they got up and applauded too. We were a hit!

Back in New York, Mary sent Bob and me an expensive bottle of champagne with a short personal note: "You are my heroes," followed by two little hearts. More importantly, she promoted us to creative directors on the Diet Rite Cola business. We were now an established team, and the word was getting around that we were pretty good. That was important as we waited for our big breakthrough.

Eating Cat Food, Swallowing Pride

In addition to our creative director responsibilities on Diet Rite Cola, Mary used us as troubleshooters on other accounts, like Ralston Purina. Their pet food division had just invented a new form of cat food, and they were eager to develop an advertising campaign that was as breakthrough as their product. They invited a bunch of writers and art directors from Wells, including Bob and me, to their headquarters in St. Louis, so we could be briefed on this taste-tempting sensation.

Upon arrival, we were invited into a conference room, where several of their top marketing guys were waiting to greet us. In the middle of an oversized conference table sat an array of colorful pouches and bowls filled with the new cat food. The VP of marketing stood up and began to speak. "Gentlemen, what you see before you is a gastronomic breakthrough for cats and the people who love them."

Really? All I saw were piles of little brown turds sitting in bowls. "For years," he continued, "cat lovers who wanted to please the palate of their beloved kitties have had only two options ... canned cat food or dry cat food. There was nothing in between. But we're about to change all that."

Then he held a pouch of cat food high over his head and announced with pride, "This is Tender Vittles!" All of the Ralston people began to clap. *Geez,* I thought, *these guys need to get out more often.*

He ripped open a pouch filled with the soft little nuggets and poured them into a tin bowl. "Hear that?" he asked as they bounced to and fro. I listened, but couldn't hear a thing. Pasqualina said, "Not really."

"Exactly!" he said. "That's because Tender Vittles are not hard little rocks like ordinary dry cat food. They're what we call 'soft-moist.' It's a first!"

"Very impressive," I said with all the sincerity I could muster. (As someone in our business once said, "If you can fake sincerity, you're golden.")

"But you know," he went on. "The real proof is in the taste." And with that, he scooped up a handful and actually popped them into his mouth. The other Ralston guys joined him, wolfing down the cat food, looking like hungry Jews at a bar mitzvah.

"Mmm, very tasty. The chicken flavor really comes through," said the brand manager.

"Yes, just the right amount of seasoning," added the marketing director. Then he turned to me and said, "C'mon, Howie. Chow down."

Every fiber of my being was screaming to get the hell out of there and run to the airport. But being the professional suck-up that I am, I joined in. I tossed a few in my mouth. The brand manager watched as I chewed, smiled, and chewed some more. I forced myself to swallow, all the while trying to control my gag reflex.

"So, whaddya think?" the brand manager asked.

They were repulsive, but I sensed that might not be the answer he was looking for. I decided to rely on a technique that has usually worked for me in my career. It's called being cute. I drew upon my experience at a recent wine tasting event and said, "The taste is immature, yet frisky, with a witty top note."

The VP of marketing lit up with pride and said, "Yes, witty top note. I love it!" All the other marketing guys chimed in, "Yeah," "Right," "Perfect." And the brand manager capped it off with, "That's why he makes the big bucks."

Epilogue: While I didn't care for the taste of Tender Vittles, apparently cats loved it. Unfortunately, the product had a high sugar and salt content that caused health problems for many of our feline friends. When Nestle acquired Ralston Purina, they discontinued the product in the United States, but I believe it's still sold in Canada and other countries. It makes me soft-moist to know that cats around the world can still enjoy that immature, yet frisky, taste with the witty top note.

Naked on Fire Island

Working at Wells, Rich, Greene meant more than just having an exciting creative job. The agency was also the center of our social universe. We hung out together, partied together, and in the summer, we even vacationed on weekends together.

Anyone who has ever lived in Manhattan knows that it's a

thrilling city, throbbing with life—except in the middle of summer when the temperature hits ninety degrees and the garbage cans make the streets smell like StarKist Tuna. That's when it's time to get the hell out of town.

For most of the people I was working with in advertising that meant escaping to a very special, out-of-the-way, amazing place called Fire Island. It was just one hour by car, followed by a half-hour ferry ride to a thin sliver of an island where there were no cars allowed and the motto was, "No shirts, no shoes, no problem."

Riddle: How many successful young professionals did it take to rent one Fire Island house? In the late sixties, the answer was twenty. There were twelve guys and eight girls, mostly in the ad business, and all of us were fun-loving people in our twenties.

A full summer share cost $400, while a half-share cost $200 and entitled you to come out every other weekend. I bought a half-share, but in my own delusional mind, I felt that I added so much to the weekly fun that halfway through the summer I started coming out every weekend. Some might say that's not fair. But would it have been fair to deprive my friends of all my humor and Jewish charm? I don't think so!

Fire Island was a let-your-hair-down, kick-off-your-shoes, sexy paradise. And as the summer progressed, everyone got close. Very close! One of our fellow housemates was a guy named Jay, a successful lawyer whom I knew from high school. He was dating a pretty copywriter, another housemate named Kaye, and they were "hot and heavy," which everyone knew about because the bedroom walls were very thin.

Jay was a guy who loved to expand his horizons and his mind

by playing chemist on the weekends. One Saturday night, he was conked out on the couch after experimenting with marijuana and some mysterious blue pills. Kaye tried to wake him, but he was out like a light with a big smile on his face. She was obviously miffed and decided to join the rest of us for a romp on the beach.

At midnight, a bunch of us ran down to the ocean, threw off our clothes, and jumped into the water, laughing and splashing by the light of the full moon. I would call it a "six moon" night because we were all flashing our proud white butts to each other. When we got back to the house an hour later, Jay was still lost to the world. That's when his girlfriend, Kaye, had a bright idea. "Let's take off all of our clothes again, stand directly over Jay with it 'all hanging out,' and wake him up." *Really Kaye? You really want to do that? Nah, we can't do that.*

We did!

We shook Jay, and when he awoke and looked up and saw all of our paraphernalia hanging down, his eyes practically popped out of his head. He said something like, "Wha ... huh?" grunted, and then passed out again. We all laughed hysterically. The next morning, over hot coffee, scrambled eggs, and *The New York Times* Sunday edition, Jay asked, "So, what'd you guys do last night?" Oh, nothing. Nothing at all.

Taking One for the Team

Our agency comradery also extended to extracurricular sports. Every summer, the agency competed in the advertising softball league. I donated my athletic skills, which had been finely honed playing stickball on the streets of The Bronx. My specialty was playing right field (reserved for players who aren't good enough for left field or center field), where I used my blazing speed to run down fly balls (and sometimes even catch them).

One day, a ball was hit long and hard to right center. Like a souped-up hotrod, I peeled out and ran like the wind with my glove outstretched, going faster and faster to make the catch. Unfortunately for me, the bigger, taller center fielder was headed full speed to the same spot. *BAM!* We collided with maximum impact, and I heard an audible crack as I went flying through the air and crash-landed on the ground. As I lay there not moving, I felt a sharp pain in my shoulder. The whole team gathered around me as I looked up in a daze. "Don't move," someone said. (Yeah, like I was gonna jump up and do a victory lap.)

As I waited for the paramedics, all I could think was, "What happened to the ball?" And then came the indignity of indignities. Not only had the center fielder knocked me flat, he had also caught the ball.

It turned out my collarbone was broken in two. For the next six weeks, I wore a figure-eight strap around my shoulders to hold my collarbone in place while it healed. With a little time to think about it, I decided I wasn't cut out for softball.

With the fall coming, I turned my athletic talents to playing pickup football games in Central Park, where I could use my blazing speed to catch long touchdown passes. But when I broke my left hand trying to catch a ninety-mile-per-hour spiral, I got the message. I hung up my cleats and learned to play Mahjong.

Playing the Third Banana

In 1971, Bob and I found ourselves in L.A., staying at the Beverly Hills Hotel. We were in town to shoot the third round in the Diet Rite Cola TV campaign. (Once again, a lot of commercials, a lot of shooting, a lot of fun.)

One sunny afternoon, while we were lounging beside the pool watching the bikinis go by, I got paged over the loudspeaker. "Telephone call for Mr. Cohen. Howie Cohen, telephone call." I immediately knew this was a serious call because it was one of the few times I hadn't paged myself. When I picked up the phone, Charlie Moss was on the other end from New York. Unable to contain his excitement, he blurted out, "*We* just won the Alka Seltzer account!"

Unable to contain mine, I shouted, "Holy shit!" This was great news, not just because it was a sizable piece of business, but because Alka Seltzer had a reputation for doing incredible work—the kind of breakthrough creative commercials that set the standard in our industry. Charlie's message was that the agency was putting Bob and me to work on the Alka Seltzer account. "You're kidding, right? You're giving us the Alka Seltzer account?"

"Well, not exactly," he said. "Stan and I are going to work on it."

"Oh, okay. So you mean we're going to be the backups."

"Well, not exactly," he replied. And he went on to mention that another senior team would be working on it.

"Sooo we're the backups to the backups?"

"There you go!" Charlie said enthusiastically. "But you guys are great, so we want you to be ready, just in case."

Okay, I thought, *we can deal with that.*

In fact, we were flattered and excited. While it was clearly a long shot, we realized we might actually get a chance to create a big, visible creative campaign for one of America's premier advertisers. For the next two months, we held our breath and waited.

We were put on hold as the two lead creative teams worked up original campaigns. Charlie and Stan came up with a novel idea to talk about something that had never been talked about before—the fact that Alka Seltzer opens your pylorus. The campaign was going to tell you what a pylorus was. And since opening your pylorus would provide relief from acid indigestion, Alka Seltzer would own the solution to the problem.

Charlie and Stan did a very entertaining campaign with cute lines like, "It opens your pylorus, Morris." But the big question loomed. Did anyone care about their pylorus?

This campaign went on air with high hopes and a lot of money behind it. Meanwhile, Creative Team Number Two was preparing their backup. Their campaign was designed to be a kind of fail-safe—a tried-and-true campaign focused on intimate interviews with the chairman of Miles Laboratories. The agency shot hours and hours of footage with this kindly elderly gent. Unfortunately, his personality was not as sparkly as Alka Seltzer was, and he said candid, but unhelpful, things like, "Well, you know, a simple glass of milk works just as good as Alka Seltzer." *Oy!*

As the agency was lamenting the failure of this approach, the pylorus campaign was coming up short. After weeks of being on TV, sales didn't budge, and panic was starting to set in. The agency was now two campaigns down, and the heat was on. Mary wanted a big-time creative answer that would fulfill her promise to Alka Seltzer so we could reverse their severe sales decline. That's when we got an urgent call to come to Mary's office.

"Boys," she told us, "we're in trouble. As you've probably heard, both campaigns aren't working. Alka Seltzer is dying, and I promised to save them. Bob, Howie, I'm counting on you. Help me save them!"

Sons of Jewish Mothers

Who could be better to write great Alka Seltzer commercials than Jewish copywriters who grew up knowing, firsthand, that burning feeling in their hearts! As Bob and I approached this assignment, we had lots of inspiration from the great work of the past—much of it created by Jews we knew.

Dick Rich and Stu Greene had done the very clever "No matter what shape your stomach is in ..." TV spot where the camera focused on the stomach areas of people with very different body types: a belly dancer, a construction worker, a prizefighter ... all wiggling and jiggling to a contemporary music track that put a smile on your face. The simple line that brought it all together was, "No matter what shape your stomach is in, when it gets out of shape ... Alka Seltzer." It was brilliant and a big award winner.

Evan Stark and Roy Grace had done the hysterical, "Mama Mia, that's a spicy meatball" spot, centered on the shooting of a TV commercial where the actor has to keep eating spicy meatballs—take after take, meatball after meatball ad nauseum (in more ways than one).

Bob Schulman was a one-of-a-kind writer who crafted what I would call sixty-second screenplays. His funny, animated TV spot featuring a man having an argument with his stomach ("when your stomach disagrees with you") was one of several award-winning

Alka Seltzer commercials he wrote. By the way, the voice of the animated stomach was performed by Gene Wilder, the great comedic actor. He, like Dustin Hoffman, John Travolta, and many other movie stars, got their start in TV commercials.

Marvin Honig was another great Jewish copywriter who did inspired work for Alka Seltzer. Funny and sarcastic, he knew how to tell a human story that everyone could connect with. His classic Alka Seltzer TV spot was about newlyweds and featured a young bride trying very hard to impress her new husband by cooking him "unique" dishes. Reading from an exotic cookbook, she sees her final inspiration: "Poached oysters!" At which point, the husband's stomach turns—and he turns and runs for the Alka Seltzer. The story was funny, and it rang true because it was. It came out of Marvin's real-life experience shortly after marrying his lovely wife, Ellen— simple humor based on simple truths.

All these guys were Jewish. Coincidence? I don't think so. The reality of this Jewish connection all came together for me one snowy New Year's Eve in New York City. Carol and I went out to dinner with Marvin Honig and his wife, Ellen, and three other couples from the advertising business. For this special occasion, we had rented a private room in the back of a lovely restaurant not far from Times Square. The bill had been paid in advance for a five-course meal, beginning with an endless array of exotic appetizers, oversized dinners (mostly spicy), nonstop wine, champagne, and decadent desserts. (Jews never learn.)

Marvin always made me laugh, so I considered myself lucky to be sitting next to him. Somehow, we got onto the subject of our childhoods, and I shared what it was like growing up in The Bronx.

Not surprisingly, we discovered that our upbringings had been simi-
lar. We both had typical Jewish mothers who implored us to, "Eat!
Eat! Eat!"

As our entrees arrived, I dove into my rack of lamb and began to
tell Marvin about my relationship with my mother. She was a wonderful, nurturing woman who adored me and, as a result, I always
wanted to please her. So the more she told me to, "Eat, eat, eat," the
more I ate, ate, ate—even if I couldn't stuff another morsel in my
body. Marvin said he was just the opposite. He rebelled against his
mother. The more she told him to eat, the more he would defy her
and push the food away from the table—even if he was hungry.

At that point, I had finished eating everything on my plate, but
Marvin had barely touched his food. He caught me staring at his
chicken parmesan and said, "Howie, I want that, but I'm not going
to eat it."

"Marvin," I told him, "I don't want that, but I have to have it!"

With that, he slid his plate over to me, and I finished his entire
dinner on top of my own. For me, it was a six Alka Seltzer kind of
night. My Jewish mother would have been very proud.

THREE

Breaking Through

Try It, You'll Like It

Finally, this was our shot. How exciting, and yet, how terrifying. With all of the great award-winning Alka Seltzer advertising that had been done over the years, the creative bar was set high, and the business stakes were even higher. Could we measure up to the excellence of past Alka Seltzer campaigns? Bob developed a small but noticeable tic. I broke out in hives. I felt a Jewish flu coming on. Finally, we settled down, took some Alka Seltzer, and got to work.

The strategy for our advertising campaign was that Alka Seltzer provides fast, effective relief for your upset stomach and head-ache—good promise, but hardly earth-shaking. What made Alka Seltzer stand out as a brand were always the clever and funny creative executions that brought the product to life—and into the hearts and stomachs of America. However, by the time the client came to Wells, Rich, Greene, their previous advertising wasn't working so well anymore. One theory was that the entertainment value had overpowered the product message.

Another was that in a world that was moving quickly to thirty-second TV spots, Alka Seltzer was still doing 60s, basically cutting viewing frequency in half. Bob and I took note of all this as we closed the door to our office and began to work.

The first thing we did was talk about our own Alka Seltzer moments. We've all had them, and Bob and I were no exceptions: those moments when you just eat too much or eat something too spicy or weird. We shared stories with each other of friends and family who had gone overboard and paid the price with a moan or a groan or a sleepless night, listening to their stomachs churn and feeling the burn. While there was pain in those stories, there was also the potential for humor. And since we knew that everybody loves a good story, and everybody enjoys a good laugh, we decided that's how we would connect emotionally with our target customers.

Bob and I liked to work in a kind of improv style. Instead of me sitting on one side of the room writing words and Bob sitting on the other side drawing pictures, we liked to talk and riff and make it up as we went along. I would take on the role of a character, he would embody another character, and we would build from there.

For our first story, we decided it would be about a guy who ate the wrong thing, something he didn't want to eat but did.

"How could that happen?" Bob asked.

"Well, maybe he's in a restaurant he's never been to before, and the waiter recommends a dish he doesn't like, and the food hits him the wrong way."

Okay, interesting place to start. What could this guy be saying?

The first line that came to mind could easily have come out of my childhood. My mother was a dear lady but a terrible cook, and I remember her trying to get me to eat her burnt liver and onions. "Try it, you'll like it." Did she ever really say that? I don't know, but just saying the line sounded funny.

Bob picked up on it and added, "How about if the guy is in a restaurant, and he's telling the story right to the camera? (I'm not sure that had ever been done before, sort of like breaking the fourth wall.) He tells us how this waiter convinced him to eat this really awful thing."

Okay, good. The waiter tells him, 'Try it, you'll like it.'" I continued to pace as I said, "Came to this little place, the waiter says, 'Try it, you'll like it.'" Bob laughs. I can't think of the next line, so I pace and I pace. And while I'm trying to think of a good next line, I fill the silent gaps by repeating, "Try it, you'll like it." And Bob laughs some more. So I keep going. "Try it, you'll like it!" And Bob jumps in with the next line. "So I tried it." And without missing a beat, I said, "Thought I was gonna die!" And we both broke out in hysterical laughter.

The next line was easy. "Took two Alka Seltzer." We ended the spot with our actor repeating the line one more time and putting an exclamation point on the spot: "Alka Seltzer works! Try it, you'll like it."

And there it was, a simple, humorous story with a problem solution, all laid out with Alka Seltzer as the hero. The mini-breakthrough was the repetition of the main line.

It was really just a happy accident. Nobody had ever taken one line of dialogue and repeated it four times in one commercial. This made the line, the story, and the product highly memorable. And since it was the perfect punchline for any situation involving indigestion and lots of other situations, it went viral. In fact, long before there was a thing called the internet, "Try it, you'll like it" was one of the first lines to spread like a virus (in a good way) across the country.

When we had our script all together, Bob drew up a few simple pictures for a storyboard and we presented "Try it, you'll like it" to Charlie and Mary. They liked it. We also shared it with many other senior creative people we respected around the agency to get their feedback. The consensus was, "Cute. Not a breakthrough, but cute."

"Try it, you'll like it" made everyone a comedian at the dinner table

Everyone felt good about it because it was safe. The truth is, if there hadn't been such a desperate need to get something on the air, "Try it, you'll like it" might never have seen the light of day. But there wasn't any time to waste. This would be a good placeholder until someone came up with the big idea and "the real" campaign.

In 1971, the spot went on the air. However, Bob and I didn't have time to sit around and watch. We were heading off to London to shoot the next round of commercials in our Diet Rite Cola campaign. Sitting beside me on the plane was the beautiful young lady I had been dating for almost two years at that point, Carol Trifari. As it turned out, she would play a very important role on this trip—and in my life.

How to Ruin a Perfect Bachelorhood

My story would be totally incomplete without talking about the woman who has been by my side through all the years. Who knows why or how romantic relationships happen? Not me. But I do know exactly how this one began.

There was a newly married couple that worked at Wells, Rich, Greene named Julie and Gary, and they decided to make me their matchmaking project. I think they felt I was just too cute to be single. And since they had found wedded bliss, they wanted me to experience the joys of matrimony too. (Never mind that they got divorced just two years later.)

Of course, I had no intention of helping them fulfill their project. I was perfectly happy pursuing the mindless, hedonistic, semi-decadent life of an advertising bachelor in the Big Apple. I was twenty-seven years old, irresponsible, and free. Wells, Rich, Greene was paying me far too much money, and I was putting it to terrible good use.

When most of my friends were renting apartments for $250 a month, I was the first one to break the $400-a-month barrier. I found myself a gorgeous one-bedroom apartment in a classic 1930s building on 56th Street and First Avenue. My bachelor pad was on the seventeenth floor, with two balconies, a fireplace, and a floor-to-ceiling bookcase built into the wall that actually swung open to reveal a hidden bar. Since the building had been erected during prohibition, the bookcase was a great place to hide illegal bottles of liquor. And since there was still a prohibition against marijuana, it was a fabulous place to hide my weed.

I kept a red 1964 TR4 convertible in the building's garage, right beside my 650cc BSA motorcycle, for the times when I needed to get around town in a hurry. I was having fun, and the last thing I was looking to do was to get tied down in a "meaningful" relationship. To me, partying was meaningful; being creative was meaningful; mindless sex was meaningful.

Then this couple came along and ruined it all. They introduced me to Carol Trifari. It wasn't an actual date. We hadn't met or talked to each other on the phone. It was sort of a semi-fix up. They had told her about me and told me about her. And when I asked what she was like, here's what they said, "Carol is beautiful, she comes from a rich jewelry family, and she's super smart." Okay, now I was intimidated. If I ever met her, I would have to use every ounce of my Bronx charm to impress her.

I could hear the dialogue in my head: "So, Carol, I hear you've skied in Portillo, Chile, and Davos, Switzerland! Great, but did you ever go sledding on a Flexible Flyer down the hills on Mosholu Parkway? I didn't think so.

"And oh, you grew up sailing your own sailboat in Newport? Nice. But did you ever do belly flops in the pool at The Bronx YMCA? That's so sad.

"And Carol, you graduated *magna cum laude* from Smith?

Impressive. But I'll bet you never attended a fraternity vomit party at the University of Miami! Poor girl, you've led such a sheltered life."

Yep, if I ever met the beautiful and smart Carol Trifari from a rich jewelry family, I would have her eating out of the palm of my Jewish hand.

Then one night, I met her. Julie and Gary invited us both to a private screening of an MGM movie at a little theater in Manhattan. When I arrived, there were about fifty people schmoozing outside the theater as we waited to get in to see the movie. That's when I saw a tall, striking brunette (as in "holy shit, she's gorgeous") wearing a red jacket and black miniskirt wrapped around a long, willowy body. (Intimidation!) As she stood there talking to a big, dumb guy, I sauntered over to join the conversation.

"Hi, I'm Howie." She turned away from the brute she was talking to and said, "Oh hi, Julie and Gary have told me so much about you." Carol went on to tell me that she was working at BBDO, one of the largest ad agencies in the country. She said she was working in the research department but was bored and really wanted to be a copywriter. She told me she had put together a portfolio of spec ads and had an appointment the next day with a guy named Nat Russo at Gilbert Advertising. Seeing an opening, I leapt into action. "Nat?" I said. "I know him very well. I used to work at Gilbert, and he was my copy chief. Be sure to mention my name." She looked impressed.

Then she said she had another interview the following week with a guy named Leon Meadow at Doyle Dane Bernbach.

Oh, this is just too easy!

"Leon?" I said. "I know him very well too. DDB was my first job in advertising, and he's the guy who hired me. Be sure to mention my name." I was pretty confident I was making a big impression on Ms. Trifari, and I hadn't even brought up the vomit parties yet.

But as the group began to file into the theater, Carol drifted away from me. And when I sat down, I noticed she was sitting next to the big dumb guy. What! She was choosing him over me? There could only be one of two reasons—she liked geeky guys with overactive pituitary glands or she was yet to discover the wonders of *mensch-y* Jewish men. I made a mental note and turned my attention to the screen.

As the movie started, I quickly realized it was some kind of experimental "art piece" shot entirely on a seamless, white background with young, overacting non-actors. It was the most boring movie I had ever seen (and it was never released, by the way). As I fought to stay awake, I subtly glanced back at Carol, who was sitting three rows behind me. She was staring straight ahead, looking mortified. The big dumb guy was out like a light, snoring his head off and drooling all over her lovely shoulder.

When the movie was mercifully over, we were all invited back to Julie and Gary's apartment, where we were treated to cocktails and canapes. I was sitting on a couch sipping a manly dirty martini when a tray appeared over my shoulder and a woman's voice said, "Canapes, Howieee?" (I later learned she had never said the name "Howie" before, and it was awkward for her, almost like meeting your first Jew.) When I turned and looked up, it was Carol. *Wow, maybe I did make an impression after all!* I said, "Thank you," and grabbed a shrimp. She sat down next to me, and we began a conversation.

She was nice and smart and very pretty, kind of like she had been advertised. There was no getting around it. I was attracted.

Should I make a move? A woman of this caliber can really screw up your whole single life. "Don't do it!" I said to myself. "Don't do it! Don't do it!" I did it. I asked Carol for her telephone number, and, dammit, she gave it to me.

What I didn't know at the time was that this was the beginning of the end of my perfect bachelorhood. I was smitten, and on our second date I invited Carol over to my bachelor pad to treat her to a steak dinner, grilled by me on a Weber kettle on my seventeenth-floor balcony. I also made corn on the cob and prepared a lovely chilled salad.

As we sat down to eat, Carol paused, cleared her throat, and said, "I don't think I've ever seen anything like this."

I proudly puffed out my chest and said, "You mean my antique Victorian dining table?"

"No, your two cats sitting on it while we eat."

"Oh, we're a very close family," I said.

After we had shared a big, beautiful chocolate cake, I pulled out all the stops. I whipped out the *Wall Street Journal* article, "The Rich Kids," and said, tongue in cheek, "Have you read any good *Wall Street Journal* articles lately?" Carol began to read it, and suddenly a look of amazement came over her face. "Oh my god!" she exclaimed. "I know this! When this article came out, my mother sent me a copy, special delivery, with a note that said, 'Why can't you meet a guy like this?'"

For anyone reading this who believes in karma, I guess that was it, no? It was the beginning of the Howie and Carol story, and my whole descent into a meaningful relationship. Over the course of the next few months, we got to know each other very well, and I became close with her vivacious little daughter, Cristina.

In summer, we enjoyed the surf, sand, and freedom of Fire Island together. I was also discovering that relationships can be expensive. Whereas my original half-share in a house with twenty people cost only $200, the three of us now shared an entire house on the bay that was costing me $3,500 for the summer. But, as they say, "What price love?"

Carol and Howie, now an official couple, on the ferry to Fire Island

Fall arrived in New York with a bracing chill, and I loved driving the three of us up to the country in my TR4 with the top down. Carol would rest her head on my shoulder and Cristina, huddled in the back seat, would squeal with glee as my car scattered the leaves of crimson and gold.

The seminal moment in our relationship, however, arrived with winter. Carol, who had skied all over the world in faraway places like Chile and St. Anton, kept telling me, "We have to go skiing together. You'll love it. I know you will."

I had never skied before, and I really didn't like the cold, so I would always change the subject. She kept pressing me, and finally, I relented. We reserved a room at a ski lodge in Sugarbush, Vermont, and began the long trek to get there. In the middle of a raging snowstorm with temperatures dropping to twenty-six below zero (no exaggeration), I cautiously (fearfully!) drove my car, creeping along the winding roads, desperately trying not to skid off the embankment. When we arrived at the hotel in the middle of the night, I schlepped our bags up to the room, feeling grubby, grumpy, and dog-tired.

Determined not to ruin our romantic ski getaway by acting like a whiny Jewish wimp, I jumped into the shower to wash away the day. When I came back into the room, Carol was already in bed, tucked under the covers. The room was lit by a small lamp on her side of the bed that cast a warm amber glow across her face. She is Italian, and in that light, I couldn't help thinking she looked like a Madonna. My heart began to flutter as I slid under the covers and moved closer to her.

I looked into her eyes and said with a smile, "Hi." Carol smiled back and shyly replied, "Hi." I reached across the bed, discreetly shut off the lamp, and for a moment, we lay there in the dark breathing in the stillness. Then, Carol pressed her body tight to mine, put her lips right up to my ear, and whispered, "Don't you just love skiing?"

I Can't Believe I Ate the Whole Thing

They say the best lines come from the heart. "I can't believe I ate the whole thing" came from my stomach. Here's the true story of how that line came to be. Okay, so now "Try it, you'll like it" was breaking on TV in the states, and we were in London to film our new Diet Rite Cola commercials.

It was probably one of our most fun and glamorous shoots. For this production, our director was none other than Milos Forman, long before he would win best director Oscars for *Cuckoo's Nest* and *Amadeus*. And since this version of the campaign involved a big original song, we brought along our favorite composer and musical director, Steve Karmen, otherwise known as the King of Jingles. And, as I mentioned before, I had Carol by my side to share it all.

On the sixth day of production, we were shooting at the world-famous Albert Hall (like I said, it was glamorous), when I got a long distance call from Charlie Moss in New York. "Guys," he said. "Something's going on back here that you should know about."

What can it be? I thought to myself. *Did the agency get the Coca-Cola account? Did someone get pregnant, even though Mary had specifically ordered us not to dip our quills in the company ink?*

"What's going on, Charlie?" I asked.

"Everywhere you go in New York people are saying, 'Try it, you'll like it.' I mean, it's nuts! The spot has only been on the air a couple of weeks, and it's taking off!"

"Wow," I said. "That's great."

And then he hit us with a huge surprise. "Listen, why don't you and Bob start thinking about your next Alka Seltzer spot?"

Our "next" Alka Seltzer spot? Did he mean we were actually going to do another one? Remember, this commercial was supposed to be a stopgap until someone came up with the real campaign—the big idea.

"Oh," he continued, "and Mary asked me to relay a thought to you. She thinks there may be something powerful in repeating a line, like you did with this one. It makes it contagious. People want to use the line in their everyday lives. They make their friends laugh. They become a hero. *Kapeesh*?"

"We get it, Charlie," I said. "Thanks for the call. We'll get going on this."

A week later, the Diet Rite Cola footage was in the can, and it was time to celebrate. On our last night in London, Milos hosted a big wrap party at a classic Italian restaurant. There were about twenty-five of us sitting around a long table, and Carol and Bob were sitting next to me. Milos was holding court. He instructed Senor Giovanni not to give us menus. Instead he ordered for the whole table—an endless array of amazing Italian dishes—antipasti, chicken, veal, fish, steaks, lobsters, salads, and nonstop desserts.

And amidst all the laughter, music, loud conversation, and Milos's cigar smoke, I ate—I mean *I ate!* Remember, I'm a nice Jewish boy from The Bronx. Finishing everything on my plate isn't what I want to do; it's what I *have* to do!

And when I couldn't stuff one more thing in my body, I leaned back in my chair and said, "I can't believe I ate the whole thing." Suddenly, Carol's eyes lit up as she said, "There's your next Alka Seltzer commercial." *BAM!*

That's how the line was born. And soon Bob Pasqualina would help make it into a classic. Upon our return to New York, that was our number one priority. Bob instinctively knew it needed to be simple.

"We need to isolate the line, like we did with 'Try it, you'll like it,'" he said. "Howie, what if it's late at night? Isn't that when you really feel it? We could have him sitting up in bed. He can't sleep, he's eaten so much."

"I like it," I said. "And maybe he's keeping his wife up with his groaning." We started to smile because we were both getting the same picture. I started pacing and Bob started doodling.

"I can't believe I ate the whole thing," I said. "You ate it," popped out of Bob's mouth. Bob was now playing the part of the wife.

I kept going, doing the repetition thing. "I can't believe I ate the whole thing."

"No, I ate it," Bob said sarcastically, and we were starting to laugh.

I said it again. "I can't believe I ate the whole thing."

"Take two Alka Seltzer," Bob said.

And there it was—our next big Alka Seltzer commercial.

"You ate it, Ralph," said the wife with sweet sarcasm

As Bob drew up the storyboard, we decided it would add more personality if we gave the guy a name. We considered Sam (my father's name), Lou, Murray, and even Moishe, but the client was from Elkhart, Indiana, and they didn't know a Moishe from a moose. We finally arrived at our everyman name: "You ate it, Ralph."

When it hit, it hit big. Everyone in the country had been going around saying, "Try it, you'll like it," and now they were also saying, "I can't believe I ate the whole thing."

And suddenly, the phenomenon leapfrogged the advertising world and became mainstream news. In a coup for the agency, *The New York Times* requested an exclusive interview with the guys who were responsible for creating these funny and infectious lines. That would be Bob and me.

A date was set for the interview. But, while we were pretty good at coming up with viral commercials, we knew nothing about how to conduct ourselves in a *New York Times* interview. This led to a near disaster.

Don't Get Caught Telling the Truth

The reporter from *The New York Times* came to our offices in the General Motors building and spent several hours getting up close and personal with Bob and me. He asked seemingly innocent questions like, "Does the client always get the joke?"

"Well, not really," we said. "A lot of it is Jewish humor, and these guys are from Elkhart, Indiana."

Oops! There were two or three comments like that in a four-page article—nothing horrible but not exactly the stuff that contributes to a warm and fuzzy client-agency relationship.

The piece broke on a Sunday in *The New York Times Magazine* section. Friends and family called from everywhere to congratulate us on our newfound fame. Suddenly, we were more than just a hot, creative team and more than just advertising stars. We were celebrities. That Sunday was the biggest, most exciting day of our lives. Then came Monday—and all hell broke loose.

Scary Mary

Bob and I were out of the agency editing our Diet Rite commercials when an urgent call came from Mary's secretary. "Drop everything! Mary wants to see you right away."

"But we're editing," Bob said.

"It doesn't matter what you're doing. Mary wants you here, and I'd advise you to get your asses back to the agency ... now!"

We jumped in a cab and sped uptown to the GM building, took the express elevator up to the twenty-fourth floor, and in less than twelve minutes we were standing outside Mary's office.

When the door swung open, we were surprised to see Mary sitting on a couch directly across from two of the top marketing guys from Alka Seltzer. She had a dire look on her face as she beckoned us into the room. In a hushed tone, she said, "Sit down, boys."

We had no idea what was going on, but we knew it wasn't good. Mary held a copy of *The New York Times* article in her hands. Looking directly into the clients' eyes, Mary began to speak in a passionate tone. "For the past year, we've worked so hard to build a relationship of trust. Working, caring, trying ..." (She went on like this for about five minutes.)

"We've broken our backs for you because we care so much ... about your business ... and about you! Rudy, George," she continued, "I think you know how much you both mean to me, personally." (Not quite since she had met them only once before. Mary always interfaced at the chairman and CEO levels. But they were impressed.)

With that, she contorted her face into an angry mask, pointed her index finger in the direction of Bob and me, and said, "To think that this relationship could be jeopardized by the stupid, irresponsible remarks of these two." Then her voice reached a fever pitch. "I'll hang these guys out the window by their heels if you want me to!"

Bob gulped. Rudy and George looked down at the floor. My foot began to twitch. I honestly thought it was over for the two of us. A few naïve remarks and everything that we'd worked so hard for was about to be flushed down the toilet of advertising history.

At that point, Mary reached across the coffee table and handed the article over to Rudy and George. In an almost inaudible whisper, she said, "All I can say is … I'm sorry."

Rudy and George began to read the article. They glanced at each other once or twice and continued to read. The room was totally silent except for the sound of the acid gurgling up in my throat. If there was one thing I needed more than anything else at that moment, it was Alka Seltzer.

Finally, when they had finished reading, Rudy looked up at Mary and said, "Well, Mary, I don't see anything so bad here."

George added, "We really like working with Howie and Bob and the work has been great."

And Rudy ended with, "So … it's okay, really."

Mary reached across the table and shook their hands. At that point, we all stood up as she escorted them to the door. Mary stood in the doorway and bid them goodbye. And, as they disappeared down the hallway, she slowly turned back to face Bob and me.

In very soft, contrite voices, Bob and I said in unison, "I'm sorry, Mary." And then came the biggest surprise of our careers, as Mary's face lit up with a big smile. She then puckered her lips, blew us a big kiss, gave two claps of her hands, and walked out the door.

Our mouths dropped open. What had just happened suddenly hit us. *Holy shit!* Mary had staged the whole thing. She knew the comments we made in the article could be a threat to keeping the account, and she decided to head them off at the pass. Instead of waiting to go on the defensive, she went on offense. She blew the whole thing so far out of proportion that our comments seemed harmless to the point of being insignificant.

This was one more example of Mary's brilliance and another valuable learning experience for us. I just wish she had let us in on the act. That was scary, Mary.

From an article in *New York Magazine*: "Bob and Howie, The Cliche Kings."

Kisses, Kisses, Hugs

As tough as Mary could be when she needed to be, that's how sweet and generous she was when she wanted to be. Many ad agencies reward their best talent with raises, bonuses, and expense accounts. Mary did all that. But she also showed her generosity in unique and personal ways.

The agency was hot, and lots of new business was pouring in, in part thanks to our hard work and highly visible creative work. This was not lost on Mary, and she began to express her appreciation. It started with little "love notes."

"Howie, Bob, nifty," Mary xoxo

And when our Diet Rite Cola campaign won awards, we got another one.

"Boys, you're my shining stars." Mary xoxoxo
(She must have been really pleased—
we got 50% more x's and o's.)

And when Hush Puppies awarded their account to Wells on the condition that Bob and I work on their business, we got another one. "Bob and Howie, Momma is proud of you!" And this time, she went even further. She verbalized it: "Kisses, kisses, hugs, Mary."

This may seem like a small thing, but this was Mary Wells Lawrence! For us to hear it coming from her was a huge emotional shot in the arm. Mary didn't just love our work, she loved us!

One day, she decided to make it a little more tangible. Mary called us into her office, sat us down, and said, "Boys, I know how hard you've been working ... on Alka Seltzer and Diet Rite and all this new business … so I think you've earned a break." Okay, that sounded good. Maybe take Friday off? Go away for a long weekend?

"Boys, I want you to take a nice, long vacation. You pick the place. Take your wife, your fiancé, your families, and go … anywhere in the world! Take two weeks, all expenses paid. Do it, boys … you deserve it!" Wow, did you ever want to kiss your boss? Fortunately, I held back. But I did give her a hug.

Bob got right on the phone with his wife, Janet, and I couldn't wait to tell Carol. The big question was, "Where do we go?" Carol said, "Machu Picchu! I've always wanted to see the ruins." But Janet said, "I know the most heavenly place on earth. It's called Villa D'Este on Lake Como in Italy."

And she went on to describe a fifteenth-century castle that had been transformed into a Grand Hotel in the nineteenth century and stood beside a pristine lake that shimmered in the night under a canopy of a billion stars. *Nuff said, let's go!*

People ask me what the "golden age of advertising" was like. This is what it was like. There was more money in the business then. And there was more time then. Time to think, time to create ideas, time to perfect them, time to travel, and time to live!

To drive home the point, we didn't even go directly to Lake Como. We had arranged to shoot our next flight of TV spots for Diet Rite Cola in Paris. So we spent a week and a half shooting commercials on the streets of Paris. After which, our significant others joined us for a couple of romantic days in the City of Lights. From there, we headed down to Lake Como to spend two romantic weeks at Villa D'Este.

At that point, Carol and I had been dating for almost two and a half years and had been living together for the past year. Since we both believed in marriage, the fact that we were not married yet raised questions. *Are we committed to each other or not? Am I the one for you and you the one for me?* Put more simply, *Am I going to pop the question or not?* In my heart, I knew the answer. I just had to get up the courage to commit. And so, halfway through our idyllic vacation, I told Carol I needed to talk to her.

On a warm Saturday night, with Lake Como glistening in the light of a full moon, I took Carol by the hand and led her up a long hill past the ancient stone walls of Villa D'Este. "What's all this about?" she asked. "Oh, I just want you to see the view from up there," I muttered.

When we reached the crest of the hill, I stopped, took a deep breath, and just like I had seen it done in Hollywood movies from the thirties and forties, I dropped down on one knee. With my heart in my throat I said, "Carol, I love you. Will you marry me?"

Carol was shocked. She had no idea this was about to happen. How could she? I hadn't known either. Tears welled up in her eyes as she delivered her answer. "Yes," she said. "And it's about time!"

Two months later, in a small but lovely ceremony, we were married in the Blue Room of New York's Plaza Hotel. Since we lived just fifteen blocks away on 74th Street and Fifth Avenue, we walked home, hand in hand, for the first time as husband and wife.

The Dumb Shoe

The last campaign that Bob and I created at Wells before starting our own agency involved a huge creative challenge. The people who make Hush Puppies shoes had come to the agency and said, "If you give us the guys who did 'I can't believe I ate the whole thing,' you can have our account." Their sales were hurting, and they were looking for some kind of breakthrough to make them relevant again.

Their unique pigskin shoes were famous for being soft and comfy to wear. People loved the feeling, but the styles were nothing to write home about. In fact, they were pretty dorky. This was a particularly thorny problem because their older customers were dying off, and Hush Puppies wanted to appeal to a broader, younger, hipper target.

Bob and I felt we couldn't just focus on the softness and comfort of the shoes. We had to find a way to make people look at their shoes in a whole new way. The term "disruptive" didn't exist then, but our instincts told us our campaign needed to be a little "in your face."

One day, as we were batting ideas around, Bob picked up one of the Hush Puppies sitting on his desk and said, "It's a dumb shoe." The expression "dumb shoe" struck a nerve with me. The shoe wasn't fancy or pretty or phony or trendy; it was just a nice dumb shoe. It was a negative statement that maybe we could turn into a positive.

We began to draw comparisons to the irreverent Volkswagen campaign, which I was very familiar with since I had been lucky enough to start my career as a copy trainee on that account. In an America where everyone worshiped "big," Doyle Dane Bernbach was irreverent enough to say, "Think small." And in one of their most famous ads, they even told a quality story by calling one of their cars a "lemon." We felt there were strategic parallels here.

"Hush Puppies aren't a fancy shoe or a phony shoe. They're just a nice dumb shoe." We felt it was a disarming way to communicate with our younger audience. Give the shoe a kind of anti-status status. And if they bought into it, after a while this dumb shoe might be the smartest shoe on the market. And for the folks who had been wearing Hush Puppies for years, the campaign could be oddly validating.

Bob and I got excited and began scripting a campaign using multiple vignettes to create repetition for the line. People from all walks of life (no pun intended) proudly showing off their dumb shoe.

TEENAGE GIRL: Gee, your Hush Puppies are dumb.
TEENAGE BOY: Thank you.
OLD GEEZER: I was wearing Hush Puppies before anybody knew they was dumb.

My favorite vignette featured the Japanese actor Pat Morita before he became famous for *The Karate Kid*. In those days, Japan was the China of today—a place famous for making cheap stuff. In this scene, Pat portrayed a Japanese shoe manufacturer standing next to a Japanese associate who was very big and bald.

PAT MORITA: We can make it cheaper ... but I don't think we can make it dumber!

Then they both cracked up, which made everybody watching it crack up.

Everyone working on this account, including Mary Wells Lawrence, was excited about the campaign, but understandably very nervous. How do you tell a new client you want them to spend $10 million to call their product dumb? You tell them the Mary way.

On presentation day, the president of Hush Puppies and a smart young marketing executive named Bill Doyle came to the agency and were escorted into the big conference room. Mary; our creative director, Charlie Moss; and two of our account people greeted them. Bob and I came in with the storyboards under wraps. Before we showed the client a thing, Mary got up and spoke in a very emotional tone.

"You have come to us and entrusted us with your brand. We take this very seriously. You have told us that you have a 'relevance problem,' and we've confirmed it with our own research. You need a big idea or you wouldn't be here. The campaign we're about to show you is controversial, of that there is no doubt.

But it's a big idea … the right idea … and if you have the courage to run it, it will turn your business around. I guarantee it!" (Wow, an ad campaign that came with a guarantee.) This was Mary at her best. She then gestured our way, "Howie … Bob …"

I did a quick setup about how you can't fool young people. If you want to sell them something, you have to disarm them and speak their language. With that, we revealed the line, "Hush Puppies, the dumb shoe."

I think I saw the president's jaw drop, but he didn't get up and leave. We went through every storyboard and every vignette, and we heard a few chuckles in the right places. Now it was decision time. Mary stood up and said, "This is important. Give yourselves some time to talk. We'll wait outside."

Following Mary's lead, all of us agency folk left the room and hung out in the hall. We held our breath as we waited … five minutes … ten minutes … fifteen minutes. Finally, the door opened, and we rejoined the clients in the conference room.

The president of Hush Puppies said, "Mary, we know how to make shoes, not advertising. This campaign makes us very nervous, but that's probably a good thing. You're the experts, and if you say it's going to work, well … hell … let's go for it."

It was another great moment for the agency, for Mary, and for us. We flew out to L.A. to shoot the campaign, with Stan Dragoti as our director. He took our funny stuff and made it funnier. My favorite spot of all, though, turned out to be an unscripted one. On all of our storyboards, Bob had drawn an end frame that showed their signature droopy-eared dog sitting next to a Hush Puppy shoe. We thought it would take us about fifteen minutes to shoot this shot. It took over an hour. Every time Dragoti called "action," the dog started behaving like a puppy. He would stand up, put the shoe in his mouth, drag it across the frame, bite it, shake it, and wiggle it … and the whole time the camera kept rolling.

At one point, a grip reached in to put the dog in his place, and you could see a big tattoo on his forearm. It was priceless. We had to make a spot out of this. And we did, at no extra charge. The idea was so simple. Our music guy, Steve Karmen, had written a terrific little bouncy ditty that was so fun, we decided to let the footage roll and listen to the music. And we added one more thing. The lyrics ran across the bottom of the screen with a bouncing ball timed to each word of the song. It went like this:

"Hush Puppies aren't such a fancy shoe or a phony shoe
They're just dumb
Soft and cool, you're gonna love 'em
Pigskin too, they're just the dumbest
Hush Puppies aren't such a fancy shoe or a phony shoe
They're just dumb
Put 'em on your feet, give your toes a treat
Hush Puppies are dumb!"

The campaign caught on quickly. The expression "the dumb shoe" had some people scratching their heads, but everyone was talking about it. And that gave the product the buzz it needed. Stores that had rejected Hush Puppies as an outdated brand suddenly saw it as a great new thing. The campaign helped sell the shoes into stores and helped them sell out. Mary had come through on her guarantee.

The Dumb Shoe Campaign was the last hurrah for Pasqualina and me at Wells, Rich, Greene. One month later, we left to open our own ad agency and pursue our dream. We had come into the agency seven years before as young Turks. We left doing the old soft shoe.

◌

FOUR

Taking the Leap

Rumors, Lies, Destiny

Bob and I had a deep desire to open our own ad agency, chart our own course, and *control our own destiny*. So, starting in late '72, we began living two lives.

We needed to fulfill all of our responsibilities to the agency that paid our salaries while doing everything we could to leave it. At the top of our to-do list were rounding up investment capital (we had no accounts lined up) and finding a great third partner—the business guy, the suit, the grown-up who would do all the business-type stuff. The whole process was exciting and harrowing at the same time.

Little by little, rumors of our impending defection began to seep out. One day, Charlie Moss cornered me in the hall and asked me point-blank, "Are you guys leaving? I'm hearing rumors that you're planning to start your own agency."

I was carrying such guilt around with me that I wanted to confess right there on the spot. "Yes, yes, you found out. It's true. I confess, we're leaving." But what I said instead was, "Where do you hear this crap? It's ridiculous!" What else could I say, really?

It went on like that for months until we finally had everything in place. We got investors who gave us the startup money we needed, and we found our third partner, the account guy, in the form of Burt Lowe—a smart, nice guy with a great resume that included being a Harvard grad and having previously worked at Procter & Gamble and Royal Crown Cola. We were confident and ready to go. Now it was time to come clean. *Gulp!* One night, Charlie Moss invited Bob and me to dinner at his lavish apartment in Gracie Square, and we agreed this would be the night to do it.

After a wonderful dinner, Charlie sat us down and began to share a vision for the future—ours. He said that Mary and he had discussed this at length and they had outlined a plan. In the coming year, Bob and I would be promoted to co-creative directors of the entire agency, a role that Charlie currently held. That was fine with him because he would be moving up to become president. The titles and responsibilities would be big, and so would the money. *OMG!* I had never even considered that possibility, but I don't think it would have changed my mind or Bob's at the time. We just wanted to have our own ad agency.

The more Charlie talked, the more silent Bob and I became. We just couldn't bring ourselves to tell him. Then, at about ten thirty, Bob looked at his watch, stood up, and said, "Thanks for a great dinner, Charlie. Sorry, I've got a long drive back to The Island. See you tomorrow." And he left! I mean, *He fucking left the apartment!* There I sat, thinking, *I've got to say something because this cannot go on.*

Finally, after a couple of brandy snifters, I was feeling no pain, and I blurted out, "Charlie, I can't take it anymore … it's true, we're leaving. I'm sorry!"

His mouth dropped open, and he said, "Fuck, I knew it must be true. Everyone's been talking about it." Then he asked, "Is there anything we can do to change your minds?"

"No, Charlie," I told him. "We love Wells, but this is just something we have to do."

"God. Mary isn't going to like this," he said, looking a little frazzled. "And I guess I'm the one who has to tell her."

That made me feel even worse. Mary had done so much for us, especially in the past year, rewarding us with an extravagant trip to Europe, all expenses paid. In a way, I felt like I had cheated on her. Yet this is how the advertising business works. Mary did it when she left her former agency, Jack Tinker & Partners, and Bill Bernbach did it when he left Grey Advertising. Bob and I were just two guys in a long line of upstanding and honest ad people who had to tell sneaky little lies with the honorable goal of starting our own agency.

Three weeks later, Cohen, Pasqualina & Lowe made its debut in Phil Dougherty's ad column in *The New York Times*. We left on good terms, and Charlie and I kept up our relationship. One day, I bumped into him on the street and couldn't resist asking him what Mary's reaction had been when he told her we were leaving. He said that Mary was out of town at the time for some much needed R&R. Charlie left an urgent message for her to call him as soon as possible, and when she called back, she said, "Well, Charlie, this must be bad news or you wouldn't have called me here."

"Mary," Charlie told her, "the rumors are true. Howie and Bob are leaving to start their own agency."

"Is there anything we can do to keep them?" Mary asked.

"No, I already tried," Charlie explained.

Charlie said there was a long pause, and then, in her own inimitable way, Mary did what she does best. She turned the whole thing around. "You know, Charlie, it's the best thing. It never would have worked out anyway. Thanks for calling. Gotta run!" And she hung up.

Mary had built a tough protective shield around herself that was essential for survival in this crazy business. It's something Bob and I would need to learn if we hoped to avoid being advertising roadkill. We were about to start an agency and compete with the most powerful agencies in New York.

The reality of my inexperience was not lost on me either. At that point, I had been in the advertising business for a grand total of seven years. With just one week to go before the opening of our agency, I couldn't help but wonder what it would have been like if I'd stayed a little longer at Doyle Dane Bernbach and Wells, Rich, Greene—watched, listened, and learned a little more maybe? There was still so much I didn't know. Yet Bob and I were about to take a giant leap into the void of ad agency ownership. And there was no parachute.

What the hell was I thinking?

Jewish Men of Steel

Ironically, I wasn't supposed to go into the advertising business to begin with. My real destiny lay in the steel business, like my father and his father before him. I was supposed to be an ironworker.

In 1933, my Grandpa Joe Cohen started a company called

Northeastern Fabricators. It specialized in taking raw steel and fabri-
cating it into essential things for buildings, like stairways and hand-
rails and iron gates. When my father, Sam, took over the business
during the construction boom of the fifties, the company played an
important role in erecting big buildings in New York City, including
the Americana Hotel, the Hilton Hotel, the Lunt-Fontanne Theater,
and many landmarks from Manhattan to Staten Island.

Business was so good that my family finally moved out of our
tiny Bronx apartment with one bedroom, one bathroom, and the
train going by the window. We moved to a brand-new split-level
home in New Rochelle, New York, where I discovered the wonders
of having my own bedroom and enjoyed something completely new
to me—a little thing called "privacy."

Given the success of the family business, it seemed only natu-
ral that I would one day become an ironworker. So during summer
breaks from NYU, that's where you would find me—in a crappy
industrial section of The Bronx, wearing dirty coveralls and steel-
toed boots, painting steel beams, welding, torching, and punching
holes in steel beams.

I was trying to like it; I really was—until a moment of truth
hit me over the head. One day, I arrived at work at the usual eight
o'clock in the morning, pulled on my coveralls, shoved my feet into
my stiff boots, and got to work. I worked and worked my butt off for
what seemed like forever. And when I was sure it was three o'clock
in the afternoon, I looked up at the clock. It was only eleven in the
morning. *Holy shit!* I thought. *How can I possibly do this for the rest
of my life? I'd rather put a rivet in my head.*

On the other hand, I had always liked to write. In particular,
I had a thing for advertising that went back to age thirteen. As a

bar mitzvah gift, three of my aunts—Aunt Minnie, Aunt Esther, and Aunt Ruth—chipped in and bought me a Wollensak reel-to-reel tape recorder. Other than the little red wagon when I was six years old, it was the best gift ever!

I immediately started writing and recording silly commercials with weird characters. I did all the skits with funny accents. Jackie Gleason playing an Italian chef. "You-a gotta try-a Momma Malluci's Mozzarella Cheese-a!" I wrote a lot of silly stuff that made me laugh. Little did I know it was the prelude to a lifelong career of writing silly stuff that would make lots of other people laugh too.

When the time came, I decided to forego the family business as an ironworker and pursue a career as an advertising copywriter. But how do you get started? Fortunately for me, I had a secret weapon— my cousin Dick Tarlow. He's a couple of years older than me and was already doing very well as a copywriter at a big advertising agency. He told me, "The best way to get a job as a copywriter is to show them how you think. You've got to dazzle them with your creativity."

He encouraged me to put together a book of spec ads. "Go through magazines and pick out the ads that suck. Then do your own ads," he said. "Come up with your own big ideas. And don't worry about pretty pictures. Stick figures will do. What matters most is the idea. Agencies want to see if you're creative or not. They want to know if you 'get it.'"

So I began at my mother's kitchen table, writing day after day and late into the night. I would start at 8:00 a.m. and get totally lost in my creative musings, entertaining myself with clever headlines and made-up visuals. And here was my moment of truth. When I was sure it was still only about eleven in the morning, I would look up at the clock and realize it was already dinnertime. *Wow!* Creativity made time fly. I had spent the whole day doing something I loved. That's when I knew I wanted a career in advertising. And so I poured myself into it. I read books on advertising, I sought more help from my cousin Dick, and I wrote ad after ad with hard yellow pencils until I got dents in my finger.

Then I sent out hundreds of resumes to every ad agency in the city. I got a few interviews but no job offers. I pounded the pavement looking for my first advertising job from September of '64 to March of '65. Nothing, until one day when I got a big break. Doyle Dane Bernbach, the most creative ad agency in the business, called me in for an interview.

I met with Leon Meadow, a sweet older man who was the agency's screener for fresh talent. Leon told me they were looking for a copy trainee, and he had literally seen hundreds of resumes. He liked some of my ideas, but he felt others missed the mark. He wasn't sure what to make of my work, but he knew there was something he liked about me. (Never underestimate the power of cute.) He asked me if I was willing to take a creative test.

"Hell yeah," I said. "You better believe it, I'm ready! Um, what's a creative test?"

It turned out to be a creative assignment. My job was to come up with a new campaign for *Webster's New World Dictionary of the American Language*. What made this dictionary unique was that it included all of the American slang and colloquialisms you wouldn't find in a proper English dictionary.

I worked day and night for a week on this problem and finally hit on an idea. I decided to focus on the people who used the words. People! If there's a common thread to most of the work I've done throughout my career, it's been about people and creating a human connection. So here's one of the ads I did for my creative test.

JEWISH GRANDMA IN KITCHEN MAKING CHICKEN SOUP. SHE SMILES AND HOLDS ONE HAND TO THE SIDE OF HER TEMPLE.
HEADLINE:
Fanny Bernstein says things like, "Oy vey!" We put them in our dictionary.

Nice idea, I thought. But was it too *kitch-y*? Too simple? Too Jewish? I showed the idea to my cousin Dick, and he liked it, which was a huge shot in the arm for me. But what would Leon Meadow think? I made an appointment, and on a chilly morning in early March, I showed up in his office. I sat down on the other side of his desk, slid my little portfolio over to him, and watched as he opened it to the first ad.

My heart was in my throat as I tried to read the reaction on his face. Was that a smile? He turned the page to the next ad. Yes, he was smiling. Leon looked up at me and began to nod his head in approval. "This is very good, Howard." He liked the work ... but he wasn't hiring me yet. Then he looked up and stared me in the face. "Howard, you're a very young man, and this is a very challenging business. Are you sure you're up for it?"

That's when I started talking, fast and furious. "Leon, I love writing copy. It's my dream, my passion. I could go into the family business ... the steel business ... it's very successful, and I could make a lot of money ... and they really want me ... and it would be easy for me to just say 'yes' and do it ... but this is what I love ... and if you hire me, I'll make you so proud and—"

"Howard!" Leon said, stopping me in my tracks. "You can stop talking. You've got the job."

I jumped out of my chair. "Thank you, thank you, Leon. You won't be sorry ... this is the happiest day of my life." Leon shook my hand and said, "Welcome to Doyle Dane Bernbach."

And that is how the world lost an ironworker—and gained a copywriter. On Monday, March 15, 1965, I began my advertising career at Doyle Dane Bernbach, the creative agency that was the inspiration for all creative agencies to follow. At the ripe old age of twenty-two, they hired me for a whopping salary of $6,200 a year.

I was really just a kid who looked, acted, and felt young—a little boy with peach fuzz on his face working in the big grown-up world of "the man in the grey flannel suit." I was a study in contradictions—cocksure and clueless, gregarious and shy, a dragon slayer without a sword. So, how did I manage to make it? By soaking up the genius all around me. I was rubbing shoulders with some of the greatest creative writers and art directors of all time: Bill Bernbach, Helmut Krone, Julian Koenig, Ron Rosenfeld, Len Sirowitz, Phyllis Robinson, Bob Levenson, Roy Grace, Bob Gage—to name a few. These legends didn't just create great advertising. They defined it.

I also had the good fortune to be assigned to the amazing creative group that was responsible for the famous Volkswagen advertising campaign. To help me develop "an ear" for the brand, my supervisor handed me a big fat book of ad slicks containing page after page of inspiration. I studied the brand voice (smart, self-deprecating), the style and cadence of the copy (every sentence was a paragraph), the little sentence connectors ("after all," "but then," "of course"), the ironic headlines that complemented but never duplicated the photos,

```
                                   March 12, 1965


        FROM:  Leon Meadow

        TO:    Copy and Art Departments


        Howard Cohen is joining the Copy Department Monday,
        March 15, as a trainee assigned to Bob Levenson's
        group.

        This young, young man brought us in some fine spec-
        ulative ads on the Peace Corps and followed this up
        with some excellent copy on our Dictionary Test
        (this is getting pretty hairy---any of you writers
        got some new copy test ideas or situations?)

        Howard will be in Office #35---the half of it, that
        is, being vacated by Gail Shanik who will now be
        in Office #19 on the 24th Floor.

        I can remember when a person standing in the hall
        and speaking his normal loud voice could be heard
        by every writer in the place.
```

The actual note that introduced me to the agency

and the clever last lines that always left you with a smile and a warm feeling about the brand.

The first ad I ever did that actually made it into print was for the VW Bug convertible. My art director and I noticed how strange the car looked when the top was down. The whole canvas top stuck *wayyyy* out of the car. What a peculiar sight. But that was perfect fodder for a VW ad in a campaign built on humor and self-deprecation. Instead of avoiding this weird physical characteristic, we exploited it with a headline that had a cute double meaning:

WHY IS OUR TOP SO WAY OUT?

It was my first published ad—a full-page in *The New York Times*, no less. Okay, maybe it wasn't the best VW ad ever done, or the cleverest, but (for me) it was a breakthrough. I was officially a published copywriter. And all of a sudden, I was getting backslaps from the other Doyle Dane creative people I admired. "Nice work, kid." "Good ad, kid." They all called me "kid" because I was the youngest copy trainee in the place.

I was so excited that I decided to throw a party at the apartment I shared with a friend on 86th Street and First Avenue. I invited all the creative people I had met, including my two supervisors. Much to my surprise, they all came. As they walked into my apartment, I had just one requirement before they could knock back a drink. They had to autograph a copy of my ad that I had taped to the wall. The signatures scribbled all over my ad that night could have made it a great collector's item. I just wish I hadn't lost it. I'm sure it would be worth a few bucks today—as if I would ever sell it.

FIVE

~

We Have Liftoff

In 1973, we launched Cohen, Pasqualina & Lowe and set ourselves up in a suite at the Beekman Towers on the east side of Manhattan. It was just me, Bob, Burt Lowe, and an amazing woman named Sally who served as our secretary, receptionist, Jill of all trades, and resident mother hen. We were lucky to have her. In addition to being smart (she graduated *magna cum laude* from an Ivy League school) and talented (she was an accomplished violinist), Sally also had the rare distinction of having been a *Playboy* centerfold. *Yowza!* When she spoke, we listened—and looked.

Sally's desk was set up near the front door of our suite to welcome all the people who never seemed to come. Burt Lowe made the bedroom into his private office. And Bob and I shared the living area as our creative workspace.

Thanks to our recent fame, we thought the phone would ring

off the hook with big important clients eager to throw their ad business our way. Instead, all we heard was silence. At one point, I even picked up the phone and shook it to see if it was still connected.

Oh well, we decided, if clients weren't coming to us, we would go to them. That's when we started digging for new business. Shoveling was more like it. This led to a series of silly, misguided, and sometimes humiliating new business pitches that made us wonder what the hell we were doing in the ad agency business at all.

Sausage Heads

We heard on good account that a Boston company famous for making tasty sausages was unhappy with their agency and up for grabs. We made a cold call to their marketing director, and impressed with our credentials, he agreed to grant us a meeting.

When we arrived in Boston, we rented a car and followed a map to what I would call the sausage side of town. There were bleak, old, and ugly warehouse-type buildings everywhere, and in the air was the distinct odor of rancid Italian sausage. Like typical ad *schleppers*, we arrived carrying a big black portfolio with ads and case histories in it, plus a reel of our TV work on 16-millimeter film and a big bulky projector that must have weighed a hundred pounds. Remember, in those days we didn't have the luxury of laptops, DVDs, iPads, or PowerPoint.

The first thing we noticed was that their waiting room was not designed to impress. It was just made to wait. It was a smallish room with a security guard sitting behind an old steel desk. Just then, a young man came out to greet us—a very young man ... as in twenty-three-years-old young. He said, "Hi, I'm Kurt. Mr. Hollis asked me to express his apologies ... he couldn't make it today. But I'd love to see your presentation. I've heard about you guys ... you're cool!"

I felt my heart sink, as the photos of sausages and the smell emanating from the factory were starting to make my stomach turn. Where was the Alka Seltzer when you really needed it?

Then came the indignity of indignities. Kurt noticed our hundred pound projector. "Oh, you've got film," he said. "Well, we don't exactly have a conference room, but I can set you up in the room down the hall."

It turned out that the room down the hall was actually a storage closet with barely enough room to fit the mops, brooms, and detergents, let alone three humbled ad execs and a sausage head named Kurt. I looked over at Pasqualina. He looked over at Lowe. Lowe looked over at me. Anyone with a brain would have cut their losses and gotten the hell out of town. Not us. We had come all the way to Boston to make a presentation, and by god, we were going to make it.

So there, in the darkened closet of a rinky-dink sausage company on the outskirts of Boston, we projected our Clio award-winning commercials on a peeling white wall with the shadow of a broom down the middle of the images. We listened to the clickety-clack sound as our reel spun through the projector, showing off the proud campaigns we had created for Alka Seltzer, Diet Rite Cola, Ralston Purina, Hush Puppies, and more. With each commercial, Kurt laughed and showered us with compliments. "Cool. I love that one. Oh 'Try it, you'll like it' ... my mom says that all the time."

And when our presentation was mercifully over, we shook hands with Kurt, packed up our big black bag and projector, and drove to the airport in a car filled with silence. Then we downed a few martinis and flew home with our Clios between our legs. We vowed, then and there, that this would never happen again. It took just three weeks to break that vow.

Carpet Man

One day, I was searching through *Redbooks*, an ad agency tool used to find new business prospects. I desperately turned the pages, poring through category after category, and then ... *Eureka!* I found it. An unknown account spending $4 million on advertising! A diamond in the rough: Carpet Jungle (which is not its real name).

I called them up and actually got through to their head guy, who I will call Murray. I told him about our triumphs with Alka Seltzer and said we could do the same thing for their wonderful carpet business. Our advertising could put them on the map. To my delight, Murray invited us out to Long Island to make a presentation to him and his partner, Abe.

Bob and I were so excited over this new opportunity that we decided to hire a freelance creative team to work on it too. As it turns out, they came up with the "big idea": a superhero called Carpetman, complete with a flowing red cape and a big "C" on his chest.

The idea was that for all your carpet problems, Carpetman was there to save the day. Bob and I must have been drinking the same Kool-Aid because we got really excited over this stupid campaign. Feeling totally confident, we drove out to Long Island to present this gem to the owners.

Upon arrival, we were greeted by Myrna, their receptionist, who I guessed was Murray's great aunt because they had the same nose. She escorted us out the back door to a carpet warehouse that stretched the length of two football fields, with carpets piled to the rafters as far as the eye could see. And standing there in the middle of this miracle of plush-dom were Murray and Abe with hands outstretched to greet us.

"You're Mr. 'I can't believe I ate the whole thing,'" Murray said.

"Yes, thank you," I said. "I'm Howie Cohen, and this is my partner, Bob Pasqualina."

They shook our hands vigorously, and Abe said, "Brilliant! I say, 'I can't believe I ate the whole thing' all the time. You would too, if you knew my wife's cooking!" as he let out a big laugh.

Since they didn't have any formal conference rooms, Murray and Abe guided us across the cavernous floor to a quiet corner in the back where we unwrapped our storyboards and got to work presenting. Bob held up the first storyboard and took them through the visual part of the story. Now it was time to present the words and music. Filled with adrenaline, I leaped up onto a huge bolt of carpet, so that I was actually looking down at Murray and Abe with a clear view of their bald spots. I acted out every character in the stories, every carpet problem, every moment of their carpet woes.

Now it was time for the big moment when Carpetman came to the rescue. I pretended to fly as I sang the Carpetman theme song. And just as I was about to reach the crescendo, I jumped down off the big carpet roll, landed right in front of Murray and Abe, and belted out the final lyric: "He's Carpetmaaaaaan!" Then I stopped and looked into their faces, waiting for a reaction. That's when Abe turned to Murray and said, "Murray, is this *schlock?*"

The road back to Manhattan was long and uncarpeted.

Memos from the Bedroom

At Cohen, Pasqualina & Lowe, our problems were deeper than just
making stupid new business pitches. We were beginning to question
the wisdom of partnering with Burt Lowe. Burt's business style was
very corporate, regimented, and slow-moving. This can be deadly in
the fast-paced creative advertising business. We began to see signs
of bureaucracy early on.

One morning, I arrived at work at our suite at the Beekman
Towers, said "hi" to Bob and Sally, poured myself a cup of coffee, and plunked myself down on the couch. As I checked the mail
sitting on the coffee table that served as our desk, I noticed a very
formal document with lots of writing on it and wasn't sure what the
hell it was. I showed it to Bob, and he didn't have a clue either. Then
I saw the salutation at the top: "From BNL to HC and BP."

"Bob, who's BNL?" I asked.

"I think it's Burt," he responded.

"You've got to be kidding me. Burt is sending us memos from
the bedroom?"

I think that was the first big tipoff that something wasn't right.
Burt's style was much more suited for a big corporation like Procter
& Gamble than a small startup ad agency like us. We liked Burt and
dreaded having to confront him about this situation. Fortunately (or
unfortunately because we wasted valuable time), we were able to
put off dealing with this.

Suddenly, we got lucky with a series of small new business
wins. And where did this new business come from? The best source
of all—high school buddies!

My father always used to tell me, "Howie, it's not what you
know. It's who you know." I always fought him on that because I felt

it diminished people's talents—namely mine. In this case, however, my father's words were right. Out of the blue, an old friend of mine named Chuck Weiss, who I knew from New Rochelle High School, came through. He was a rising star in the marketing department at Alberto Culver in Chicago.

I had called to ask him if anything was going on, and he said the words that were music to my ears. "Howie, your timing couldn't be more perfect." He went on to tell me that his boss, Leonard Lavin, the infamous owner of the company, known for his package goods brilliance and for being an old prick, had been talking about going outside their normal agency circles (and making his current agency sweat).

BOOM! They assigned us a product called Calm Deodorant with a $2 million TV budget. Within a month, we were shooting an original TV campaign with the catchy theme, "I'm Calm under the arm." The idea was simple and cute. No matter what stress you're going through in your daily life, it was no sweat because you can be "Calm under the arm."

Within a few weeks of that, another old friend from New Rochelle High School named Dan Fellman (who went on to become head of film distribution at Warner Brothers, where he ruled the roost for many years) called to say that he was part of a company that owned Carrols, a fast-food chain. They needed an agency for their $4 million account.

Dan put us in touch, and lo and behold, we won the business. We got off to a great start with Carrols by coming up with a cool, creative idea for their new fried chicken product. The chicken was made country style, crispy on the outside and juicy on the inside. Our idea was to give the chicken a catchy name and then use the name to create a memorable campaign. The moniker we came up with was Carrols Crunchy Country Chicken and the alliteration became the hook for our TV theme: "Carrols Crunchy Country Chicken. You can't say it, but you'll love it!" We had a lot of fun challenging people to say the name three times fast. The flubs and gaffes and giggles were infectious, and the chicken took off (no pun intended).

These were nice business wins. But by our second year in business, reality was setting in. We had won accounts, done good work, kept the clients happy for a while, and then lost them, one after another. The reason was that we were babes in the woods who didn't know how to run an agency. Because we didn't staff up properly for the new accounts that were coming in, we did a poor job of servicing them. Bob and I didn't know how to do it, and the grownup thinking we expected from our business partner never materialized. We were in trouble, and it was clearly time for a change.

It was sad and uncomfortable, but we were forced to confront Burt and eventually come up with a plan to part ways. We would find a new third partner, and Burt would gracefully phase out of the agency. But who would be his replacement? We needed a strong business guy, and this time we resolved that it would be someone who had a big-time ad agency background. One day he walked in the door, all six foot four inches of him, looking like a Hollywood leading man and bearing a strong resemblance to the actor Lee Marvin.

His name was Tim Timberman, and he was a former alum of Colgate Palmolive. Tim had also been chairman of a big ad agency, Kenyon & Eckhardt. But if his physical presence was big, his personality was even bigger. Tim was a showman who did things on a grand scale. Instead of wearing suits, he dressed casually in jeans, corduroy sports jackets, and cowboy boots that made his big frame even more imposing. Tim had lots of ideas on everything from how to get new business to how to position brands to how to get publicity for our fledgling agency.

Bob and I decided that he was our guy. Eventually, we changed the name of our agency to Cohen, Pasqualina & Timberman. From day one, Tim injected a new sense of life and hope into the agency. We needed it—desperately. By the time Tim arrived, we were down to our last $40,000 in the bank. We needed to make something happen, fast.

Desperation and Detroit

Sometimes, when the economy is bad, it can open doors that would normally be slammed shut. In 1974, the country was in the midst of a huge recession, and car sales had come to a screeching halt. When companies are desperate, oftentimes they will do drastic things they would never consider doing when times are good—like hire us, maybe? We saw this as an opportunity and sent telegrams to three major car companies, telling them that the guys who did the famous Alka Seltzer advertising had a big idea for them.

Two of the car companies declined, but one bit. A young and enthusiastic advertising director named Ham Schirmer at Chrysler Corporation was intrigued. He called me and said that he was going to be in New York the following week and asked if I was available for lunch. My heart leaped. This was it, I was sure.

The following Wednesday, he arrived in the Big Apple, and I took him to a fancy alcohol-fueled lunch at Lutece, one of New York's finest and most expensive restaurants, which I paid for with our agency's shrinking bank account. We immediately hit it off.

Ham talked nonstop about how much he loved our commercials, our creativity, and our humor, and how exciting it would be to work together. *Yes, yes,* I thought. *Let's do it. This could be the beginning of a beautiful relationship!* I asked the waiter to bring another round of drinks.

We talked some more and drank some more, and Ham was effusive in his appreciation of our work and our talent. Then his face turned glum, and he got very serious. "Howie, you guys are exactly what Chrysler needs to climb out of this shithole we've gotten ourselves into. But (and here was the big but!) it's never going to happen." Ugh, my heart fell into my shoe. "What do you mean?" I asked. "Why not?"

He went on to tell me all about Detroit inbreeding: of the WASPy insiders who played golf and drank and went to church together (not necessarily at the same time), and how Chrysler Corporation had long-standing relationships with three huge agencies (whose CEOs they'd gone to school with and pledged the same fraternities with), and how their kids were now pledging these same fraternities. It was starting to sound a little like Appalachia. Did they also marry their cousins?

"You're getting the picture, right, Howie? I'm sorry. This is what I hate about my fucking job, but hooking up with you guys just ain't gonna happen." Then he shook my hand and turned to leave. "But I gotta tell ya, you're a great guy and I never knew Jews could drink like that." He laughed and left.

I walked out of that upscale restaurant feeling like a downscale loser and $220 poorer to boot. Our agency was going down the tubes, and I was beginning to think all hope was lost. One week later, however, I got the surprise phone call of my career.

"Howie, it's Hammy. You won't believe this, but my boss, Pete Dow, was just at a marketing conference where they talked about the benefit of hiring outside creative agencies to bring a fresh perspective to your advertising. So I told Pete, 'Funny you should say that. I just met this great guy in New York, Howie Cohen, and he and his partner did the famous Alka Seltzer stuff and ...'" he went on like that, all leading to the words my heart was aching to hear. "So, Howie, is there any chance you guys can come to Detroit for an assignment?"

And that's how we got into Chrysler Corporation, as their fourth agency assigned to corporate projects. And when Chrysler needed the big idea to get cars moving again, we came up with something that would actually change the way car companies did business.

Super Baby and the Super Bowl

In our sixth month of being an official Chrysler agency, the entire car business was in trouble, and Chrysler was no exception. Cars were sitting on dealer lots gathering dust and interest payments. The call went out to all four of Chrysler's ad agencies—including us—to come up with a big idea that would get cars moving again. They needed a very big idea, and we were determined it would be ours. But what could it be?

Bob and Tim and I holed up in our offices for days, banging ideas around. Clearly, something dramatic was called for, and it had to go beyond just being clever and cute. We needed something powerful to appeal to the car buyer's pocketbook. So we started by brainstorming different kinds of offers. "Buy a Plymouth, get a second one free!" (Put down the vodka, boys.) "Buy a Dodge truck, and make no payments for four years!" (Fastest route to Chapter 11.) "Buy a Chrysler, and we'll throw in a house!" (We were getting punchy.)

Then we hit on something really interesting. The guys at Chrysler had mentioned the idea of a "cash back" deal. And here's what was cool about it: the cash would be paid to the buyer directly from the factory, not the dealer. This was particularly meaningful because car buyers never knew if they were getting a good deal. This way, they could make their best deal at the dealer level and then get an additional $500 cash back from the factory. We took this simple concept and ran with it.

Our idea was to create an entire cash back or, as we called it, "rebate program," on all Chrysler vehicles that would run for several months. To give it a positive spin, and avoid sounding like the company was in trouble, we gave it the festive theme that made it sound like a party: "Chrysler Corporation's Car Clearance Carnival."

This was "the big idea"; we were sure of it. And we wanted to make sure none of the other three agencies beat us to the punch. We wrote scripts, quickly booked a meeting with Chrysler, and within two days we were racing to the airport to catch our plane to Detroit. The only problem: it was a cold, stormy December, and the wicked forces of nature were conspiring to ruin our grand plan.

"We're sorry, sir," the counter person at the airport said. "There's a snowstorm in Detroit, and all flights are grounded."

"But we have to get to Detroit. It's important," I said.

"Sorry, sir. We can't fly in a snowstorm."

In a moment of humor that probably made me sound like an a-hole, I said, "You don't understand. We have to save the American economy!"

Of course, the comment was way over the top. But it wasn't so farfetched. The success of the American economy was so connected to the automobile industry that if this rebate campaign could get cars moving again, the overall economy could start moving again too.

After several hours and just as many martinis, the snow stopped, the skies opened up, and the plane finally took off. We arrived late that night, got a few hours of sleep, and early the next morning, we found ourselves facing twelve members of Chrysler's executive committee.

In a hushed and tense room, we presented our idea to guys who were pulling down six- and seven-figure incomes. The scope of the campaign was enormous, involving multiple deals across all of their car lines, delivered in waves of TV commercials over the course of several months: rebates on Chryslers, Plymouths, and Dodges of $300, $400, and $500, with the big launch set for the Super Bowl, which Chrysler had already bought for some other campaign.

They sat raptured as we brazenly told them that the Super Bowl was perfect for our launch—scrap everything else (their other agencies loved that) and introduce the rebate campaign to America on the day of the big game. "This will turn your business around," we told them. Go big or go home!

When we stopped talking, everyone looked around the room at everyone else, and no one seemed eager to say a word. Then, one by one, they began to drive spikes into the heart of our idea. Their head of finance said, "This will cost so much money, it'll kill us." An ad exec chimed in, "It'll cheapen our image." An operations guy piped up, "No way. It's December already. We'll never pull it off."

And then, in a wonderful Capra-esque moment, the biggest of the biggies in the room got up out of his chair, looked every man in the eye, and said, "Gentlemen, you've told me all the reasons why we can't do this. Now tell me how we're going to get it done!"

Holy crap, just when you think this kind of thing only happens in the movies, a Detroit-born Gary Cooper restores your faith in the American businessman. Suddenly, the debate was over, and everyone became mobilized. On December 9, 1974, we got the green light to shoot a package of twenty TV spots, with the first three to be launched on the day of the 1975 Super Bowl, just four weeks and four days away. It was exciting, it was thrilling—and it was fucking terrifying. How were we going to pull this off?

Your Check is in the Quail

Fortunately, we knew who to call. Barney Melsky was a friend, and one of the best producers in town. We began by having lengthy logistical meetings with Barney and his talented director partner, Neil Tardio.

The shoot required that endless fleets of brand-new vehicles— Chryslers, Plymouths, Dodges, and Dodge trucks—be shuttled in and out of Los Angeles. We also needed to cast scores of actors, both principals and extras, to play the roles of enthusiastic car buyers as the whole carnival of rebates swirled around our ringmaster, Joe Garagiola.

By the way, we were really lucky to have Joe. He had been under contract to Chrysler Corporation, and when we sold them our campaign, they suggested that we use him as our carnival barker. We agreed but were very unsure. After all, he was just an ex-baseball player and TV broadcaster. Could he pull off an extravaganza of this magnitude? As it turned out, any concerns we had were totally off base, and we knew it on the very first day of production.

Joe walked up to Pasqualina and me and said, "Guys, I know what a big deal this is, and I just want you to know I'm going to give it my all. Trust me, I've got your backs."

What a great guy and a great trooper. The pressures of the coming weeks would prove to test his patience and sanity, but he never got pissed off or blew his bald top. He did a fabulous job with energy and enthusiasm, and it made all the difference. Joe Garagiola truly had our backs.

To get the whole thing off the ground, Barney rented one of the largest sound stages in the world, where they had shot *Gone with the Wind,* and he booked it for over a month.

To pull off a production of this magnitude takes a steady stream of money. This came in the form of checks delivered almost weekly from Chrysler Corporation—$110,000 here, $125,000 there.

Barney was in the uncomfortable position of continually having to ask us for the money so he could pay the crew, the extras, the facility, the rentals—the whole shebang. Sometimes, the checks didn't arrive on time, and Barney would get a little tense. To take the edge off, my partners and I began to play a little game of "surprise" on him.

It began one Friday night after the second hectic week of shooting. We asked Barney to join us for a late dinner at a fancy Beverly Hills restaurant. We were all drinking and laughing, but we could see that Barney was nervous. The check from Chrysler hadn't come yet, and he needed the money to keep the lights on.

After polishing off our second bottle of fine cabernet, the waiter came out wheeling a large cart with a silver-domed platter on it. I said, "Oh, the quail has arrived. Have you ever tried quail, Barney?"

"No, I'm not partial to quail. Where I grew up in Brooklyn, we ate plain, boiled chicken," he answered.

That's when all three of us chimed in, "Barney, you've gotta try the quail!"

"Okay, okay. I'll try the fucking quail," he said.

Then came the surprise. When the waiter lifted the dome, there was no quail there—just a big fat check from Chrysler Corporation for $115,000. Barney's eyes practically popped out of his head. We all laughed, and that was the first of many little surprises over the course of our long shoot.

After a while, Barney always knew something was coming, he just never knew when, where, or how. One of my favorites was the "fire in the wastebasket" gag that had Barney screaming, "Fire! fire!" A stagehand ran over and extinguished it. As Barney was breathing a sigh of relief, Bob reached into the bottom of the basket and handed Barney a check for $100,000.

The grand finale came on the last night of shooting, after four pressure-filled weeks. Bob and Tim and I were standing with Barney on a cold, dimly lit stage as the lights and energy faded from our carnival. All of the actors and extras and most of the crew had already gone home, and a janitor was sweeping up around us. Another big check was due, and Barney was hip that it was coming.

Suddenly, the janitor, who was sweeping up a pile of used coffee cups, soda cans, and cigarette butts, reached down and pulled an envelope with Barney's name on it out of the pile.

"Is there a Mr. Melsky here?" he asked.

Barney gave a knowing smile and said, "That's me."

The janitor handed him the envelope. Barney ripped it open with gusto and pulled out a dirty, coffee-stained piece of paper that said, "Sucker!" And when he turned around, Tim was holding his final check for $165,000.

Barney had been punk'd again. But no matter how pressured the situation, Barney always enjoyed our check jokes ... almost as much as he enjoyed cashing the checks.

For Pasqualina and me, the shoot was a marathon of trips from New York to Los Angeles, then on to Detroit to update Chrysler's upper ranks, then back out to L.A. to shoot and edit, then heading back to New York to take care of business.

Given the magnitude of this production, you might think it was the biggest thing in my life. Actually, it was the second biggest. Carol was eight months pregnant with our first child. And, as fate would have it, the launch of our baby was scheduled for the exact same day as the launch of the campaign.

With every trip across the country, and after every late night shoot, a little voice in my head was saying, "What if she's born early? Could this be the night? Will I miss the most important event of my life?" As it turned out, the advertising gods were smiling down on us. With impeccable timing, Carol gave birth to our beautiful daughter Johanna on January 10, just two days before the Super Bowl, and we were actually still in the maternity ward on the day of the big game.

As I sat next to Carol's hospital bed, watching her cradle our baby in her arms, I was filled with emotion. The last four weeks had been a whirlwind of shooting, writing, editing, flying, and fretting. Now the big day was finally here. Suddenly, there it was on the hospital room TV. Our sixty-second kickoff commercial was debuting on the Super Bowl. Joe Garagiola was standing in the middle of a sea of balloons and cars and car buyers with a big brass band marching as he belted out the words I had written to an audience of a hundred million people, heralding the very first car rebates.

In a moment of elation, I lifted my baby girl up to the TV screen and said, "Look, Johanna, that's Daddy's commercial!" She cried.

But there were smiles at Chrysler headquarters in Detroit because our campaign was a big success. From day one, Chrysler experienced a huge spike in sales, and their share of the market grew dramatically against their two biggest rivals, GM and Ford, who had sworn they would never lower themselves to do rebates. Within one week, both companies were on-air with their own makeshift rebate ads. The huge boost in car sales for all three American car companies created a lift in the overall American economy.

It was an amazing time when impossible dreams came true. Chrysler was on the road to recovery, and our agency was on the way to victory. Carol and I had a beautiful, bouncing, blue-eyed baby girl we named Johanna Trifari Cohen. And most important of all, in Super Bowl IX, the Steelers beat the crap out of the Vikings, 16–6.

Thanks to the publicity that followed our Chrysler extravaganza, great things began to happen. We moved out of our little suite at the Beekman and got fancy new office space in a beautiful building on Third Avenue, just above P.J. Clark's, the landmark restaurant and pub.

And we started adding valuable new help. Tom Kostro, a talented young kid fresh out of art school who had made an award-winning student film, joined us. Tom could do it all: draw storyboards suitable for framing, create visual presentations, come up with ads, and make our ads better. He filled the place with youthful energy.

Shortly thereafter, we hired a sweet little mild-mannered lady named Peggy as our bookkeeper. She could do anything with numbers, especially when she was moving money from our company into her own personal account.

Sometimes, treachery can come from the most unlikely places and the most innocent-looking people. Who knew? Not me or Bob—we trusted Peggy like she was family. In fact, in her second year at the agency, when she gave birth to her first child, Carol gave her our daughter's crib as a gift. Yep, she was family alright. And nobody can screw you like family.

As we continued to grow, we added a couple of smart account people and a really talented creative team in Frank DiGiacomo (a terrific writer who happened to be Italian) and Stan Block (a great art director who was Jewish). We were clearly bucking the trend.

Over the next couple of years, we picked up some nice accounts from Elizabeth Arden to the New York City Opera and Ballet. I loved the creative challenges, and I loved the diversity. In my career, I've worked on just about everything from cars to coffee, films to fashion, fast food to antacids. Yet, the greatest satisfaction has always come from using our talents to do some good in the world.

The Wisdom of Elie Wiesel

One day, we were approached by a little known, but very worthwhile, cause called Soviet Jewry. Some of you may remember the funny bit that Gilda Radner, a.k.a. Emily Litella, used to do on *Saturday Night Live*. She said in her funny, whiny New York accent, "What is the problem with Soviet jewelry? I mean, if I want to buy jewelry, why would I go all the way to the Soviet Union ... isn't there enough good jewelry right here?"

She continued this humorous rant until someone off camera finally corrected her and said, "Uh, it's Soviet Jewry. Not jewelry ... Jewry!"

"Oh!" She paused and then delivered her famous punchline, "Never miiind!"

It was very funny, but the problems that the Jews were suffering in the Soviet Union were anything but. The Soviet authorities were systematically persecuting Jewish people, who were being denied the ability to leave the country. Their synagogues were being closed down, and there were reports that hundreds of Jews had been imprisoned or executed.

That's what led to the creation of the organization called Soviet Jewry, headed up by the great humanitarian and Holocaust survivor Elie Wiesel. And when they needed an ad agency, Cohen, Pasqualina & Timberman jumped at the chance to help, donating our talents to help raise awareness of the problem and get as many Jews out of the Soviet Union as possible.

Then, one day, tragedy struck. In Israel, Palestinian terrorists sneaked into an Israeli grammar school and murdered twenty-three children in cold blood. We got an emergency call from Elie Wiesel.

"We have to do something quickly. We need to speak out about this unspeakable tragedy. I want to do a full-page ad in *The New York Times* ... tomorrow!"

We immediately met with him to discuss a strategy for the ad. He was a small man with a big presence. You could feel his passion, his intelligence, and his incredible humanity. As he spoke, my eyes wandered to the small tattoo with blue numbers on his arm—a chilling reminder of the concentration camp he had survived.

As he spoke, he stressed the need to get the facts right and, just as importantly, to get the tone right. This was as important an ad as we would do in our entire careers. And we needed to do it in one day.

The news of this contemptible act had already spread through the media, and Americans were outraged. We needed to provide the unique perspective of the Jewish community, as represented by Soviet Jewry. Bob and I huddled, and before the afternoon was out, we had our ad. It was going to be a simple all-type ad with a huge headline that took up 70% of the page. Bob did up a comp and hand-wrote the headline using his own chicken scrawls. It read:

> While you were sleeping,
> 23 innocent Israeli
> children were murdered
> in their classrooms
> in cold blood.
>
> Wake up!

This huge headline was followed by two short lines of copy, imploring people to not look the other way, to speak out and get involved, and to help end the persecution and the savagery.

We rushed over to Elie Wiesel's apartment on the west side of Manhattan to present the rough comp of the ad. He loved it and only had one issue with my copy. He asked why in the headline I referred to the victims as Israelis and not Jews. I said, "Given that it happened in Israel, it might be more relevant." He looked at me with his dark, soulful eyes and said, "Howard, what is more relevant than being a Jew?" I changed the copy on the spot.

We rushed back to the agency to do a mechanical so we could get it to the newspaper in time. Bob picked a strong bold typeface to drive home the power and emotion of the message, and we raced back to Eli's apartment to show him the finished mechanical.

"What's this?" he said. "This isn't what we agreed on!" What? We were shocked because it was exactly what we had shown him that morning. "No," he said. "Why did you change the type? It was perfect the way it was." He had fallen in love with Bob's chicken scrawls and didn't understand that we wanted to run a "professional-looking" ad. "No," he said. "What you showed me was perfect. Children have died! And that handwriting felt exactly the way a child would write it."

Damn, he was right! We had "out-slicked" ourselves. Elie Wiesel was able to see the true power of the ad with the innocence of a child. We changed the ad back, and it ran the next day with Bob's childlike handwriting. It totally stood out among all the other ads in *The New York Times*, not just for its shocking subject matter but for its unique look. And Soviet Jewry began to emerge as an important leader in raising awareness of the persecution and injustices leveled against Jews around the world.

There will always be detractors of the ad business. To many people, we promote mindless materialism and encourage bad values. Some of that is true. There's a lot of bad advertising with bad intentions out there. That's why most of the way we communicate today has moved out of advertising and into social media, where people can share with their friends and be believed because they don't have an agenda. But there will always be a place for advertising. And I believe it's still one of the best methods we have in a free society to inform, educate, entertain, and help people make better choices about the stuff they buy.

And once in a while, as with Soviet Jewry, we create something that fights injustice and helps make the world a better place.

Good Car, Bad Jew

Now our agency was picking up more clients, and our ads were getting noticed in a variety of categories. We were on a roll, and for the first time, Bob, Tim, and I started making some good money. I felt it was time to reward myself with something special, and I knew exactly what I wanted.

It was my dream car—the one I'd promised myself I would buy one day when I finally "made it." It wasn't a new car that I wanted. It was a couple of years old and very classic in its lines and elegant in its shape. (Yes, an older car. Was Pasqualina having a positive effect on my taste?) I started my search for it in earnest, eagerly looking for anyone who had one for sale. One Sunday, there it was in the used car section of the Sunday edition of *The New York Times*. Carol and I hopped in a cab and raced uptown, where we met a man named Muhammad.

He was about fifty years old and had a thick middle-eastern accent. He took us down to the garage, and as we rounded a corner, the car revealed itself to me and literally took my breath away. It was a 1972 Mercedes Benz 300 SEL 4.5, chocolate brown with a rich honey leather interior. It was top of the line, and I immediately fell in love from the bottom of my heart. We made a deal right on the spot, and I drove the car home that night.

I affectionately called it The Brown Bomber. And whenever anyone got in the car, I used the same clever (some would say obnoxious) line, "Please pardon the leather smell."

Everywhere I drove that car, it got "oohs and ahhs," and everyone seemed to be happy for me—except one person—Tommy, the Orthodox Jewish kid whom Julio and I had treated to his first lobster dinner.

Tommy had always looked up to me, almost with hero worship, but now he was sulky and seemed very pissed off. Finally, I confronted him and asked what the hell was going on. That's when he unloaded on me.

"Howie, I can't believe you! You, a Jew, bought a German car … from an Arab, no less! It's a *shonda*!"

"Yes," I responded, "but I'm very hard on it."

He didn't laugh. I'm sure he went to temple that night to pray for me.

The Brown Bomber on a trip to Napa with a very pregnant Carol

I drove my beloved Mercedes for fourteen years, shipping it out to Los Angeles on the furniture truck to keep my German baby feeling safe and loved. I finally wound up selling it when it got old and cranky and I realized that my German auto mechanic, Gunther, was making more money fixing my car than I was making in advertising. Sometimes in life, you have to know when to say *"Auf Wiedersehen."*

No Daddies in Business

For about half of the five years that Cohen, Pasqualina & Timberman was in business, we were a success with a lot to be proud of—a Super Bowl campaign, new account wins, profitability, and a bunch of creative awards. So how did we screw it up so badly in the end?

By not being fully engaged in the business of our own business. The truth is that Bob and I relied mostly on the expertise of our business partner for all the grownup stuff, preferring instead to focus on what we loved best—coming up with big-time creative campaigns. We naively thought that someone else would take care of all that pesky business stuff—a grownup who would take care of us. When all was said and done, we just wanted a daddy. We found out too late that daddies don't exist in business. While Tim was super smart, we learned that he didn't want to run the business side either. He wanted to be like us.

Unlike any management person I'd ever seen, he wore ostrich cowboy boots and big fancy belts with rhinestones. And instead of being at the agency managing our business relationships and our money, he was flying out to L.A. to be with us on our TV shoots. He would arrive in stretch limousines looking like Mr. Hollywood and take groups of people out for big fancy dinners. Meanwhile, back in New York, we were running out of money. And, as I mentioned before, our sweet little bookkeeper, Peggy, was stealing from us to the tune of thousands of dollars!

If it sounds like I'm pointing the finger at our business partners, I am. But Bob and I have to take our share of the blame. We were foolish and naïve. After five years, our agency triumph had become an advertising tragedy. By 1978, we were on our last legs.

That's when Charlie Moss called. That's when we met with Mary. And that's when we agreed to come home to Wells. Only now, it would be a fresh new start in the glitz and glamour of L.A.

A whole new level of excitement was about to start, and along with it, a whole new level of troubles. California, here we come.

SIX

La La Land

See You at the Polo Lounge

The Beverly Hills Hotel holds a special place in my heart. It was the hotel where Carol and I stayed in the early days of our courtship. In 1971, she accompanied me to L.A. for a TV commercial shoot. That trip was especially memorable because at 6:01 a.m., while we were fast asleep, the city was rocked by a magnitude 6.6 earthquake.

It was the first time Carol and I felt the earth quiver and shake beneath our bodies (no sex jokes, please), and it rattled us to our cores. But after the rumbling stopped, we rewarded our courage by having room service deliver us eggs Benedict in bed.

For the next seven years before we moved our family out west, every time I came to L.A. on business I returned to the Beverly Hills Hotel. Sven was the lifeguard at the pool; Nino was the maître d' in the Polo Lounge, who was succeeded by Dino (or was it the other way around?); and Alex Olmedo was the tennis pro at the hotel's courts who helped improve my backhand. Poolside was a place for posturing, and you could always expect to hear someone "self-page" themselves to emphasize their importance. It was kind of an obnoxious thing to do, and I can't imagine any grownup actually doing it—unless that grownup was me.

At a prearranged time, following my instructions, a friend would page me at the pool. "Paging Mr. Cohen. Paging Mr. Howie Cohen. Telephone call." As they brought me the phone, people would turn and stare, and I would shrug, as if to say, "Ugh, can't they do anything without me?" I'm sure everyone thought I was a very important person—or maybe just a *schmuck*—but it was fun.

In June 1978, when Mary Wells Lawrence hired Pasqualina and me to be co-creative directors of the fast-growing West Coast office, they put us up at the Beverly Hills Hotel for over a month until we could find a house to buy. Carol was still back in New York with our cat and our kids, Cristina and little Johanna, getting organized for the big move. She had lobbied hard to get me to leave New York, and now she was beginning to worry that I might hate it and never forgive her for ruining my life.

On the first morning, the phone rang in my room, and Carol spoke in a hushed tentative tone. She was obviously nervous. "Howie? Are you okay? Is it alright?"

"Well, let me see," I said. "I just took a nice long run through the streets of Beverly Hills, I ordered up a brie omelet with a side of bacon and coffee from room service, and the real estate agent is sending a limo to pick me up in half an hour to look at houses to buy in Bel Air. I think I'm adjusting."

My love story with the Beverly Hills Hotel continued over the years, with occasional meetings in their fancy bungalows and champagne brunches at the Polo Lounge. It reached a pinnacle in 2001 when our daughter Johanna, now a beautiful young woman, married Charlie, the man of her dreams. They were looking for the perfect place to celebrate their union, and in our hearts, we knew there could only be one place. So, with 125 of our dearest friends and family from the West Coast, Midwest, Southwest, and New York in attendance, I walked Johanna down the aisle on the lush green lawns of the Beverly Hills Hotel.

The wedding was a bit of an extravaganza, and unfortunately, this time Mary Wells Lawrence wasn't paying for it. But it was a wise investment that yielded a rich dividend. On January 24, 2009, Johanna gave birth to our amazing granddaughter, Zoe Elizabeth Weirauch.

We had come full circle. Our experience with the Beverly Hills Hotel began with a colossal earthquake. And it ended with a beautiful granddaughter, who is a 10.0 on the Richter scale.

Killing the Clown

Bob and I were now co-creative directors of Wells, Rich, Greene/ L.A. Our offices were on the twentieth floor of a soaring modern building in Century City. Just as Charlie Moss had advertised, Bob and I had a big corner office with floor-to-ceiling glass windows that looked out to a golf course to the north and the Pacific Ocean to the west.

But if we thought that life would be easier in La La Land, we were in for a rude awakening. The agency's accounts were big and troubled. And Jack in the Box, which represented one-fourth of our business in L.A., was in dire straits. Their sales were slipping rapidly because they didn't have the food quality or the reputation to compete with McDonald's and Burger King.

To complicate matters, Jack in the Box had just hired a new marketing director, whom I will refer to as Bubba. Anyone in our business knows what most new marketing directors do: they fire the incumbent agency and start over. The situation was tense.

Jack in the Box and Wells had crafted a new business strategy built on new, great-tasting adult products. But when the agency tested its patented cute advertising to announce the new, great-tasting food, consumers mocked it. They couldn't believe that this great-tasting, new food could be coming from a place they referred to as "Gag in the Bag." As a result, we modified the strategy of just introducing delicious new adult products to also announce that Jack in the Box had changed. It was a big task and was cause for tension around the agency. We needed a big creative idea.

One night at around 2:00 a.m., fueled by several tumblers of Dewar's on the rocks, I had one of those Eureka moments. From the beginning, Jack in the Box was known for its colorful clown, which was a big draw for kids. But now we were coming up with adult products and positioning the chain to grownups. So we didn't need that silly symbol anymore. In fact, the clown would potentially detract from our promise of delicious, grownup tastes.

So here was my idea: Let's blame all of Jack in the Box's problems on the dopey clown. All that mediocre food—that was his fault, not Jack in the Box's. And if we got rid of the clown, it would be proof that we had changed. So let's do it in dramatic fashion. Let's blow him away! Based on this idea, Pasqualina and I wrote a

TV script that told the world, in no uncertain terms, that Jack in the Box had changed.

> *OLD LADY PULLS UP TO JACK IN THE BOX IN A 1940s PACKARD. SHE SEES TWO JACK IN THE BOX EMPLOYEES STRAPPING DYNAMITE TO THE CLOWN*
>
> *OLD LADY: What are you doing to the Jack in the Box clown?*
>
> *EMPLOYEE: He's going bye-bye, lady.*
>
> *OLD LADY: But he's so cute!*
>
> *EMPLOYEE 2: Cute was the old Jack in the Box. Now we stand for great new food.*
>
> *(CUT TO LUSCIOUS FOOD AND BUILDING A SANDWICH)*
>
> *EMPLOYEE: Like our new Hot Ham & Cheese Supreme. Tender ham and tangy cheese on a toasted poppy seed roll. The food is better at the Box.*
>
> *(HE HANDS SANDWICH TO OLD LADY, AND SHE TASTES)*
>
> *OLD LADY: Mmm, the food IS better at the Box. WASTE HIM!*
>
> *(THE CLOWN BLOWS UP IN A MILLION PIECES AS SONG ERUPTS)*
>
> *SONG: THE FOOD IS BETTER AT THE BOX, JACK IN THE BOX, BETTER AT THE BOX ...*

It was bold, and maybe a little crazy, but ideas like that have the potential to do dramatic things. Now if we could just sell the idea to the client. The day we were scheduled to present to Bubba, we had the opportunity to present it first to Mary. She had flown into town because she was very aware of the turmoil we were experiencing on Jack in the Box and knew the account was in jeopardy. I was actually a little nervous to present to her. This was a big one and, even after all these years dealing with Mary, I wasn't sure how she might react. How silly of me.

She instantly got the power of the idea, loved the script, and radiated confidence. "Howie," she said, "I think you guys may have just saved the business." What a shot in the arm. If Mary thought it was a winner, it was a winner.

But what would Bubba think? That afternoon, we presented to him in our main conference room. Much to our surprise, he said, "This is exactly what the business needs … something dramatic, a breakthrough. Terrific work, guys!" It was a great moment of victory and made us wonder what we had been so worried about. Bubba was a smart client and a good guy. *Not so fast.* The very next day, he came to the agency and fired us.

We were in shock. What the fuck was that all about? One day he says the campaign is great, and the next day he fires us? Who *is* this guy? But we weren't going to take this lying down. Mary Wells Lawrence was still at our Los Angeles offices, and when she heard that Bubba had fired us, she went ballistic.

She immediately typed up a letter to her buddy, the chairman of Ralston Purina, the parent company of Jack in the Box. She ranted and raved. She told him how unfair this firing was. She said she had seen the creative idea that would turn their business around. In fact, she said that she was so confident it would work that the agency was willing to pay to produce the TV spot with our own money as well as test it. She proposed that if the spot scored well, then Jack in the Box should agree to let us keep the account. She ended her letter with a personal remark to the chairman, "See you at the Bogey Club." Relationships matter!

Well, Mary had a way of being *very* convincing, and that was an almost impossible offer to pass up. The chairman of Ralston Purina graciously accepted and instructed Bubba to UN-fire us. Naturally, this totally pissed him off, but he couldn't do anything about it. We were going to produce and test the spot and let the chips fall where they may. Now the pressure was really on! The account was on the line, agency money was on the line, and Mary's reputation was on the line.

At that time, the most popular research methodology was administered by Burke Marketing Research, which measured day-after recall. One day after a commercial was aired, Burke would conduct telephone interviews with a sample audience to see if they remembered seeing the spot and what, if any, selling points they could play back. The results were then translated into a score.

The average recall score for a fast-food commercial was twenty-two. Any score seven points higher was considered above average, and if you scored in the thirties, you were golden. So that was what we were shooting for and praying for. A decisive score of thirty or better would ensure that we kept the Jack in the Box account. Now it was time to produce the spot.

Naturally, we wanted every advantage we could get. We wanted our go-to guy with a reputation for comedy to direct it. We wanted Stan Dragoti. Yes, the same Stan Dragoti who had been Charlie Moss's creative partner was also now a full-fledged commercial director.

At this point, I have to stop to tell you a little more about the legend of Stan. He was tall, dark, handsome, talented, and funny, with leading man looks that made him a chick magnet. That would be enough to intimidate other creative people in the agency, and it did, including yours truly. But since I was sort of a young, cute agitator in those days, his reputation made me want to get up in his face and make him aware of me. He may have been god's gift to mankind (and womankind), but what was I, chopped liver? (Yes, I was somewhat delusional.)

For several months after I first arrived at the agency, I had been hearing about the legend of Stan. Then one day, we found ourselves walking toward each other down a narrow hall at Wells, Rich, Greene. I was instantly aware that he was a superior specimen: better looking and about five inches taller than me.

I just didn't believe in Greek gods (or, in his case, Albanian gods), and I wanted to prove I was every bit his measure. Now was my chance to use my Jewish boy charm and sarcastic humor to disarm him. Stan walked towards me; I walked towards him, closer and closer, until suddenly we were standing face-to-face. We circled each other like two prizefighters looking for an opening. Suddenly, we stopped. I looked up at him—way up—and delivered the line he would never forget, "Five more inches and it would be all over, pal."

He chuckled, shook his head, and walked away, no doubt thinking to himself, "Who was that little *schmuck*?" But I obviously made an impression.

For the next thirty years, every time I saw Stan, the first thing he said was, "Five more inches and it would be all over, pal."

With Stan's movie star looks, you can imagine how envious all the guys at Wells, Rich, Greene were, especially when he started dating and then married supermodel Cheryl Tiegs. They were madly in love. I remember Stan saying to me, "There's no worm in this apple," meaning he couldn't find any faults. Cheryl Tiegs was as beautiful on the inside as she was on the outside.

One night, after Carol and I had moved to L.A., Stan and Cheryl invited us out for dinner at a swanky Beverly Hills restaurant. The setting was magical, and the wine and food were superb. However, the conversation was practically nonexistent because Stan and Cheryl spent the whole evening holding hands and gazing into each other's eyes.

Stan Dragoti looking every bit the Hollywood director

Unfortunately, as with most flames that burn too brightly, their marriage didn't last. But while it did, it was one for the ages. Stan went on to conquer Hollywood with two hit movies that he directed, *Love at First Bite* and *Mr. Mom*. Yet he never let fame go to his head. He was always just Stan.

If I had one bone to pick with him, it was over an incident some time in the late seventies. People magazine decided to do a special article on Cheryl and Stan, in which they talked about their glamorous lives, living in a Bel Air mansion, and driving matching Mercedes. To my surprise, the article stated that Stan Dragoti was the guy who wrote, "Try it, you'll like it" and "I can't believe I ate the whole thing."

Carol was outraged by this and said, "Howie, you have to call *People* magazine and tell them they've made a huge mistake. They're giving him credit for your and Bob's work!"

While I was obviously not happy about this, I said, "Look, it's an honest mistake. I'm sure Stan will call the magazine and tell them to correct it."

But he didn't. A few months later, *People* magazine did another article on Stan and Cheryl, and *again* they gave him credit for our Alka Seltzer commercials. Carol went ballistic.

She sat down and dashed out a scathing (with charm) letter to *People* magazine that began like this: "Dear *People* magazine, the writer of 'Try it, you'll like it' and 'I can't believe I ate the whole thing' lives in Bel Air and drives a Mercedes, but his name is not Stan Dragoti, and he's not Cheryl Tiegs's husband. He's mine!"

Some time later, I was talking to Charlie Moss, and he shared what had happened. He said, "I got a call from a panicked representative of *People* magazine. He told me they had received a letter from a woman named Carol Trifari Cohen, saying Stan did *not* write those commercials."

"That's correct," was Charlie's reply.

"What!" he said. "How can this be? We've printed this twice … it has to be right!"

"Well," Charlie said. "You're obviously victims of your own media bullshit … if you print it, it must be true."

"Jesus," the representative said. "If Stan didn't write those commercials, who did?" To which Charlie replied, "I did." Of course, he told me he was kidding.

For the next two years, I checked every *People* magazine to make sure that if they ever did an article on Alka Seltzer again, they would give credit where credit was due. (To Charlie Moss, of course.)

In any case, we needed a great director for our Jack in the Box spot. Given his comedic talent and our history together, Stan was the perfect guy, so we were happy when he read the script and loved it.

Over the next month, Stan threw himself into the production, pushing for the perfect casting, hiring the best cameraman, and shooting take after take to get the perfect performances. We edited it, polished it, perfected it, and submitted it to Burke. Then we waited for our score. Tensions were high at the agency. A lot of jobs were on the line. Several excruciating days went by. And finally, on a gray December day in L.A., the results came in.

Pasqualina and I were sitting in our Century City office, staring out at the Pacific Ocean, when the door flung open. It was the account guy on Jack in the Box.

"We got the score!" he shouted.

I leaped out of my chair. "What was it … did we hit thirty?"

"No," he said coyly. "We didn't hit thirty."

"Damn," I said.

And then he shouted, "We got a seventy-fucking-two!"

"Holy shit!" I said.

He started talking fast and furious—how it was the highest scoring fast-food commercial of all time. And not only that, viewers remembered everything about the spot. The explosion … Jack in the Box is changing … the food is better. Everything!

By now, our fellow associates were starting to pour into our office and someone was popping the corks on some fine champagne. Then Charlie Moss was on the phone from New York, calling to congratulate us. He said that when Mary heard the score, she literally screamed, leaped out of her chair, and did a jig around the room. This was why Pasqualina and I had gotten into the advertising

We changed Jack in the Box's image with a bang

business in the first place—to do great work, heroic work in this case, and share the victory with the people we cared about.

The exploding clown was more than just a TV spot—it was a dramatic social event. News channels up and down the California coast featured it every night for a full week; the clown exploded hundreds of more times on their news shows, giving us free exposure and adding to the power of the campaign. This simple idea immediately turned Jack in the Box around, delivering double-digit sales increases. And, just as importantly, the image of the brand and what it stood for changed overnight.

In the interest of full disclosure, there was a bit of negative backlash. It came from mothers of young children whose kids were somewhat traumatized by the violence inflicted on their beloved clown.

One complaint letter said, "My poor five-year-old daughter ran screaming from the TV. What kind of evil, sadistic person would do this to a poor clown? He must be gay or a Nazi … or both!" Wow, that hurt! I could live with one or the other, but Howie Cohen, a gay Nazi? That's just cruel.

The reality was, when your fast-food client is getting their asses kicked by McDonald's and Burger King, you gotta do what you gotta do. For Bob and me, this was a great victory. Nothing could have been better—except for one thing. One month later, Bubba announced he was voluntarily leaving his job at Jack in the Box to "pursue other interests." In other words, he was fucking fired. It couldn't have happened to a nicer guy.

Movie Madness

If dealing with Bubba had been a bad dream, the guys at Columbia Pictures were a minor nightmare. When we first arrived at the agency, we sat down with the head account guy on the business, a guy named Bob Wolf, to get the skinny on what our movie clients were like.

He immediately launched into a true story. He said that one day he and a senior copywriter drove out to Burbank to present a new ad campaign to their marketing director for one of Columbia's up-coming films. This client had always insisted that the work we do be edgy and irreverent, and this campaign was that in spades. When they presented the work, the marketing director agreed. In fact, he was blown away. However, since this guy was still an underling, Bob Wolf asked him, "But what will your bosses think? You know how conservative they are."

Much to his surprise, the marketing director puffed up his chest and said, "I don't give a shit what my management thinks. This is fucking great! I promise you this campaign will run. And if they don't buy it, I'll fucking quit!"

Wow! Feeling elated, Wolf and the writer drove back from Burbank to the agency in Century City, listening to the Eagles and singing along at the top of their lungs. But one hour later, when they arrived back at the office, there was an urgent message waiting for them from the very same marketing director: "Call me!"

Wolf got right on the phone, and the marketing director didn't waste time telling him, "The campaign is dead. We need new work!"

"What? What happened? An hour ago you were ready to stake your entire career on this campaign."

"I know," the client said. "But my boss thought it was too risky, and I couldn't bring myself to fight him."

"Jesus," Wolf said. "Where do you get your integrity?"

Without missing a beat, the client said, "Where do I get my integrity, Bob? Let me tell you a story. George Segal was a big star whose movies made a lot of money for this studio. Then he developed a little cocaine problem. So one day, George gets stoned out of his mind and decides he wants to see our president. Our president can't see him because he's at lunch with some important people. So George gets offended and goes apeshit. He barges into the president's empty office, knocks over plants, rips pictures off the walls, dumps cigarette butts onto the floor, and rubs them into the fancy *shmancy* carpet with his shoe ... he really trashes the place. And when our president gets back from lunch and sees what George has done, he becomes enraged and says to the entire executive committee, 'George Segal will never work for this studio again!'

"Well," he continued. "It seems that a short time later, George cleaned up his act, and he went on to have a colossal hit movie with another studio. I mean, he was back on top again! And one year to the day later, our president personally hired George at an outrageous salary to star in Columbia's next big blockbuster. Where do I get my integrity, Bob? Right from the top!"

Bond, James Bond

It was a telling story and a vivid reminder of our own past experiences with movie studios when we had our own agency. After the highly publicized success of our Super Bowl campaign for Chrysler Corporation, our agency was hot and the movie studios came calling. If there's anything that can give a movie exec a big woody, it's being associated with hot talent, whether it's movie stars, producers, directors, or ... ad guys.

One of the most glamorous projects we worked on was a campaign for the James Bond movie *The Spy Who Loved Me*, starring Roger Moore, with Barbara Bach (the future Mrs. Ringo Starr) as the Bond girl. In high-level meetings with the MGM/UA marketing guys, they told us they needed something fresh because the Bond franchise was losing steam. The same old advertising just wouldn't do.

Up to that point, every Bond movie had featured the image of James Bond holding a gun with scantily clad girls in the background. "We want to lose the gun," they said. "It's getting old. We need something more creative … that's why we're bringing you guys in."

"Okay," I said. "But Bond holding the gun is your icon. Everybody recognizes it, and you own it. Are you sure you want to walk away from that?"

"Fuck the gun," was the eloquent response from their ad manager.

I took a chance and said, "Bill, you have to learn to say what you really feel." He didn't laugh.

"We need something fresh," he stated. "Give us a breakthrough idea … that's why we hired you."

Soon, Pasqualina and I were flying off to London to meet the producer of all the Bond films and attend one of the most extravagant Bond publicity parties of all time. A limo driver behind the wheel of a big cushy Daimler Benz greeted us at Heathrow Airport. As we got into the car, we were both handed envelopes containing £300 in spending cash. We were driven to the exclusive Dorchester Hotel, where we unpacked and decompressed for a couple of hours. Then we were picked up and driven to Albert R. (Cubby) Broccoli's exclusive London Townhouse.

He was the highly successful producer of all the James Bond

films. (Trivia: While it may sound strange for a man to be named after a vegetable, it was actually the other way around. His ancestors were Italian horticulturalists who crossed cauliflower with rabe to create the veggie that bears his name.)

We were ushered into a rich wood-paneled study, where we were served hot tea and scones as Cubby shared the history of the James Bond franchise and his vision for the new movie. Then he invited us to a little party with a thousand of his closest friends.

To publicize the movie, MGM threw a Hollywood-style extravaganza. Everyone who was anyone was there: famous actors, actresses, and assorted dignitaries, including members of parliament and the prime minister of England. The party was held on the largest soundstage in the world at the time, built specifically to house two mock nuclear submarines central to the movie's plot. The finest food, wine, champagne, truffles, cheeses, cakes, cookies, and brandies stretched the full length of the stage. It was glamorous and thrilling, and we stayed past 1:00 a.m. before returning to the Dorchester Hotel.

The party was first class; however, what was going on at the hotel was not. It seems that London was going through a recession, and the once grand hotel had slipped in quality. Security had become a little lax, and unsavory characters were roaming the halls at night.

Sometime around 3:00 a.m., I was awakened from a deep sleep by a knock on my door. I heard high-pitched giggling in the hall. When I opened the door, there were five young "ladies of the night" standing in front of me, and one said, "Hey, Yank, want to have a good time?"

Before I could slam the door shut, they pushed their way into my room (okay, it was a gentle push from a very lovely hand) and laughingly shoved me toward the bed. I was still trying to emerge from a jet-lagged sleep and didn't really understand what was going on, let alone know what to do about it. As the high-pitched laughter of these young, nubile nymphets filled the room, I felt hands running all over my body and heard them saying things like, "C'mon, handsome, we're going to have some fun," and "You know you want it."

Now, most men I know, at one time or another, have had fantasies about enjoying multiple sex partners at the same time. Maybe it's a ménage à trois with two girls and a guy; or two guys and a girl; or if you're really kinky, a guy, a girl, and a cute sheep. But five to one seemed a little over the top. I finally remembered who I was and what I was supposed to be doing. And, oh yeah, that I happened to be married to a woman I love.

I began to push them toward the door, and as I did, I felt a strange conflict that maybe only a neurotic Jewish guy could feel. I felt guilty about rejecting them. Words like, "It's not you, it's me," came to mind. Finally, I said, "Look, you're all very charming, and this has been fun, but I'm going to have to ask you all to leave now."

"Aw, don't be a party-pooper," (pronounced poopah).

"Sorry," I said, "I have to get up early to fly back to New York. But let me pay you for your time."

They had been in my room for about ten minutes. "Here," I said, as I reached into my wallet. I gave all five of them the equivalent of a ten-dollar bill in English pounds. "Alright," they said, as they marched out the door and headed for the elevator to find their next "mark."

"But it could have been fun," one said, looking back over her shoulder.

It was a nice shoulder. However, if I had any second thoughts about missing out on this, they were quickly squashed as I remembered the words of my Italian wife, whose roots go back to Napoli and the land of the Cosa Nostra. She stated, and I quote, "If I ever catch you cheating on me, I will cut off your Jewish penis and stick it in the trash compactor." *Ouch!*

At that point, all I really wanted was a few hours' sleep. Pasqualina and I would be leaving that morning for New York to create the next generation of incredible James Bond advertising— without the fucking gun.

We flew home inspired and excited. If these guys wanted a breakthrough, we were going to give it to them. We jammed for three solid weeks, coming up with tons of fresh ideas. And we weren't the only ones. As is typical in the movie business, at least four other creative shops were working on this same project. Money was no object; it was all about coming up with the big idea.

Finally, we presented our work to the powers that be. We presented ad after ad, and with each one, the client nodded with delight. We were a hit!

After that, we waited to get the green light to produce our campaign. A full week went by, and when the news finally came, it wasn't good. They had decided to go a different way. *Shit!* Some other shop must have come up with the big idea. We were crushed.

Then we saw the winning campaign. It was James Bond, holding the gun, with scantily clad girls in the background. Nothing had changed. They had spent hundreds of thousands of dollars on campaigns from five different ad agencies to do what they had always done before.

I was shocked and needed to find out what had caused this seismic shift in their thinking. I called their marketing director and asked, "Jim, what gives? You're doing the same stuff you did before. I thought you were committed to change. Aren't you the guy who told us, 'Fuck the gun'?"

"Howie," he said, "you just don't get it. That image of Bond holding the gun is our icon. We own it, and everybody recognizes it. Why would we ever want to walk away from that?"

Damn, why didn't we think of that?

Here's J-a-a-ack

I'd be lying if I said that working with movie people was all angst and pain. After all, it's still Hollywood with all its glitz and glamour, and I must confess to sometimes being starry-eyed—especially when it involved a huge star.

The first time I saw Jack Nicholson, he was an unknown starving actor sleeping on the floor of Harry Gittes's apartment in New York. Harry was a talented copywriter at Wells, Rich, Greene, and Jack was his best friend in the world.

When Jack's star started to rise, Harry decided to join him in Hollywood and pursue a career as a film producer. By the way, you might remember that the name of Nicholson's character in the film *Chinatown* was Jake Gittes. Guess where they got the last name?

Anyway, these guys always remained very tight, and when Nicholson decided to make his debut as a movie director in 1978, Harry agreed to help promote the film. That's when I got a call from Harry.

"Hey, Howie. I see you guys have been doing some movie advertising."

"Yeah," I said. "We've done a bunch of stuff."

By that time, we had worked on campaigns for all kinds of movies for different studios, ranging from *The Spy Who Loved Me* to the Richard Dreyfus film *Inserts* to *Nickelodeon* to *Mr. Billion*, a film that marked the American debut of Terence Hill, Italy's number one movie star.

It was a strange and diverse mix of films from several different studios. Pasqualina and I had apparently developed a reputation for being troubleshooters. They would bring us in on the tough ones because we always came up with something unexpected. And that was why Harry called us at our agency in New York.

"We've got an interesting little movie here," he said. "Jack decided to make a period piece ... a Western called *Goin' South*. It's good, but it won't be an easy sell. I know all the crap campaigns we'll be getting from all the usual suspects. I'd love to see what you guys would come up with. Are you interested?"

"Well, we're really busy, Harry. But for you?" Of course, I was being facetious. We would love to work on a movie project, especially for Jack Nicholson. Despite the craziness of the movie business, we still loved the glamour, and at that particular time, we needed the money.

"Great," he said. "I'm going to set up a special meeting with Jack. I want you to hear his perspective on the movie firsthand ... I think it would really help."

"Perfect," I said. "Pasqualina and I will see you guys out there."

When I got home that night, I decided to have a little fun. I told Carol I was going to be working on a new movie assignment and had to fly out to L.A. to meet with some guy ... an actor ... oh, what was his name again ... you'd probably know it if you heard it ... uh ... Jim ... Joe ... Jack? "Oh yeah, that's it, Jack Nicholson."

She said, "You're flying out to L.A. to meet with Jack Nicholson? Not without me, you're not!"

And so we arranged for an extra creative genius to attend the meeting—my wife.

One week later, in a conference room at Paramount Pictures, we met with Jack and Harry and a slew of people who either worked on the movie or were tasked with promoting it. There were about eighteen of us sitting there, with Jack at the head of the table. Carol was sitting directly next to me, but she wasn't looking at me. With Jack Nicholson in the room, there was only one place anyone could look—at Jack. He was that charismatic.

For about an hour and a half, he shared all of his feelings about the movie: why he'd made it, what it was really about, what it meant to him, who the movie was for, and why he thought people would care. He was passionate and very convincing. We asked a few questions and threw in a few comments to try and impress him with our smarts, and that was it.

Everyone got up to leave, and Jack positioned himself at the door. As we all filed out of the room, Jack shook everyone's hand and thanked them for coming. Carol was right behind me as I got to the door and it was my turn to say goodbye. Jack looked me in the eye, shook my hand with a firm handshake, and said, "Nice meetin' ya, Howie."

And then, being the incredible (some would say insufferable) flirt that he was, he turned to Carol. With me standing right there, he grabbed her hand with both of his hands, looked her directly in the eye, and said in a long, slow drawl, "And it was re-a-ll-y nice meetin' *you*, Carol!" He held the look and held her hand and didn't let go ... *beat ... beat ... beat ... release.*

Carol is a grown, mature, sophisticated woman, but her face blushed a deep ruby red. When we got to the car, I turned to Carol and said, "That was interesting." She smiled back at me, not saying a word.

To this day, both she and I remember that moment. And if I ever fall into the trap of acting a little full of myself, she reminds me of the time Jack Nicholson practically made love to her with his eyes. And it shuts me up, fast.

Blood and Fangs

Flash forward. It is now 1979, and we're at Wells, Rich, Greene/ L.A., and one of our monster responsibilities is to do the advertising for Columbia Pictures with a schedule of twenty-five movie releases a year. *Holy shit!* Three or four would be a lot. Ten is a monster. But twenty-five movie campaigns a year can bury you—and it almost did. What's more, we quickly learned that the Columbia Pictures people were cut from the same cloth as all the other movie people we had worked with—nervous, neurotic, and slightly nuts.

Here's one example. In 1979, there was great anticipation for a new movie called *Nightwing,* which the marketing guys at Columbia saw as a "classy" film because it was based on a bestselling book and was being produced by Martin Ransohoff, a big-time independent Hollywood producer.

Frankly, we didn't understand all the "classy" talk. *Nightwing* was about bats. Bats are creepy little creatures that hang upside down in dark caves and suck blood from people's necks. How classy is that?

I naively brought this up at a strategy meeting, and the marketing director jumped down my throat. "*Nightwing* is based on a bestselling book involving Indian lore (he pronounced it "law," because he was an ex-New Yorker), and it stars the great actor David Warner … I'm talkin' Shakespeare heah!"

"Very well then," I said. "We've got two classy teams working on it back at the agency, and Kupchick and I are going to work on it personally." I was referring to Alan Kupchick, my good friend and a VP associate creative director at the agency.

Alan and I had been through the movie wars together and managed to maintain our sanity by finding humor in wacky situations. By the way, he went on to become a talented photographer, and I collect his highly original photographs.

Since I was the first to tell him that he is a true artist, we developed nicknames for each other. He is Artisto, and I am his Patroni. But I digress.

One of the fresh ideas we came up with for *Nightwing* was to shoot an original TV spot rather than cut together a commercial using footage from the film, like everyone else in the business always did. Instead we would capture the essence of the film without showing scenes that gave away the story.

Some of the best movie campaigns of all time have capitalized on this simple creative principle, such as the original *Alien* movie, showing an iconic cracked egg with green light seeping out and the line, "In space, no one can hear you scream."

Our script called for a dramatic actor to deliver a monologue in an eerie setting lit only by a campfire in the desert at night. To ensure that it would be "classy," we recommended that the actor be none other than David Warner. The Columbia guys flipped over this idea. Get the star of the movie, one of the greatest British actors of our time, to deliver our TV commercial—classy, real classy! They booked David Warner, and in the interest of getting the perfect performance, we knew exactly who we wanted to direct it. We hired Stan Dragoti.

The opening line of the spot was a killer, in a good way. It was meant to be delivered by David Warner with Shakespearean gravitas:

THEY ARE THE QUINTESSENCE OF EVIL

Or, as he would say it, "EEEEVILL."

We were very excited; this was going to be classy, real classy.

On the day of the shoot, David Warner was locked in his trailer as teams of production people scurried around the soundstage, making it look like the desert at night, with ominous dark mountains in the background subliminally shaped liked bat wings. Dragoti was a stickler for detail, and the scene would take five hours to light and set up. In the first hour, David Warner came out of his trailer and approached Kupchick and me. (Hmm, was that liquor we detected on his breath?)

"I must talk to you, loves." Yes, he actually called us "loves."

"Sure, David, what is it?" Kupchick asked him.

"I am a classically trained actor, not a commercial actor. I know how you people do commercials. You do take ... after take ... after take."

"You're right, David," I said. "It's because we want to get it perfect."

"Sorry, loves," he told us. "I caaaan't do it. I caaaant! I caaant! I do one take!"

Oh boy, this was going to be a long afternoon ... or maybe a very short one.

Then he disappeared back into his trailer. A couple of hours later, he came out again. (Hmm, was that the smell of single malt scotch?)

"I hope you understand, loves, I want to give you what you want. It's just the idea of take ... after take ... after take. I caaaan't do it! I caaaan't!"

With a lot of careers on the line, I wanted to say, "You can. You can and you will!" but I didn't. Kupchick, the grownup, jumped in and said, "You're the great David Warner, and we have the utmost faith in you. It will be great!"

He slowly nodded and returned to his trailer.

Finally, Dragoti was ready, and it was time to place David Warner into the scene. He came out of his trailer and glided easily to the campfire, as if he were freshly oiled (and we suspected he was). Dragoti walked up to David, said a few words in his ear, then ran back behind the cameraman, and called, "Action!" The camera slowly dollied into David's face, as he began, "Theyyy are the quintessence of eeeevilllll!" (Oh god, that was perfect!) And he went on to deliver a magnificent performance of Shakespearean caliber. It was amazing, and I thought to myself, *Thank god we got it because we'll probably have to wrap now.*

That's when David called out to Dragoti, "Did you get it, love? I think I could do that first line a little better. Can we give it a go?" So much for, "I do one take." Two hours and seventeen takes later, Dragoti said, "It's a wrap," and we had a great original spot in the can.

When we screened it for the guys at Columbia, they wet their pants. This was the classy commercial they wanted for their classy film. Of course, nobody was talking about the quality of the movie, which was seriously in question as the early reviews started to leak out. Still, we launched our classy spot, and we launched big. We ran the campaign with heavy media money behind it for ten days leading up to a Friday opening—which was as quiet as a bat in a cave. Nobody came.

By Sunday, we were getting panic calls from the client. "We need new advertising ... fast!

"Okay," I said. "What do you have in mind?"

Suddenly, he went batshit! "What do I have in mind?" he shouted. "I want bats ... I want fangs ... I want blood! The movie is called *Nightwing*, dammit!"

Classy, really classy.

One week later, we launched our bloody fangs campaign, but no amount of gore could save this sucker. *Nightwing* bled out.

Get Outta Town

Sometimes you need to get away from it all to refresh your thinking and recharge your batteries. I must admit, my glamorous job wasn't always so glam, given the pressure to create shiny, new ad campaigns for twenty-five Columbia releases a year, hawk new burgers for Jack in the Box, and constantly pitch new business. Carol realized how stressed I was and decided to do something about it. She planned a quick getaway for the two of us to Mexico's Cabo San Lucas, just a short flight from L.A. No big deal—leave on Thursday morning, come back on Sunday night. Get some much-needed R&R in the Mexican sunshine.

But the day before we were supposed to leave, I got a panicked call from Carol. "Howie, it's terrible. I just found out that we need passports to get back into the country!"

"So? We have passports," I said.

"No, we don't. They've expired. We're screwed!"

Oh well, I thought to myself. I hadn't been sure this trip was a good idea in the first place. We could go some other time. However, I underestimated the resourcefulness of my wife. Just a few hours later, she called back. "Forget what I said. I've got it worked out. We're going!"

So, on a Thursday morning, we took off for the crystal blue waters and white sand beaches of Cabo and spent three and a half wonderful days relaxing in the Mexican sunshine. And when it was time to leave, I almost didn't want to come home. But, of course, we had to. There was a lot going on back at the agency.

When the flight landed at LAX, we were standing in line going through customs, and all of a sudden I remembered we didn't have passports. I turned to Carol and asked, "How are we getting back into the country?"

"No problem," she said. And she shoved an official little document into my hand. "Just show them this."

When I reached the head of the line, I handed the document to the customs inspector. He looked at it. Then he looked at me, looked at it, and looked at me again. I was getting nervous. Then he let out a little chuckle and waved me through.

We were greeted by a limo, and after Carol and I were comfortably in the car, my curiosity got the best of me. I pulled the document out of my pocket and was shocked to see what had gotten me back into the country. It was my certificate of circumcision (yes, there really is such a thing). And on it was a photo of Rabbi Rosenblum with a thick beard and a tall black rabbinical hat. He was the holy man who had given me what some call the cruelest cut of all. Carol, by contrast, who had grown up Catholic, had used her Certificate of Communion as proof of citizenship. It was a case of the Jewish husband with ancestors from Poland and Ukraine coupled with the Catholic wife with roots in Napoli, giving added meaning to why they call America "the melting pot."

I laughed and gave her a hug. Nobody but Carol could have gotten me back into the country with such surgical precision.

Winning Is the Only Thing

Like every other agency on the planet, Wells needed new business. The pressure was always there to grow. In fact, the ad business is all about new business. If you're not growing, you're shrinking. If you're not winning, you're losing. New business brings in new money, fresh talent, and tells the world your agency is still viable, which means you're still viable. That's why ad men will do just about anything to win a new account—as evidenced by this classic joke.

Marvin was the president of a medium-sized agency with ambitions of being a large agency. Their big opportunity came when they were invited to pitch a huge automobile account. Marvin's agency pulled out all the stops, did a big dog-and-pony show, and when the presentation was over, there were back slaps and applause from a very enthusiastic audience. The president of the car company gave Marvin a wink and told him he'd be hearing their decision on Wednesday.

Well, Wednesday came and went, and so did Thursday. By Friday morning, Marvin was beside himself with worry. He stood in the bathroom mirror shaving his face, and with each stroke of the razor, he became more agitated. "They should have called by now.

They told us we were great. What went wrong? They're probably calling another agency right now to discuss compensation while I'm standing here like a schmuck."

Suddenly, there's a loud *POOF!* and the devil appears in the mirror.

"Marvin," the devil says, "you really want that account, don't you?"

"Yes, yes, I do!" Marvin says.

"Well, Marvin, I can get you that account."

Marvin snaps to attention, hanging on the devil's every word. "It can be yours, signed, sealed, and delivered this very afternoon. But Marvin, if I do this for you, I will need something from you in return."

"Anything," Marvin says, "I'll do anything. What do you want?"

The devil says, "I want the souls of your wife and children for all eternity!"

Marvin says, "What's the catch?"

The Dinkum Dawg Debacle

Given the pressure to win new business, every agency in L.A. was on the lookout for a live one. And then one day, the word spread that an exciting new account with huge growth potential was coming to L.A. from Australia and looking for an ad agency. Its name was Dinkum Dawg.

According to the scuttlebutt, it was a new and unique sausage product with a portable cooking method that allowed it to be set up in malls and on street corners in high traffic areas all around town. Furthermore, this simple concept was hugely successful in the Land

Down Under, thanks to high sales volume and zero real estate costs.

Upon hearing this, one of our young copywriters said, "You mean like a hotdog stand?" What a wiseass! It was quickly decided that he would not be allowed to participate in the pitch. This opportunity was just too big to blow.

According to sources, Dinkum Dawg was planning to spend $10 million for an initial launch on the West Coast, with intentions to increase spending to $100 million as it sold franchises and rolled out across America.

L.A. agencies, large and small, went all out to get a meeting with the Aussies. One agency videotaped man-on-the-street interviews to get reactions to the product idea. Some did spec creative campaigns for a product they had never seen. One little agency even roamed the Qantas Air Terminal with signs saying, "Wifkin and Pifkin welcome Dinkum Dawg!" Hundreds of thousands of dollars were run up by dozens of agencies to pitch this hot new account.

Then came the big shock. The week that the Dinkum Dawg execs were supposed to arrive in L.A., nobody showed up. That's when it all came out. There was no Dinkum Dawg. It was all a hoax—a colossal joke on the L.A. ad community.

Sitting here now, I ask myself, "How could so many sophisticated people in our business have been so gullible?" And then I'm reminded of how Bernie Madoff duped all those smart, unsuspecting people out of their life savings. Why did they believe? Because they wanted to. And it was the same thing with all of us. The possibility of getting a $100 million account made everyone suspend disbelief and abandon common sense. One thing I know for sure: this town will never fall for a hoax like Dinkum Dawg again ... until the next time.

He Got Rome; I Got Cucamonga

On the other hand, going after new business can be thrilling, especially when you win. In early 1982, the agency pitched a fashion account called Brittania Sportswear, makers of stylish, casual clothes. Bob and I helped win the day with an original creative campaign based on the theme, "Live in Brittania." The words were made memorable by a rousing piece of music, which served as the backdrop for sexy fashion-forward TV spots.

Since the brand name was Brittania, we decided to give the campaign a European flair. Our kickoff spot featured a young Italian stud living *la dolce vita* on the streets of Rome and up-tempo romantic situations designed to show off the guy's clothes. The client was so excited over this idea, he signed off on a European shoot with a $250,000 production budget. Bob and I were excited too—we were heading to Rome!

Not so fast, Howie. The shoot dates happened to conflict with an important convention for one of our other new clients—the much less glamorous Handy Dan—a home improvement chain that predated Home Depot. These handy dandy guys were throwing a "first class" bash for all their managers and salespeople in beautiful Rancho Cucamonga—yes, there really is such a place—about an hour and a half outside L.A., and they fully expected one of their agency creative directors (me!) to present their new ad campaign to get the troops fired up.

What! Are you telling me I'm not going to Rome? I fretted. I sulked. I tried to come up with an excuse—any excuse—not to go to Cucamonga. "My cat died, and I have to give the eulogy"; "I was diagnosed with C.R.S. (Can't Remember Shit)"; "My wife just left me for my best friend's ... wife!"

In the end, there was no getting out of it. Bob was flying to Rome, Italy. And I was driving to Rancho Cucamonga to eat rubber chicken dinners and laugh at off-color jokes from guys with tool belts and bad comb-overs. Life just wasn't fair.

When Bob got to Rome, he was kind enough to keep in touch via colorful Italian postcards. "Bongiorno, Howie! Went to The Vatican today and met the Pope ... having dinner with Sophia on the Via Veneto ... miss you!" *Bastard.*

Three weeks later, Bob returned with miles of gorgeous, sexy Italian footage that came together beautifully in the edit. However, when we screened the commercial for the client, there was dead silence.

"What the hell is this?" the client said.

"What?" Bob said. "It's exactly what we showed you on the storyboard! Rome ... sexy guy ... hot babes … beautiful scenery … great clothes ... Brittania!"

"You told me we were going to have an Italian stud wearing my clothes," the client said. "This guy's short! Look at him … he's a head shorter than the girls are!"

I tried to lend some moral support. "Hey, he's handsome. Look at that classic Roman nose. And he looks great in the clothes."

"He's five foot five, goddammit!" the client roared. "We give you $250,000 to shoot a campaign in Rome, and you come back with a fucking midget?" With that, the client stood up from his chair ... all five-feet-five inches of him ... and stormed out of the room. A short time later, we lost the account. When all was said and done, Bob got Rome, I got Cucamonga, and the agency got the shaft.

Guy Walks in with a Beard

But then we got lucky. Really lucky! The easiest piece of new business we ever won at Wells, Rich, Greene/L.A. was when a guy with a $10 million account walked into our offices and said, "I want to meet Howie Cohen and Bob Pasqualina."

He was Barry Reis, the VP of marketing for Hills Bros. Coffee, and we liked him from the first moment we met. Barry was a no-bull straight shooter who knew exactly what he wanted, and he had flown down from San Francisco to get it. Barry looked and acted less like a VP of marketing at a packaged goods company and more like a *menschy* creative guy. He sported a beard, dressed casually, and had a great sarcastic sense of humor.

When we asked why he was looking for a new agency, he didn't pull any punches. He said that their ad agency was BBDO in New York and it wasn't working out. In the early years, BBDO had done some nice work for them, but things had changed, and in his words, Hills Bros. was "tired of all the bullshit." The creative work was spotty, it was always done last minute, and the agency kept changing the staffing on their business. (Other than that, it was a dream relationship.) It also didn't help that BBDO was 3,000 miles away in New York. Apparently, Barry and the other senior management folks at Hills Bros. had decided they'd had enough.

Fortunately for us, Barry knew about agencies, having spent several years as an account executive at Doyle Dane Bernbach. He knew about Bob and me and our work for Alka Seltzer, and he decided that he wanted that level of creative work for the Hills Bros brand. So, after chitchatting for a while, he got right to the point. "We're changing agencies and we'd like to give our account to you guys."

How often do ad guys hear golden words like that from a perfect stranger in the first meeting? No pitch. No RFP. No spec work. Not even a little sucking up.

Barry had just two stipulations. The first was that we had to promise that Bob and I would work on the business. Not just supervise it or play creative directors but actually work on the account and come up with the creative campaigns.

"No problem," I said. "That's why we're here, and that's what we love to do." And it was absolutely true, especially since this was a package goods account and we hadn't done much of that kind of work in a while.

The second stipulation was that we not reinvent the wheel. He wanted us to use their iconic Hills Bros. Bean Buyer character created by BBDO. He said that this approach had worked very well for them, but now it was getting a little stale. He wanted us to freshen it up and make it vital again.

Those were the two stipulations. Our answer was short and to the point. Yes and yes! And that was it—a two-hour meeting and a great new client and friend. It doesn't get any better than that. Besides, how can you not love a cute Jewish guy with a beard?

Golden Stream of Consciousness

Every year a bunch of us from the agency were invited to the Hills Bros. Gala Christmas Party. It was always an extravagant bash held in a huge ballroom with a live band and food and drinks as far as the eye could see. Our relationship with Hills Bros. was so tight that we were the only outsiders invited to these events. We always partied into the wee small hours, laughing, drinking, dancing, joking, drinking, eating, and ... did I mention drinking?

One of these parties stands out most in my mind for what happened afterward. At about 1:00 a.m., as I was heading back to the Mark Hopkins Hotel in the middle of the foggy San Francisco night, I found myself walking in lockstep with Paul Miller, the president of Hills Bros., who's a fantastic guy with a great sense of humor. We couldn't seem to find a cab, and all of a sudden the urge hit us both of at the same time. We needed to take a piss, badly.

So right there at curbside, in the dark and the fog, we unzipped to do the deed. And as the double stream began, Paul launched into a stream of consciousness. "You know, Howie," he said. "I've been thinking about our new Bean Buyer character."

"Uh-huh. What do you think?" I asked.

"I like him. You know, he's got a great look, and he puts a great new face on the brand."

"Yep," I said.

By the way, in moments like this, it's important to maintain proper piss etiquette. Stare straight ahead, avoid eye contact, and never look down.

Paul continued his line of thought. "I've got an idea," he said, almost apologetically. "And you can tell me if I'm off base here because you're the creative guy, you know?"

"Sure, what's the idea, Paul?" I asked.

"I think it would be great to put the guy in a hat. You know, like Indiana Jones. That would really make him stand out."

Now, a lot of creative guys might reject a creative idea coming from a left-brained CEO, just on principle, but that was never the way Pasqualina and I worked. We always believed that creative ideas can come from anywhere, and if you're smart, you'll listen and not let your ego get in the way.

I thought for a minute and said, "Paul, you know, that's not a bad idea. I can see it." The whole storyline of our campaign was that our Bean Buyer goes to the ends of the earth to find the best coffee beans. He's demanding, he's rugged … kinda like Indiana Jones. The hat would make our guy look more iconic. I said, "Paul, I like it!"

"Great, great," he said.

In that moment, I couldn't help but marvel at how productive the two of us had been. We hadn't just taken a piss, we'd taken a meeting—one that would result in a successful ad campaign that would run for the next nine years. Paul and I finished our business, zipped up our flies, and as we said goodbye, we gave each other a big hug. But we didn't shake hands.

Sucker for a Snuggie

After all my years in the advertising business, you'd think I'd be pretty sophisticated and immune to hype. Not me. What keeps me turned on to advertising is that I'm a Pollyanna. I want to believe.

One day, while I was watching TV, I snapped to attention when a commercial came on for the best thing I had ever seen in the world—a Snuggie! How did I ever get by all these years without one of these? There, before my eyes, was a bright royal blue Snuggie providing comfort and warmth to a smiling woman on a cold, wintry day. I can hear all of you doubters saying, "Can't any old blanket do the same thing?" Silly you.

A Snuggie is a miracle product that not only covers your body like a blanket, but it also has sleeves so your arms don't get cold. And not only that, you could even order this product with pockets. "Who needs pockets?" you ask. You do! Because pockets can

hold everything you need while you're watching TV—like your re-
mote, your used tissues, or even a small paperback mystery if you're
the intellectual type. You see, the Snuggie people had thought of
everything.

But before I would allow myself to order one, I had to know the
price to be sure I wouldn't get ripped off. They didn't disappoint!
The Snuggie was just $19.99 plus shipping. But wait, there's more!
They said, "If you order your Snuggie right now, we'll send you two
Snuggies for the price of one!" Well, I got right on the phone to a
helpful lady who asked if I would like to order two Snuggies. I remembered that the TV ad said I could get two for just $19.99, so (of
course) I said I wanted two. Little did I know I had just ordered four.

Then she asked me if I would like to add the convenient pockets,
and I thought, *What idiot would order a Snuggie without pockets?
Not me.* What I didn't realize is that I was ordering two pockets for
each of the four Snuggies, for a total of eight. And when she asked
if I wanted them to rush my order, I said, "Of course!" How could I
live another day without it?

After taking my credit card information, the nice lady thanked
me for my order, went down my list of add-ons, confirmed my total
price of ... $99.99! ... and hung up. I had just been Snuggied. But I
was still excited.

When my four Snuggies arrived, I was thrilled to curl up in front
of the TV, all warm and toasty. Never mind that I live in L.A. where
the temperature is seventy-two degrees. I loved my Snuggie, and I
decided I would put the extra ones to good use as personal gifts.

When my friend Steve and his wife, Lynne, were visiting, I said,
"Hey, since you're our special friends, I want you to have this." But
when I unveiled the bright blue Snuggie, they seemed to hesitate.

"Oh, how nice ... thanks so much, but ... it's very blue, isn't it ..."
(as they started to back out the door).

I was getting the impression they didn't appreciate the Snuggie as much as I did. No problem. I decided I would give one to someone with taste—my daughter Johanna. She took it and thanked me. But the last time I visited their home, I was somewhat surprised to see her husband, Charlie, wiping down his car with a bright blue rag—such disrespect for such a beautiful product. How could he?

That did it! I was not going to waste any more precious Snuggies on tasteless ingrates like family and friends. I packed up my last two Snuggies and schlepped them to our condo in Aspen, Colorado. I kept them safe and warm in a storage closet to save for a rainy day— or, as it would turn out, a very snowy one.

SEVEN

Slings and Arrows

Beware of Sweet-Talking Strangers

Does evil lurk in the shadowy halls of the ad business? Are there really sneaky, conniving people who are out to steal your job and ruin your reputation? Nah, can't be. Or so I thought.

One day, Pasqualina and I were introduced to a guy named Ray Townsend who ran a successful ad agency in Orange County, aptly named The Townsend Agency. Ray was a charming guy who looked and sounded uncannily like the Ted Baxter character on *The Mary Tyler Moore Show*. This prompted us to do cute little imitations of him using a booming voice with Ted Baxter inflections. "This is Ray Townsend with *The Evening News*!" It was harmless fun, but what was about to happen in our lives was far from harmless.

It seemed that Ray had built a successful career by cultivating just one account, Century 21, the largest franchised real estate company in the world. In fact, Ray helped to build the organization, one franchise at a time. In the early days, he traveled around the country convincing independent real estate companies to join Century 21 as franchisees, so they could benefit from the media clout of a national organization. As they grew, their members numbered in the hundreds, which generated huge profits and an impressive $30 million advertising budget. And guess who handled the advertising for them? Ray Townsend, of course.

But the account was getting too big for the little Townsend Agency of Orange County. So Century 21 politely asked Ray to look for a bigger ad agency to acquire them. That way they'd still get the benefit of Ray's experience, but they'd also have the resources of a big national agency. Wells, Rich, Greene was one of several national agencies interested in doing the deal. Like Wells, all of the agencies were big, smart, and capable. But none of them had our secret weapon—Mary Wells Lawrence. She flew out to California to meet with Ray and the management of Century 21, and, not surprisingly, her charm and brilliance won them over.

Within a month, the acquisition was complete. The Townsend Agency was now the Orange County office of Wells, Rich, Greene/West, and Ray was our chairman. No problem. Pasqualina and I liked Ray. He seemed nice and sort of harmless. Unfortunately, that wasn't the case with the creative director he brought along with him.

In the interest of protecting the guilty, I will call him Jocko. This guy looked like he came out of Central Casting, Orange County style. He was a tall, smooth, good-looking glad-hander. He billed himself as a creative director, writer, producer, poet, and creative genius extraordinaire. The truth was, he was a genius at only one thing—self-promotion.

In our new setup, Jocko remained the creative director on the Century 21 account, working out of the Orange County office. Bob and I worked out of L.A. and were given the expanded titles of co-creative directors of the West. As such, it was understood that Jocko would report to us. What we didn't know was that Jocko had bigger plans for himself. He was hell-bent on becoming the *uber* creative director of the West, and there were only two things standing in his way: Cohen and Pasqualina.

Jocko Measures the Drapes

Jocko always greeted Bob and me with a big slap on the back and a "Hiiiiii. How are youuuuuu!" We bought the whole charade when we first met him, showing him around our offices and introducing him to all the creative people. Then, strange things started to happen. Jocko began to show up at our L.A. offices, unannounced.

I first realized there was a problem when one of our art directors pulled me aside and said, "Jocko stopped in my office today and closed the door."

"Really?" I asked. "What did he want?"

"Oh, he just asked me questions about my life, my marriage, and where I wanted to be in five years."

Hmm, that was strange. About a week later, a copywriter stopped me in the garage. "Hey, I just thought you should know, Jocko says he's looking forward to working with me. Is he moving up here?" And then from another writer, "Jocko says there are going to be some changes around here. Is everything alright?"

From the beginning, Bob and I thought this guy was a joke. Now we realized if we didn't do something quick, the joke might be on us. I got on the phone to Charlie Moss in New York. "Hey, Charlie, we need to talk."

"No problem," Charlie said. "I need to be out there this week. Why don't we have dinner Friday night?"

"Great," I answered. As I got off the phone, I had a feeling of relief. Once Charlie knew what was going on, he'd take care of it. Jocko was screwing with the wrong guys.

On Friday night, Bob and I showed up at Charlie's bungalow at the Beverly Hills Hotel. Flames flickered in the fireplace and warm feelings permeated the room. Wine was poured and poured again. We talked about old times and shared a few good laughs. Then the clock struck ten, and the mood changed. "Look, guys, we've got a problem," Charlie said. Was he beating us to the punch about Jocko? "There are concerns about the Jack in the Box account."

"What? Their business is fine," I said. "What concerns are you talking about?"

"It's about the relationship," was Charlie's reply. "It's about you guys."

"Are you kidding me, Charlie? We're heroes down there. What about our exploding clown commercial that saved the account and got a seventy-two Burke score and turned their business around!"

"You guys came through, but that was a year ago. (As they say in this business, you're only as good as your last campaign.) We've been hearing things," Charlie continued. "Ray Townsend says the client feels they're not being listened to ... that the agency doesn't respect their opinions."

"That's bullshit, Charlie," I told him. "Ray doesn't know what he's talking about. Ray doesn't know what he's talking about. Ray has zero involvement with the Jack in the Box account. The only guy from down there who's even met the client is

Jocko!" And that's when it hit me. Jocko wasn't just going behind our backs in L.A.; he was spreading venom down at Jack in the Box and using Ray to sabotage us in New York.

"I'm glad you brought up Jocko," Charlie said. "Mary's not happy with what you guys have been doing lately. She feels we need a change, and I have to agree with her." My heart leaped into my throat.

"Charlie, are you telling me you want to make Jocko the creative director on Jack in the Box?" I asked.

"No, creative director of the West."

I thought I was going to have a heart attack.

Suddenly, there was a knock on the door and in walked our friend Bob Wolf, who had become the head account guy on Jack in the Box. 'Hi, guys," he said in an almost cheery tone, totally inappropriate for the situation. We had gotten to know Bob on the Columbia account and, being an ex-New Yorker like we were, we had considered him a friend. I wondered why he hadn't let on that he knew about all of this.

Charlie turned back to us. "Listen, this could be good for you guys … take some of the pressure off. Jocko could come in fresh on all the accounts. And think about it, he's perfect for Jack in the Box. They're in San Diego, and Jocko's from Orange County. (Translation: They're *goyim*; he's *goyim*.) He looks like them, he talks like them. (Translation: He's not a swarthy Italian or a Bronx Jew.) This could solve a lot of problems for the agency," Charlie added.

At that point, I felt a large vein pulsating in my temple. "Charlie, are you saying you want to trade a Cohen and Pasqualina for a Jocko?"

And in a very somber tone, Charlie said, "Yes."

I was ready to blow. "Charlie, he's a fucking hack! He'll ruin everything. You can't let this happen."

Suddenly, Wolf piped up. "Guys, don't let your egos get involved. We need a change and this could be good for everybody … for the agency and for you guys." (Yeah, humiliating demotions are always good for a man's self-esteem and career.)

I started to raise my voice. "I'm telling you, this is a crazy idea. Jocko is a fucking hack, and if you make him creative director, our advertising will go down the tubes. If you do this, I will quit. And Bob will quit!"

I looked over at Bob, who was sitting right beside me, looking absolutely shell-shocked. I knew he was fuming, but he did it in his own quiet way: the Italian way. Like, "I'm not saying anything now, but I will get my revenge." His style was "Shoot me with a gun, and I will blow you away with a howitzer."

"I hate this," Charlie said. "It's the worst part of my job. Look, Howie, this is what Mary wants."

Oh, Mary, I thought to myself. *How can you do this to us? Do you really believe these guys? Don't you remember who we are? Where is the love?* I got up out of my chair and angrily said, "Fine. You can have your Jocko, but I'm gone," and I started toward the door.

Charlie groaned. He didn't want us to quit because it would create too much disruption and turmoil in the L.A. office.

Bob Wolf stood up and said, "Whoa, Howie. I know exactly where you're coming from … this is rough. Maybe there's another way." I turned and stopped.

He looked at Charlie, and I saw an almost imperceptible nod

pass between them. I guessed they had discussed a default position. Wolf said, "How about if we just make Jocko the creative director on Jack in the Box, and you guys stay creative directors of the West? That way, you can keep your jobs and Jocko would 'theoretically' report to you."

Theoretically? Well, I guessed that was better than the alternative. I looked at Pasqualina, and he looked at me. The whole thing sucked, but this seemed like a solution that would at least allow us to retain our responsibilities and our dignity.

Pasqualina and I tried one more time to convince Charlie and Wolf that this whole thing was nuts, but it was too late. The poison had already taken effect. Jocko had won the first battle in his personal crusade to become creative director of Wells, Rich, Greene/West. In doing so, he had declared war on Bob and me. It was a war we did not intend to lose.

Hack City

Jocko was now creative director on the Jack in the Box account, and as his first official creative act, he proved just how much of a miserable hack he was (and I say that with the greatest amount of respect). He created a TV campaign that came across with the freshness of five-day-old sushi. There was no idea. It was just people biting into the food, smiling at the camera, and exulting, "Deee-licious! I love it!" It was like a bad *Saturday Night Live* skit, only the laugh was on Jack in the Box—and Wells, Rich, Greene and us.

Unfortunately, we couldn't do much about it. Jocko was in his honeymoon period with the client. Over the next several months, we continued to hear whispers about how Jocko was preparing everyone for "the new regime." The tension was mounting and, sooner or later, something had to give. Then one day, something gave.

Along Came a Kangaroo

In a shocker that rocked the company, kangaroo meat was found at Jack in the Box. It was mistakenly shipped from Australia by one of their beef suppliers, and it found its way into their burgers. You can't make this stuff up, right?

TV and radio stations had a field day with it. "Feeling a little bounce in your burger? Hop on over to Jack." Overnight, their sales fell off a cliff, and they were the butt of everyone's jokes. At the time, we were running a jingle on the radio with a rousing chorus, "The food is better at the Box, Jack in the Box, better at the Box ..."

One afternoon, a popular DJ played this track and added his own sound effect. On every downbeat, you heard, "BOING! BOING! BOING!" It was actually quite funny—unless you happened to be Jack in the Box. Suddenly, there was a mad scramble to come up with a big creative idea to save the company.

Jack in the Box turned to Jocko, but he was like a deer in the headlights. Remember Ralph Cramden in the Honeymooners? "Homma, homma, homma." Jocko didn't have a clue what to do. Ironically, he turned to Pasqualina and me. "Heyyy, guyyys, let's all get together and come up with a big idea for J-a-a-ack, okayyyy?"

Yeah, right! The real Jocko was finally being unmasked for the no-talent hack that he was, and Bob and I were not about to toss him a lifeline. Instead, we did what we do best. We got to work.

Our creative solution was simple, if a bit counterintuitive. Rather than go on the defensive and apologize for kangaroo meat, we decided to go on the attack. We focused all our efforts on a brand-new burger that Jack in the Box had on the drawing boards— a Bacon Cheeseburger Supreme. It was big, it was delicious, and it had real bacon—something no other fast-food burger had at the time. There was absolutely nothing like it in the fast-food business. We decided to go right up against McDonald's to prove that when it came to great burgers, "There's no comparison."

The script called for a youthful, somewhat irreverent spokesperson who could persuade the audience without hitting them over the head. We found him in a new, undiscovered talent by the name of Dan Gilvezan (who went on to achieve success in big-time animation as the voice of Spiderman). As we were rushing into production on our new TV spot, Jocko made an important contribution. He left on vacation.

Since the product was so far superior, the script needed to be simple and smart. It was just Dan Gilvezan interacting with a large group (who remained unseen off camera).

> **DAN: Let's compare the Bacon Cheeseburger Supreme from Jack in the Box to McDonald's bacon cheese …**
>
> **CROWD INTERRUPTS: Whaa? Can't do it!**
>
> **DAN (WITH FALSE SURPRISE): Oh, they don't have one?**
>
> **VOICE IN CROWD: (TRYING TO BE HELPFUL): They got a Big Mac.**
>
> **DAN (SARCASTICALLY): Close enough.**
>
> **CUT TO BEAUTIFUL BUILD OF OUR NEW BURGER**

*DAN VO: The new Bacon Cheeseburger Supreme is
100% beef with melting cheese and real, sizzling crispy
bacon on a toasted bun.*

*VOICE IN CROWD (INDIGNANT AT THE UNFAIR
COMPARISON): Wait a minute! You can't compare a
Bacon Cheeseburger Supreme to a Big Mac!*

DAN: (WITH SARCASTIC SMILE): Precisely!

*BEAUTY SHOT OF FOOD AND ANNOUNCER:
The new Bacon Cheeseburger Supreme from Jack in the
Box. There's no comparison.*

When the spot was launched, it had a tremendous impact on
Jack in the Box's business. Sales bounced back (so to speak) to pre-
kangaroo levels and then continued to rise from there.

The folks at Jack in the Box invited Pasqualina and me down
to San Diego for a celebratory dinner and welcomed us back onto
the account. Charlie Moss called to congratulate us and said, in no
uncertain terms, that our little Jocko problem was about to end. Our
"no comparison" TV spot became a full-fledged campaign that was
used to introduce fifteen new products and helped Jack in the Box's
sales outpace the industry. Sadly (mock tears go here), Jocko was
not around to see it.

Upon his return from vacation, he started getting the kind of
respect he deserved—none. And it seemed to affect him, both emotionally and physically. He developed a slight stammer and a facial
tic. He began to show up at work looking a little disheveled. He
started coming in late ... and then he played hooky ... and then he
disappeared. Some people down in the Orange County office said he
had left to "pursue other interests." Others said the poor guy had a

nervous breakdown. All we knew for sure was that Jocko was gone from Wells—forever.

If there's a lesson in this Machiavellian soap opera, it's that this business is all about creativity and ideas. That's what clients want, that's what they need, that's what they pay for. Jocko thought he could succeed on the basis of big white teeth, a gift for gab, and deceit. He soon found out he was wrong. Dead wrong.

Pasqualina and I didn't hate the guy, but we despised what he stood for. When he finally did himself in, we showed that we were above being petty or vindictive. We sent flowers.

Secret Calls with Ken

Bob and I survived the craziness of the Jocko plot, but the whole thing rattled us. How could New York have been so wrong about this? And how could Bob and I have been so clueless?

I decided I needed more contact with our home base so they could hear from my perspective what was really going on at the agency. I found an eager and willing ear in Ken Olshan, the recently appointed chairman of Wells, Rich, Greene in New York.

Ken was a delightful guy who came to Wells after the agency acquired his marketing consulting firm. He quickly rose in power because he showed great leadership abilities and helped run the Procter & Gamble business, one of the agency's most important accounts. Ken was a smart strategist and a caring leader who understood people and the politics of the business. In times of gnashing teeth, he always seemed to come up with solutions that were good for individuals as well as the agency. But Ken had a problem with the L.A. office.

It seemed that our president, a guy named Peter Johns, was a bit of a wild card, an unreliable prince with a huge ego who didn't want to be told what to do by New York. This guy was trouble, and Ken couldn't get through to him to find out what was going on. It was clear that Ken was his boss, but he resisted taking Ken's calls.

Since Ken and I were getting pretty close, he asked me to set up a twice-a-week call, where I would fill him in on all the goings-on at the L.A. office. In a business rife with turmoil, we came to look forward to those calls. Ken and I would spend about forty minutes on the phone, half the time talking business and the other half kibitzing about food and music and movies and life. We also shared old jokes.

"Howie, did you hear this one? Sadie is standing in line at the checkout counter of her local grocery store in Boca Raton when she notices a good-looking man just ahead of her. Sadie, obviously attracted to him, says, 'Well, I've never seen you here before.'

"The man says, 'That's because I just got out of prison.'

"'Really?' Sadie says. 'What were you in for?'

"'Well, if you really want to know, I killed my wife with a butcher knife, dismembered her body, put all the pieces in plastic bags, and threw them in the garbage.'

"Sadie thinks for a minute and says, 'So … you're single?'"

Ken and I laughed a lot. More importantly, I gave him my honest assessments of what was working at the agency and what wasn't, which was extremely valuable to a man who was responsible for our profitability and success from 3,000 miles away.

Ken had Mary's respect and her ear, and I knew I could trust him to relay the truth and give her good sound advice. There was something bad brewing on the Century 21 account, and I had intimate knowledge of the problems. I suspected that Ray Townsend wasn't communicating this to Ken, so I called to share what I knew.

"Ken, have you been hearing anything about Century 21?" I asked.

"No, is there a problem?"

"Okay," I said. "I want to share an interesting meeting I had the other night. Are you ready for this? It was with the head guy over at McCann Erickson."

"Uh-huh," Ken said.

As background, McCann was one of the other two big agencies we had beat out for the Century 21 account, when Mary did the deal with Ray Townsend.

"Ken, this guy called me and asked if I would have a drink with him. So I said sure. Well, you know in our business you never have one drink. And after about four vodkas on the rocks, the floodgates open, and he starts telling me shit."

"Like what?" Ken asked.

"The bottom line is, he said we are definitely going to lose the Century 21 account, and McCann is going to get it. There is no doubt; it's all set up. This will happen in one year."

"Are you serious?" Ken said. "This is terrible. Howie, do you believe him?"

"At first I thought he was just spewing bullshit. But then he went on to tell me stuff only someone with inside knowledge would know."

"Like what, Howie, what did he say?"

"Ken, he knew all about the trip that the president of Century 21 and his wife took to Mary's villa." Mary had a palatial villa overlooking a lake in Cap Ferrat in the South of France, that she used as a personal refuge, as well as to entertain close friends and valuable clients. "What pissed me off is that he said the president was making fun of it all. He said Mary wasn't like them. She was froo-froo, while they were just good old boys from Orange County. All this fancy French stuff was a joke to them."

I continued. "He said the president of Century 21 shared the whole story in a mocking way. He said that from the time they got to the villa, there were bouquets of flowers everywhere, servants at their beck and call, little bowls of candies and shit. He said, and I quote, 'If you farted, someone would be right behind you with a spray.'"

"Bastards," Ken said. "Howie, this sounds really serious!"

"And here's the capper. This guy went on to ask me if I would be interested in being the head creative guy at McCann in L.A."

"No shit," Ken said. "What did you say?"

"Ken, I wanted to say, 'Go fuck yourself,' but being the gentleman that I am, I told him I appreciated the offer, but I was very happy where I was."

"You're the best," Ken said. "Look, this is very important information, and I will share it with Mary right away. Thank you. I'll get back to you."

I later learned that when Ken told Mary about this, she was justifiably furious. But there was nothing she or we could do to save the account. McCann had their tentacles into Century 21 through a secret relationship. Exactly one year later, they fired Wells and moved the account to McCann L.A.

When all was said and done, Ken shared one more Mary anecdote. On the day Century 21 fired us, she was storming around her office spewing venom. "They slept in my beds ... they ate my food ... they drank my wine ... how could they do this to us?" But she was still Mary, and it didn't take her long to get over it. Two hours later, she said, "Screw 'em, we'll replace them in a month!" How could you not love her?

Not long after the loss of Century 21, I got a call from Ken. "Howie, what are you doing tomorrow?"

"Um, Bob and I will be working on a new TV spot for Jack in the Box to introduce their new steak sandwich."

"No, you won't," he said.

"I won't?"

"No, you're coming to New York. Mary has some important stuff we need to discuss."

This sounded ominous. "Ken, is there something I should know?"

"Don't worry about it," he said.

Okay, I trusted Ken. If he said I shouldn't worry about it, I wouldn't worry about it. Except for the seven hours, I lay awake that night.

The next day, Carol was by my side as we boarded a plane to New York. She was looking forward to being back in the city, hitting the museums, and seeing some old friends. I had no idea what was waiting for me. The problem with being a satellite office is that somewhere between New York and L.A. the truth can get distorted. As the plane winged its way toward New York, I pressed my head against the window and gazed down at the beauty of the Grand Canyon far below. I felt refreshed by the chill of the cold glass against my forehead. It helped me to focus my thoughts. The Machiavellian plot with all its drama and angst was only three months behind us.

What had really happened? Why did Mary and Charlie believe

all the crap that came their way from Townsend and Jocko? How could they have gotten it all so wrong about Bob and me? There had to be more to it. High above the clouds, I began to understand. The sneaky plot didn't just involve Jocko and Townsend. Our backstabbing president, Peter Johns, was also a culprit.

And, of course, it was obvious that Bob Wolf had been in on the whole devious plan long before he arrived at the Beverly Hills Hotel bungalow that night. Could it be that Wolf was not the friend I thought he was? Yet, if he was a friend, why hadn't he given me a heads up? Why were Pasqualina and I so blindsided that night? If they really believed there were problems with our performance, why hadn't they given us a chance to fix it instead of just coming in and trying to lop off our heads?

The truth was that Bob Wolf had some personality issues and questionable people skills. He was smart, but he had a way of outsmarting himself. He prided himself on being very direct with people, to the point of being abrasive and often hurtful. I think he saw this as a form of toughness and personal strength. But if you're pissing people off and weakening relationships, both in the agency and at the client, how could that be a strength? His approach to presenting creative work to the client was with the attitude of, "We're Wells and you're not." And he seemed to convey, "If you don't buy this commercial, you're stupid."

I guess I'm a slow learner, but I was starting to see the light. When the client complained about not feeling listened to and not being respected, it was not Pasqualina and me they were referring to. It was Bob Wolf.

When the shit had hit the fan, he did what a lot of deceptive people do. He covered his own ass by pointing the finger in the other direction—at us. Now our "no comparison" campaign was doing gangbusters and the Jack in the Box clients were loving Bob and me again. At least that's what we thought. Of course, we had been very wrong before. Something was in the air, and it wasn't just Carol and me on a plane to New York. A day of reckoning was coming.

Justice, Italian Style

When I arrived at the GM building in New York that day, I had a nervous feeling in the pit of my stomach. I just didn't know what was going to happen. Ken greeted me and steered me to his voluminous office, just across the hall from Mary's. He was very nice, but he wasn't saying much, which made me even more nervous.

"Wait here, Howie. I'll be out soon."

I sat down stiffly on his big, cushy sofa. I watched him walk across the hall and enter Mary's office. The door closed, and I was left to wait. And wait. Thirty minutes later, much to my surprise, out of Mary's office came Peter Johns and Bob Wolf. Apparently, they'd gotten a free trip to New York too, but they weren't looking happy about it. In fact, they looked pretty grim.

Peter walked swiftly past me, heading for the elevator, while Bob Wolf stopped at the door of Ken's office and leaned in.

"What's going on?" I asked.

"Not much," Wolf said. "We just got fired!"

"What?" I said, genuinely surprised.

"Yeah," he said.

"Are you alright?" I asked.

"Yeah, I'm fine, just more agency bullshit. I'll be okay."

"Good," I said. "If there's anything I can do ..." Well, wasn't that just like me. To be concerned about Bob Wolf. I guess I was still in my naïve stage. I really felt bad for him. Can you believe it? I felt bad for the guy who'd screwed me. Like I said, I'm a slow learner. Had the situation been reversed, I think he would have shown his concern for me with caring words like, "So long, sucker!"

Wolf turned and headed toward the elevator. Suddenly, Ken stepped out of Mary's office and beckoned me in. I was still processing the news and had no idea what to expect next. As I entered her office, Mary walked briskly toward me and beckoned me to sit down.

I plopped my butt down on the same big couch where Rudy and George from Alka Seltzer had sat that day when Mary threatened to hang Bob and me out the window by our heels. I wondered what was in store for me this day.

The sun was shining through the massive windows overlooking Central Park. I was trying to read Mary as she offered up, "Coffee? Water?"

"Is it too early for a good, stiff vodka?"

Mary smiled. Ken laughed. "Listen, Howie," she said. "I've been spending a lot of time with Ken, and he's been filling me in on what's going on out there. Howie, we've made some mistakes, some poor staffing decisions. (A thought flashed through my mind. *Am I one of them?*) But Ken and I have a new plan we want to share with you, and it's going to be great, just great!"

"Great!" I said. (We were apparently having a "great" fest.)

"Howie, what we're talking about is a fresh start," she said. "We're reorganizing and pumping new blood and energy into the L.A. office. We're going to build back the excitement we had before."

"Sounds great, Mary," I said. "What can I do to help?"

"Actually, there's a lot you can do to help, Howie." And then she hit me with a blockbuster. "We're making you president of the L.A. office." Lucky I wasn't drinking coffee, or I might have spewed it across the room.

"You're making me president?" I asked. "Seriously? Wow, I'm honored. But Mary, I'm a creative guy."

"Howie, you know this business better than all those phonies with the MBAs who can't come up with a strategy or make a decision. And the truth is, none of those guys are Wells, Rich, Greene-ers. You are, Howie. How long have we been together, eight years?" she asked.

"More like eleven, Mary, if you count New York and L.A."

"That's what I mean, Howie, you're family. None of the others were, and look what happened to them. Peter Johns is gone. So is Ray Townsend, Jocko, Bob Wolf ... they're all gone!"

For some reason, all I could hear in my head were the words of Al Pacino in *The Godfather*: "Barzini is dead. So is Phillip Tattaglia. Moe Greene. Stracci. Cuneo. Today I settled all family business."

Mary continued. "We're family, and the most important thing about family is that there's trust. Ken trusts you, Howie. I trust you."

Trust. I loved that. It made my heart feel good to hear it, to be together with Mary again, to be a Wells, Rich, Greene-er, and to be family. But there was a little hitch. In addition to being president, Mary and Ken insisted that I retain the title of co-creative director. That meant that technically Bob and I would no longer be equal. Things like that can change a relationship. What I would gain by becoming president could lead to a much bigger loss in my life.

I had a mix of emotions, all at once excited and concerned. As I turned to leave Mary's office, Mary shook my hand and Ken gave me a hug. And as I walked down the hall, he called after me.

"Have a great trip back ... Mr. President."

Fond Farewells Are Never Fond

On September 25, 1982, I celebrated my fortieth birthday. Midlife!

I'm told that particular milestone can be traumatic for a lot of people. Not for me. Wells, Rich, Greene had just made me president of the L.A. office, Carol and I had recently welcomed our beautiful son, Jonathan, into the world, and the sun was shining brightly in La La Land.

But Bob Pasqualina and his wife, Janet, had been experiencing different emotions for quite some time. They were feeling the irresistible tug of New York. All of the things that Bob didn't like about L.A. when we first moved there were still with him.

I remembered how frustrated and disappointed he was when the two of us were looking to buy our first homes in L.A. He was a traditionalist who loved the simple beauty of classic East Coast architecture, like old colonials, Victorians, and Tudors. So he was sorely disappointed with the homes his L.A. real estate agent was showing him. I thought back to 1978 and remembered our conversation.

"Howie," he said. "They've got fucking rocks on the roofs."

I gave him the practical reason. "It's so the houses don't burn down in the canyon fires every year." I don't think that reassured him.

"Howie, they don't have basements."

"It's a good thing," I said. "Or they would get ruined in the mudslides that come after the fires." That only made it worse.

"Howie, the houses don't even have foundations. They're built on slabs."

"It's a good thing, Bob, because it's better to have a slab in a 6.2 earthquake."

By that time, I think Bob was ready to pack up everything and head back to New York. But he didn't. Bob and Janet actually stayed almost two years longer than our original contract, and I was grateful for the extra time we had together. In the end, though, the magnetic pull of the Big Apple was just too much for them. Bob and Janet sold their house and moved back to New York, and Bob became a commercial director.

With my longtime partner gone, all of a sudden we only had one creative director who was also doing his best to be president—me. That just wasn't going to work. For almost a year, I had done my best to live up to my responsibilities as president, but if I were to be honest, I would have to give myself a grade of C+. The role just didn't come naturally to me, and it wasn't very fulfilling. I longed for the days of working on big creative campaigns.

I called Ken and told him my feelings. We talked about how Wells would be far more powerful with a fulltime, dedicated president working with me as a charged up, rededicated creative director. He agreed, and this began a two-month search for a suitable executive talent who was more than a suit. Then one day, a big solution turned up in the form of a small man. His name was Richard Kelly.

Ken introduced him to me over cocktails and a steak dinner, and I liked him immediately. Richard was a well-heeled Brit—smart and very strategic. And he had all the right credentials, having risen to high ranks in big agencies and, more importantly to me, having led a hot New York creative agency to great work and rapid growth.

Over the next year and a half, Richard and I enjoyed a tight relationship. I liked him, and we got along well, working side by side to grow the agency. Things were going well. But there was a curveball coming my way. This is the advertising business, remember?

EIGHT

~⌣~

Moving On

A Reason for Treason

I never thought I would leave Wells, Rich, Greene … again! I was really enjoying my career. We were doing some great work, I felt appreciated by our clients and the agency, and Mary was paying me a lot of money that provided my family and me with a comfortable Bel Air lifestyle. Who would want to leave a job like that? Not me. If it weren't for the strange events that were brewing in New York— things that were beyond my control—I would never have even considered leaving. The bomb dropped one sunny Friday morning.

Richard called me into his office and asked me to sit down. He offered me a bottle of water and began to speak. "You're not supposed to know about this, but I feel I need to tell you." That didn't sound good.

"What's up?" I asked.

"We may have to resign the Hills Bros. Coffee account."

"What?" I said. "Resign Hills Bros.? They're one of our best accounts. We're doing great work for those guys, and they're our friends … it's one of the best relationships we've ever had."

"I know," he said.

As a reminder, the Hills Bros. people had come to the agency for Pasqualina and me, and we had developed close personal relationships with them. When Bob left for New York, our account guy Mark Johnson stepped in to fill the void by gaining their trust and making friends with them.

Mark and I led a talented group of people who all loved working on the business. We would fly up to San Francisco and meet with them, eat with them, and party with them. It was a dream relationship. What's more, they were a prestigious package goods account, which is rare on the West Coast. And they were spending $10 million, mostly on TV advertising, which made the account highly visible and profitable for the agency.

"What can New York be thinking?" I asked.

"It's simple, Howie. You know that Wells has a lot of Procter & Gamble business in New York. Well, Folgers Coffee is a division of P & G, and Mary thinks the New York office has a good shot at getting the business. But not if we have the Hills Bros. account."

I immediately understood. Folgers was probably ten times the size of Hills Bros. It would be great for the New York office if they could win it, but it would be terrible for the L.A. office.

"It's unfortunate," Richard continued in a typically understated British way. "And I know how personally involved you are with the guys at Hills Bros. For me, too, it could be a giant step backward in terms of growing the West Coast office. That's why I wanted you to know. I'm thinking what the alternatives could be."

"What do you mean?" I asked.

He came right out and said it. "What do you think the chances would be of us taking the Hills Bros. account and starting an agency?"

Whoa! This was all coming at me very fast. "I'm not sure I really want to do that again," I said. "You know, I had an agency in New York. We did big things, we were hot, it was exciting, but in the end, it didn't work out, and it was pretty painful. Life has been good for me here."

"I understand," he said. "I like it here at Wells too. But I'm looking at what's happening now, and I'm concerned about the future of this office. If they're willing to just lop off one of our best accounts, who knows what could happen next."

He had a point. Our destiny was in New York's hands, not ours. That was something to seriously consider. He added, "Please don't say a word of this to anyone. My understanding is that no decisions are going to be made for at least a month. Let's just take a little time to think about it ... okay?"

We shook hands, and I left the office early that day to go home and think. I was glad that Richard felt comfortable enough to confide in me.

But I also felt disappointed that Ken Olshan, whom I had been so close with, didn't call to tell me this personally. Maybe he didn't want to scare me or hurt my feelings. Or maybe over the last year and a half, our relationship had just lost the magic. That was another thing for me to consider. If I wasn't important enough to be told something as potentially career-altering as this, where did I really stand with him and Mary?

Three weeks later, Richard confirmed that New York was serious about moving ahead with their quest to win the Folgers account. The time was fast approaching when we would have to resign Hills Bros.

Richard and I began to meet in secret. "Do you think Hills Bros. would have any problem going with a startup agency?" he asked.

"I doubt it. I know they love us, and we've done a lot for their business over the past five years. But Richard, I have to be upfront with you." I said. "The Hills Bros. guys don't know you very well. They came to the agency for Bob and me, and now that Bob's gone, their loyalty is to me and Mark Johnson."

As with any agency, there are just a handful of people who really matter to the client—the ones who really do the work. In addition to Bob and Mark and me, our MVPs were a young hot creative team in the form of Claudia Caplan and Jim Walker. Claudia was a precocious young writer, brainy and ballsy and talented beyond her years. Her art director partner, Jim, was a golden boy (in more ways than one). In addition to his art director talents, he was tall, handsome, blond, and boyishly *goyish*. Together, they did fabulous work on the Hills Bros. business.

I continued my line of thought with Richard. "I guess what I'm saying is that the client has a very high regard for Mark, and it may be time to get him in the loop."

Richard agreed, and that was the start of a triumvirate. Mark saw the same problems with losing this account and got excited over the opportunity of starting an agency. But could this account support three heavyweight salaries? And did it make sense to have two of our biggest expenses allocated to account management? Would we be starting out with a financial handicap? We put that concern in the back of our heads and continued to move forward, planning how we would do this.

Then, when we were just two days away from flying to San Francisco to tell Hills Bros. we had to resign their business and ask for their blessing to start our own agency, Richard called me into his office.

"Listen," he said. "I've been thinking a lot about this, and it just doesn't make financial sense. You and Mark are the key guys on this account. You can do this ... and you should. I've thought a lot more about the situation here, and I think I can make it work. And I know you guys will do great on your own."

It was a bit of a shock, but a smart decision on Richard's part. And I soon found out that he had other reasons for his decision beyond what was good for Mark and me. Apparently, Richard was having "a thing" with Joan McArthur, the most senior creative person at the agency after me. I had known Joan for a number of years, and we had enjoyed some great times creating campaigns, going off to fight the ad wars together, and partying with friends after hard-fought victories. With Mark and me out of the agency and out of the picture, Joan could rise to be creative director (and she did) and she and Richard could be together (in more ways than one) and run the whole show. Hey, why not? Everybody deserves a shot.

Mark and I were moving on to our next big challenge, and so were Richard and Joan. That week, Mark and I took the flight up to Hills Bros. for a private meeting with Barry Reis and Paul Miller. Quite frankly, we were nervous. We knew how much they liked and respected us, but trusting us to start an agency? That was a major leap of faith. Hills Bros. was a $10 million account, and a lot of their success rested on the quality of their advertising. As we sat down in their small conference room, Barry asked, "What's up, guys?"

Mark said, "This sucks, but we got the word from New York that we have to resign your account." Barry and Paul looked a little stunned.

I jumped in. "Yeah, they want to pitch Folgers. We hate this. It's not right after all the time we've put in together. We've never had such a close relationship with a client. And to think it could all go away for no good reason."

"I agree," Barry said. "This is really a surprise."

"But, guys," Mark said, "we have an idea we want to share with you." Mark paused, took a deep breath, and continued. "We'd like your blessing to take the Hills Bros. account and start our own ad agency." We could see this was all coming at them fast, but we shouldn't have been worried.

"We don't want to lose you guys," Paul said. "If this is what you want to do, we're behind you 110%."

Mark and I both exhaled and a smile came over our faces. "Let's do it," Paul continued. "Open your agency and we'll be happy to be your first client. There's only one thing I need to caution you about. This is a commodity business. You probably already know this because you've been working with us for a while, but if there's a coffee freeze in Brazil and coffee bean prices go up, we'll have no choice but to cut ad spending. I'd hate to see that happen. I'd hate to see you start out with a $10 million account and see it go down to $4 million or less 'cause I know it would hurt."

That's when Mark uttered the fateful words. "Paul, we're not worried. I mean, a coffee freeze in our first year? It ain't gonna happen."

Of course it happened.

Softly, I Will Leave You

I couldn't leave Wells without a proper goodbye. That was tough. I loved Mary. I loved Charlie. I loved Ken. It hurt my heart to leave, but it was the only thing I could do, given the circumstances.

I chose to call Ken. Damn, that was hard. As I dialed the phone, I was feeling sad, and I could feel my throat tightening up. He picked up the phone in New York. "Ken?" I said. "It's Howie."

"Oh hi, Howie, nice to hear from you. What's up?"

"Ken, this is a call I never thought I would have to make." He was silent. "Ken, I'm leaving Wells."

"Oh, Howie," he said disappointedly.

"Ken, I've known about the whole thing with Folgers and us having to resign the Hills Bros. business. That's a knife to the heart of this office. They're our closest relationship and a good profitable account."

"I know, Howie. It sucks, but you know this business."

"I do, and I don't blame you for making the decision to go after a bigger account. If you get it, it will be great for New York, but it would be terrible for us. And that's why I'm leaving, and so is Mark. We're taking the Hills Bros. account and starting our own agency."

"Wow!" he said. "Wow, wow, wow." I sensed he was a little hurt, but I also knew he was smart enough to know this was the right thing for us. "Howie, I'm not happy about this, but I totally get it. All I can do is wish you guys the very best. I'll figure out with Richard where we go from here."

"Thanks for your understanding. Please send my love to Mary and Charlie, and tell them I will miss them. And Ken, I'll miss you ... a lot!"

"I love you Howie."

He hung up. And that was it. A sad farewell to the agency I loved, the agency that had been so good to me in so many ways.

Now it was official. I was walking away from my big beautiful job at Wells. And Mark and I were announcing the opening of a brand-new ad agency, Cohen/Johnson. Here I go again.

Drink to a New Partner

The first time I ever talked with Mark Johnson at length was on a business trip, late at night in St. Louis, in a bar over drinks—lots of drinks. In fact, we closed down the bar that night, which was only fitting.

Mark and I were destined to become partners, first at Wells, working together on several of our most important accounts, and then at our own agency. And the glue in our relationship for a long time was a mutual fondness for "belting 'em down."

Mark Johnson was a totally different animal than Bob Pasqualina. To begin with, Mark was my partner in the ad wars but not my creative partner. He was not an art director or a writer. He was an account guy.

A native of Marblehead, Massachusetts, and the son of a doctor, Mark's life was a study in contradictions. He was a strategic guy, good with numbers and statistics, who graduated from Dartmouth and went on to get his MBA from the Amos Tuck School of Business Administration. At the same time, he was a devout rock 'n' roller who had played guitar in a professional rock band in the seventies. As a result, Mark was as comfortable quoting Rosser Reeves as he was Mick Jagger, and his favorite initials were not MBA but LSD.

Mark worked at Wells, Rich, Greene in New York in the mid-seventies (after I had left) on some Procter & Gamble business. He knew his stuff. So that was the basis for our budding relationship.

We both wanted to do great work. We both came at it from

different disciplines to arrive at a good place. And when the work day faded and the job was done, we both loved to reward ourselves with some tall frosty ones.

On May 6, 1985, Mark and I officially swung open the doors of Cohen/Johnson and announced that an exciting new agency was ready to take on the world. We had the good fortune to be starting out with a $10 million account, which amply paid for a staff of nine people, including Mark and myself. We had left Wells on good terms, agreeing not to poach the agency's talent pool. However, we did take some young twenty-something future stars in the form of Paula McSpadden, our junior account exec on Hills Bros., and Sue Dawson, a sharp young lady who would turn into a spitfire of a producer. We were excited, energized, and ready for anything. Well, almost anything.

Hanging by Our Thumbs

Paul Miller, the president of Hills Bros., must have been psychic. Sure enough, just as we were opening the doors of our new agency with Hills Bros. as our charter account, *WHAM!*—there was a coffee freeze in Brazil. When that happens, it creates a coffee bean shortage that causes the price of coffee to go through the roof. As a result, coffee lovers cut back on their coffee drinking and sales take a big hit.

So what do coffee companies do? They try to minimize the damage by cutting expenses any place they can. And the typical place they cut is their advertising budget. *Slash!* Suddenly, as Paul Miller had fatefully predicted, our $10 million advertising account was down to $4 million. It was just our first year in business, and it looked like our budding agency might get nipped in the bud.

A Schmaltz-y Plan B

With the setback in agency income, the pressure was on to get new business. When we weren't beating the bushes and knocking on doors, I found myself being circumspect. *What have I done? Is this the way it's supposed to be? Have I stayed at the party too long?*

From the first day I started in the advertising business, I heard the same cliché: there are no fifty-year-old creative people in this business. It was stated as a simple fact based on simple economics.

The older you get as a copywriter or an art director, the more you cost an agency in salary and overhead. At the same time, the older you get, the less willing you are to burn the midnight oil and kill yourself to come up with the big idea. You've got a wife and kids to love and spend time with, and you've developed other interests and hobbies. Your world is not just advertising anymore.

Conversely, young creative people coming into the business (much like myself when I was a young Turk) are dying to make their mark and willing to do anything to hit it big, including working late at night and bunking at the agency on weekends. Young people cost less and are willing to do more.

The bottom line is there's not much job security for older people in the advertising business. So a lot of writers and art directors spend serious time coming up with a viable Plan B, just in case they are politely asked to vacate the premises, or in the parlance of Madison Avenue, "Get the fuck out of here!"

In truth, I was always pretty confident in my talent and didn't spend time worrying about this. Yet, I did have a Plan B I was so excited about that at one time I thought it might even become my Plan A. And, although I was only in my early forties, I definitely started to think about it more as our agency was gasping for breath.

My idea was to market the first great chopped liver in America. (Don't laugh—this stuff tasted great.) My product was based on a killer chopped liver recipe handed down from generation to generation by my Polish-Jewish ancestors. I learned to make it at my mother's side in the tiny kitchen of our Bronx apartment. My mother would boil up some hard-boiled eggs, chop up onions, and fry them in a pan slathered with *schmaltz* (rendered chicken fat).

Then she would throw the chicken livers in the pan with the onions and the *schmaltz*, fry it up, and bring all the ingredients to me in a big wooden bowl. My job was to screw the iron meat grinder to the kitchen table and turn the crank. The secret was not to grind it too much. We liked our chopped liver big and chunky instead of like fine pate, which was strictly for *goyim*.

I loved the taste, even though it gave me serious heartburn. Somehow, I never made the connection between the food I was eating and that burning feeling in my chest. Like Buddy Hackett, I thought I would die if the fire went out of my heart. I loved chopped liver, and I knew how to make it. And to ensure that I would make millions on this product, I created a Clio-caliber ad campaign and even shot a test commercial featuring myself standing in the kitchen wearing a white apron and holding a meat cleaver.

The script went like this:

> **COHEN: When I was a kid, my father would come home and say, "Where's Howie?"**
>
> **And my mother would say, "In the kitchen, making chopped liver."**
>
> **"Making chopped liver! That kid's not normal. He should be out playing stickball like his brother, Jerry!"**

And she would say, "Sam, chopped liver is his life!"

CAMERA SLOWLY ZOOMS IN

COHEN: And it still is my life. I make Cohen's Famous Chopped Liver, with fresh chicken livers and fried onions and lots of hard-boiled eggs. And you know what?

CAMERA ZOOMS IN TO CATCH THE TWINKLE IN MY EYE

COHEN: I never skimp on the schmaltz! That's why Cohen's Famous Chopped Liver is so famous. So when people tell me about famous people like Robert Redford and Muhammed Ali, I say ... "What am I, chopped liver?"

FREEZE ON MY FACE AS WE DISSOLVE TO THE SAME IMAGE ON THE PACKAGE OF COHEN'S FAMOUS CHOPPED LIVER

"What am I, chopped liver?" could have been the next big viral line

I was sure that "What am I, chopped liver?" could have been bigger than "I can't believe I ate the whole thing," bigger than "Try it, you'll like it." I could just imagine people driving along Sunset Boulevard and seeing a big billboard featuring the famous Frank Sinatra ... then the famous Madonna ... then soon-to-be-famous Howie Cohen saying, "What am I, chopped liver?"

But in the end, I couldn't do it. As good as it tasted, I knew how bad organ food with lots of *schmaltz* was for people's health. As a friend said to me, "Howie, your chopped liver will kill more Jews than Hitler." In the interest of saving lives, I killed the chopped liver.

NINE

~

Hitting the Jackpot

With our reduced income on Hills Bros., we desperately need-ed new business. A big account … a medium account … any account would do at that point. Then a new opportunity popped up from an old familiar place.

Jack in the Box was in trouble again. Within three months after Mark and I left the agency, Jack in the Box decided to pull the ac-count from Wells. They moved their business to a Chicago agency, of all places. This was pretty devastating to the Wells L.A. office.

With the decision to resign Hills Bros., Wells L.A. not only lost a good $10 million account, but they had lost two of their top guys in the form of Howie Cohen and Mark Johnson. And, with Jack in the Box flying the coop to Chicago, they lost their biggest account. Jack had been spending $30 million on advertising at the time. This precipitated a series of account losses, and within two years of losing Jack in the Box, the Richard Kelly and Joan McArthur reign was over. The agency closed its doors on the West Coast, forever.

I hated to see it happen. Many of those people were my friends, and I had a strong emotional connection to Wells, the agency that had given me so many opportunities and had helped shape my talent and my career. I called a few people in New York to express my condolences. We agreed to stay in touch and wished for better times for all of us.

Wells was finished in LA., and Cohen/Johnson was on the respirator. But now, we had this opportunity.

Lucky Socks

One day, Mark Johnson popped into my office and said, "You know, I've been looking at Jack in the Box's numbers (they were a public company), and they really suck. Maybe you ought to call Jack Goodall, the chairman, and see if we can do a project for them or something."

Yeah, right, I thought to myself. *He's really going to want to take a chance on a nine-person agency with one declining account.*

"Give it a shot," Mark said. "What have we got to lose?"

I called Goodall's office and actually got through to him. He sounded happy to hear from me, like we were old friends. I told him I'd been doing a little thinking on their business (not much, but I could vamp), and I wanted to come down and talk. Much to my surprise, he said, "Okay, how about Thursday, twelve noon, in my office? I'll buy you lunch."

I flew down to San Diego, and we met privately over a salad, chips, and a Coke. To my delight, he opened up to me, bemoaning his current advertising campaign.

"Howie, all they're doing is deals. We can't keep cutting our prices … we'll kill our business. And the way they're doing it!"

Jack let out a deep sigh. Apparently, the campaign was a personal embarrassment to him because it featured a buffoonish character who looked suspiciously like himself. The TV campaign asked the question, "What do we have to do to get you to come into Jack in the Box?" And the unfortunate answer was … "Cut you a great deal." The "cute" gimmick was that the guy in the commercials would get so frustrated he would do something silly to harm himself.

In the first spot, he put his fist through a wall. In the second spot, his hand was in a cast, and he kicked a chair. In the third spot, he had a cast on his hand and was standing on crutches and … you get the idea. It was amusing, but unfortunately, the joke was on Jack in the Box. All they were doing was reinforcing a perception that the food wasn't good enough to bring people in—only cheap prices were.

"Howie," he said. "We've had three great campaigns since I've been at Jack in the Box ... and two of them were yours." A great compliment. The Exploding Clown campaign that Bob Pasqualina and I launched in 1980 repositioned them as an adult fast-food place and helped turn their business around. And the No Comparison campaign saved them from kangaroo meat and built their business from there. Then Jack said, "I keep asking myself, what would Howie Cohen do?"

Yowza. This was the shot we had been hoping for—a chance to show our thinking and maybe win an assignment. I told him I would be back in one week to show him what Howie Cohen would do.

Based on what he'd told me about their current campaign, I started to get an idea. In a world of silly fast-food commercials, the silliest being Jack in the Box's, we had an opportunity to present a different tone of voice and a new point of view—a serious point of view from a company that was serious about great tasting food.

I batted this around at our agency with the troops, and we all saw strong possibilities. It was a different approach for fast food, for sure, and one that grew directly out of their strategy to create great tasting adult food products. So we got to work and wrote an entire campaign around this idea of "serious food."

One week later, Mark and I flew down to San Diego and showed up in a big boardroom to present six storyboards in a completely new TV campaign. There were seven people representing Jack in the Box management in the room. They all had defeated looks on their faces. Their sales were down, their stock was down, and they were down. Mark and I instinctively picked up on the quiet solemnity of the room and used it to our advantage. We adopted a serious tone that was totally in keeping with our strategy. We held up a sparse whiteboard with our positioning statement on it and spoke the words, "Jack in the Box is serious food."

With that, Mark and I began to present the storyboards that told simple stories of people who were serious about the great tasting adult food at Jack in the Box. We focused on unique products that nobody else had: fajita pitas, finger foods, and Bacon Cheeseburger Supremes. There were no gimmicks, no tricks, and no jokes. What would make these spots stand out would be the charm of the stories and the credibility of the performances.

When our presentation was over, and the last script had been read, Jack Goodall asked one question. "Howie, are you sure this will work?"

In a business where nobody can be sure of anything, I said what I had to say. "Yes, Jack, I'm sure!"

I got a call at my home the next day. It was Saturday morning, and I was just getting out of the shower when the phone rang. "Hello, Howard? This is Mr. Goodall's office calling. Could you please meet Jack in his office on Monday morning at 9:00 a.m.?"

"Um, yes, sure, I can do that." (*Holy shit!*)

I got off the phone and immediately called Mark. "I don't know what he wants to meet about," I told him, "but it's gotta be good, right? I mean, he's not going to ask me to come all the way down to San Diego to tell me we sucked, right?"

Mark agreed and added, "You know what, if the meeting is at 9:00 a.m., maybe you should fly down there tomorrow night, stay at a hotel, and get some sleep. Then you can be there nice and fresh on Monday morning."

Good idea. Carol and I packed our bags and left for San Diego Sunday evening. I can't say that I slept well, but in the morning, I was pumped and ready to go. I showered and started to get dressed. I put on my boxer shorts, followed by my slacks and my nicely pressed shirt. I pulled my dress shoes out of the hanging bag and reached for my dress socks. *Oops!* That's when I realized I had forgotten to pack my dress socks. Now I was getting stressed.

"Oh, don't worry about it," Carol said. "Just wear your sweat socks from yesterday … no one will even notice."

And so, decked out in a white dress shirt and Armani tie, black cashmere sports coat, gray slacks, shiny black shoes, and bright white sweat socks with a Nike logo, I got into a cab with Carol to attend one of the most important meetings of my life.

When I got to Jack Goodall's office, his secretary invited me to sit down on a small couch near her desk. "Please make yourself comfortable," she said. "Jack will be out in a minute."

I sat there leaning a little forward, trying hard to make the cuffs of my dress pants hide the bright white sweat socks. Her fingers were flying across the typewriter keys, when all of a sudden she looked up and asked me to verify a couple of facts.

"Howie, your agency is Cohen/Johnson … C-o-h-e-n slash J-o-h-n-s-o-n, correct?"

"Yes, that's right."

"And you're located in Los Angeles at—"

Just then, Jack popped his head out and beckoned me to come in. "Sit down, Howie, want a cup of coffee?"

"No, thanks. I've had all the caffeine I can handle this morning."

He turned away, and I sneakily reached forward to pull the cuffs further down over my white Nike socks.

"Howie," he said. "We liked what you and Mark presented to us." My heart leaped. "How fast do you think we can get this going?" he asked.

"Fast," I said. "We can put a test plan together and—"

"Test?" he said. "We don't need any test, Howie. We need sales and we need them fast. Ginny is typing up a press release. You guys are going to be our new ad agency."

I was stunned. Never in my wildest dreams did I think he would hand us the whole account. Remember, we were a small agency with just nine people, a diminished coffee account, and a dwindling bank account. Jack in the Box was a $30 million piece of business!

We talked for a while longer. It was all about urgency, urgency, urgency to get things going again for Jack in the Box. Then we shook hands, and I left Jack's office feeling almost giddy.

As I walked down their long hall, I was giving high fives to everyone—the sales guys, the marketing guys, the janitor. Then, just as I reached the end of the hallway to leave the building, Jack called after me, "Howie, whoa!" He said it like a command, and it rattled me. Was he changing his mind? Was he going to tell me this was all a cruel joke? Jack smiled, pointed to my feet, and said, "Maybe now you'll be able to afford dress socks?" We both cracked up.

When Carol and I got to the airport, I couldn't wait to get to a payphone to call Mark at the office (remember, there were no cell phones in those days). When he answered, I said, "Mark! (I think I was shouting.) We got it!"

"Really?" he said.

"Yes, yes! We got it!"

"Fan-tas-tic!" he said. Then I heard him telling the rest of our people, "It's Howie, he says we got it." I heard a little cheer go up. "Great! Did they say what they want ... I mean ... do you know the scope of the assignment?"

"Mark, you don't understand. We just got the whole fucking thing! We won the Jack in the Box account!"

"We won the whole account?" I heard the whole office erupt in the background.

"Carol and I are going to make the noon flight back, so we've gotta run, but I'll tell you everything when I get back to the office."

When we arrived back in L.A., there was a limo driver waiting for us holding a big sign that said "Howie Cohen" on it. I walked up to him and asked if I was the Howie Cohen he was waiting for, and he said, "Cohen/Johnson?"

"Yeah," I told him, and he escorted Carol and me to a big stretch limo just for the two of us. Mark was showing his true classiness. And just in case we were thirsty from our long, one-hour journey, there was a bottle of Dom Perignon chilling in a silver bucket.

As we sped away from LAX, I popped the cork and poured Carol and myself a sparkling glass of bubbly. I began to fantasize about the future. For Cohen/Johnson and all of our people, this could very well be the beginning of good times, big times, affluent times. It all depended on one thing though. Jack's question came back to me.

"Howie, are you sure this will work?"

We would all find out soon enough.

Howie, Mo, and Jack

Mo Iqbal and I were brought together by fate—and a fajita pita. Our little nine-person agency, Cohen/Johnson, had just won the $30 million Jack in the Box account. And Mo had just been promoted to marketing director of Jack in the Box.

Together, we were destined to do great things—or not. The marketplace would soon tell us if our Serious Food campaign was a winner or a bomb.

Mo's background was one of those great Horatio Alger stories. He came over to this country from Pakistan with twenty bucks to his name and got his first job at Jack in the Box sweeping floors at night. He quickly moved up the ranks, working the deep fat fryer, handling the cash register, and supervising other employees. Pretty soon he knew how to do every job in the store, and they made him manager. Mo seized the opportunity and made that store one of the most profitable in the Jack in the Box chain, which got the attention of corporate.

In just a few years, Mo joined the white-collar gang at Jack in the Box's headquarters. And that's where he was, waiting for his shot to become marketing director, when Cohen/Johnson came on board.

The day we were introduced, Mo offered to drive me to the San Diego airport. As he maneuvered his car onto the freeway, he turned to me and asked, "What's the most important thing you would be looking for from me?"

That's the first sign of a good client. He cares about what's important to you, and he believes in relationships. I said, "Honesty, sharing information, and being treated as a partner."

He smiled and said, "That's what I would ask from you too."

As Bogey said to Claude Rains in *Casablanca*, "Louie, I think this is the beginning of a beautiful friendship." On the other hand, it could all go to hell in a handbasket if our campaign didn't work.

What we were about to do was dramatically different from anything else in the category. Typical fast-food advertising was fun, upbeat, and often goofy. Our campaign focused on foodies who loved the great new tastes coming out of Jack in the Box. And they were serious about it. But hey, it was still just fast food. Were we taking ourselves too seriously?

One of our first agency hires was a senior account guy named Tom Ruffino. We brought him in on the basis of his vast fast-food experience, acute strategic skills, and his ability to match Mark Johnson and me, shot for shot. Together, our team got to work shooting our first three TV spots, editing them, and getting them on air with lightning speed.

After the campaign had been on the air for just one week, it was report card time. In a somewhat ominous call, Mo asked Tom and me to fly down to San Diego to talk about the results. When we entered Mo's office, we immediately got a bad feeling. He was sitting behind his big desk, and he wasn't smiling. He had stacks of sales reports laid out in front of him, and he was slowly shaking his head.

Tom let out a nervous laugh and said, "So, should I be updating my resume?" Mo didn't laugh.

"Well, guys," he said. "I don't know what to do except read you the results. Phoenix: down 2%." He paused, looked up at us, and slowly shook his head. I glanced over at Tom, who was turning the color of an avocado. Mo went on. "Houston: down 1%," and he slowly shook his head again. Our hearts were in our throats. Then he stopped, waited a beat, and said, "Oh, but what's this? L.A.: up 8%! San Diego: up 10.5%! Seattle, San Francisco: up, up, up! Guys, it looks like we've got a winner here!"

And with that, he reached across the desk to shake our hands. "Mo, you bastard," Ruffino said as we all laughed. It was a moment of triumph … and a hell of a relief.

Month after month, Jack in the Box sales kept rising, fueled by great new products and a smart, new ad campaign. It was the beginning of a successful relationship that lasted for nine years.

Mo and I are good friends to this day. Sometime after leaving the company, he sold his stock in Jack in the Box and became one of the largest franchisees in the Hardee's hamburger chain, which was ultimately acquired by Carl's Jr. Mo now lives with his lovely family in a large mansion on a hill with a 180-degree ocean view, where he treats his guests to caviar and foie gras.

I'm still eating at Jack in the Box.

Call In the Reinforcements

In 1986, we started growing almost too quickly and became overwhelmed with work. We needed some big-time creative help, so we put the word out to our favorite headhunter, Miranda Chiu of the

Baeder/Chiu Company: "Find us a creative star." Three weeks later, she came through with a young hotshot art director from New York named Bruce Dundore.

Bruce was a rising star at BBDO in New York with a great reel that included award-winning TV spots for big-time clients like Pepsi and Dodge. So why would he want to leave the security of a big-time New York agency for a young L.A. agency with great hopes but a questionable future?

The answer was love. No, not for me. Evidently, Bruce had a beautiful girlfriend in L.A., and he was eager to give up everything to be with her. We saw that as a great opportunity for Cohen/Johnson. So I told Miranda, "Okay, I'd like to meet with the guy."

This led to an incredible boozy dinner at The Grill in Beverly Hills, a fancy-shmancy restaurant with colossal portions and prices to match (I was pulling out all the stops). Over martinis and several bottles of wine, we talked about what he wanted and what we needed. I liked Bruce immediately. He was funny and talented—and passionate about doing great work.

Just a few weeks later, he moved to L.A. to be with his beloved Maria and work with me at Cohen/Johnson as my future co-creative director. One of our first assignments together was to create a new campaign for our client, The Disney Channel. It would involve funny animated characters and accents. It was tailor-made for Bruce because he was funny and animated and loved doing accents. He latched onto this assignment like a New York rat dragging a slice of pizza down the subway stairs.

This campaign called for him to play the role of a key Disney character: Goofy. Trust me when I tell you that nobody does Goofy like Bruce. (That's a compliment.) This campaign was so important that the president of The Disney Channel decided to be there to see what we had come up with. No problem. We had a great campaign, and we had a master presenter in Bruce Dundore.

The president sat at the end of a long conference table as Bruce got up to do his *shtick*. He was big, bodacious, and the embodiment of Goofy. The words were written for the character, and his inflection was perfect as he hovered over the conference table.

As he launched into the script, he flailed his arms, wiggled his Goofy tail, and drove the humor home with the full force of his personality. It seemed like a winner from the moment he opened his mouth. However, just as Bruce was about to wrap it up, disaster struck. He had apparently forgotten to spit out the wad of gum he was chewing before he began his presentation. So as Bruce delivered his final Goofy punchline, the gum shot out of his mouth like a cannonball, and bounced really hard on the table and directly at the president of the Disney Channel—bounce ... bounce ... bounce— until it landed directly in front of him.

For a second, time stopped as everyone held their breath. Then the president let out a huge guffaw, and everyone else followed suit. And what might have been a catastrophe ended in a cascade of laughter and a campaign sold!

That was my Bruce—a big, boisterous, raucous talent who could scare the shit out of you, but who would ultimately charm the pants off you. Over the course of the next eight years, he stayed at Cohen/Johnson, then left us, then came back, then stayed with us, and finally left again. No matter what, I always respected his talent, appreciated his humor, and admired his outsized presentation skills—even if he couldn't speak and chew gum at the same time.

It Ain't Brain Surgery

With the help of Bruce and other great creative talents, our agency was growing fast. Jack in the Box liked the job we were doing for them so much that they invited us to pitch another business their parent company, Foodmaker, owned. It was a Mexican restaurant chain called Chi Chi's.

We came up with a simple idea to create a memorable icon, based on the founder of the chain—a Mexican gentleman named (surprise) Chi Chi. We envisioned him to be a lovable cross between Pancho Villa and Ricky Ricardo. We also created a sidekick for him, a foil who could be used to underscore Chi Chi's passion and commitment to keep on creating great new original Mexican dishes. His sidekick, Lupe, could never understand why Chi Chi wanted to work so hard when they could be relaxing and having fun in the sun.

We won the account based on this idea and on the faith that Jack Goodall had in our agency. Now we had the approval to cast our main characters and shoot our first TV spot. We knew this production had to be great, so we passed on the usual suspects and reached out to a director we had never worked with before—someone with a big reputation and an ego to match.

His name was Norman Seeff, and his fascinating background is important to this story. Norman had grown up in Johannesburg, South Africa, where he dreamed of someday becoming a brain surgeon. Determined to succeed, he put in the time, the passion, and the years, and ultimately achieved his goal. He was a full-fledged brain surgeon, saving people's lives. However, after a number of years doing this work, he realized that he wasn't being fulfilled creatively. So he abandoned his medical career and became an accomplished photographer, eventually moving on to become an award-winning commercial film director.

At Cohen/Johnson, we had admired his work, so we sought him out to direct our first TV spot in order to bring these important characters to life. We began casting, and from day one the chemistry felt really good, and there was a lot of mutual respect.

Everything was going just fine until one day when we had a major disagreement over who would play the part of Chi Chi. Norman felt strongly that it should be one particular actor, but I felt just as strongly that it should be a different actor. That's fine; this business is all about collaborating and challenging each other's creative viewpoints.

However, what started out as a respectful difference of opinion became a confrontation that erupted into a shouting match. "No, no," he said. "You don't know what you're talking about! I'm absolutely certain I'm right on this."

"Okay," I said. "But I'm the writer on this thing, and I also know the client. I really think we should go with the other guy."

We went back and forth like this for a while, and then he got really pissed off. He got right up in my face and shouted, "You don't know what you're talking about! I'm the director, who the fuck are you!"

Without thinking, I shouted back, "I'm Howie Cohen. *I was doing this when you were just a brain surgeon!*"

I hadn't intended to deliver a funny line, but it got a good laugh from everyone in the room, including Norman. The crisis had passed, and we were able to move on. When all was said and done, we went with his choice, and the commercial was a success. I guess I told him!

Real Men Wear Boxers

The Jack in the Box advertising was all over TV, and as a result, our agency was becoming well-known around town. But when the $27 million Mervyn's account came up for review, there was no guarantee we would be on their list.

Every agency in town would kill for that account. So we asked ourselves what we could do to stand out. Finally, after a martini-fest worthy of Mad Men, we hit on the big idea. We hired a professional photographer to take a picture of Mark and me sitting in our executive chairs, wearing nothing but our boxer shorts. (Mark wanted to look more dignified, so he also wore a tie.) To give this shameless display of male flesh particular meaning, we wrote a profound headline: "We need a clothing account."

We blew this ad up in size to an enormous seven feet tall, had it mounted on Styrofoam, and shipped it by FedEx to the advertising director of Mervyn's. Then we waited. One day turned into two and then three. Nothing. Finally, late on a Friday afternoon, we got a call from the advertising director, who began with just two words, "You're in."

One of our crack creative teams, George Roux and Beverly Chamberlain, came up with a winning campaign centered on the line, "For the clothes you love to live in," and we went on to win the Mervyn's account. As they say, when you're hot, you're hot.

With big retail accounts like Jack in the Box and Mervyn's, producing TV spots in Anglo and Hispanic versions, the agency was churning out a hundred TV spots a year, and we were listed by *Broadcast Magazine* as the largest producer of broadcast advertising in the West. That's a lot of work and a lot of pressure. Lucky for us, we had a dynamo producer who was up to the task.

Shape Your Life

Our VP of broadcast production was a guy named Joe Rein. Joe was an experienced, street smart, can-do kind of guy—a former prizefighter whose tough battles in the ring helped prepare him for the wars on Madison Avenue. But one particular production almost knocked him down for the count.

Cohen/Johnson was in the running for a plum *new* account, Bally's Health & Fitness Clubs. It was a sizable TV broadcast account, so we were the perfect agency for it. Of course, there were forty other agencies banging on their door.

Mark Johnson and I managed to get an hour-long meeting with their VP of marketing, where we gleaned an important piece of inside information. He wanted to direct his advertising at a whole new target—boomers. We seized upon this insight and decided to make it the focus of our advertising. The thinking was simple. For this older target, working out wasn't about ripped muscles or being attractive to the opposite sex. It was about living healthily, having a better quality of life, and living longer.

One morning, as I pondered this in the shower, I came up with a line: "You don't just shape your body. You shape your life." When I got to the agency, I shared it with Bruce. He immediately saw the potential in the line, and we began to discuss how we might bring it to life. Instead of just showing people working out, we would tell an emotional story of one person—an older person—who was getting the most out of life by working out and being fit.

Bruce's idea was that we could make a very dramatic and emotional commercial if we didn't reveal that it's an older guy right away. He envisioned shooting the spot with a series of extreme close-ups ... tight shots of biceps, hands on weights, legs lifting, arms rowing ... but never seeing his face until the very end. That would be the dramatic payoff. This very fit man would turn out to be a grandpa.

We shared the script with Mark. He got excited, and we all agreed—let's go for it! We would invest our own money and shoot a finished TV spot in order to win the account. The key was to find a talented director who was hungry to put a great new spot on his reel and would be willing to shoot it on the cheap.

Enter Joe Rein. He found the perfect director in New York and, as luck would have it, we were heading there to shoot some beautiful food footage for Jack in the Box. We decided to get both jobs done during our ten-day stay in the Big Apple. All we needed now was the right guy to play the key role.

No problem, right? Wrong! Our hero had to be around sixty years old and very fit, with big muscles and a six-pack. There aren't too many of those guys hanging around the streets of New York, but we weren't worried. Joe Rein was on the case.

In the middle of one of the hottest Augusts on record, Joe started pounding the pavement. Like a cheap detective, he went from gym to gym looking for our guy. He scoured Manhattan, and when he couldn't find him there, he took the train up to The Bronx, and when that failed, he hopped on over to Brooklyn. Time was running out, and Joe was getting a little punchy (poor choice of words, perhaps?), but he wouldn't give up.

One hot, humid night after a long day of shooting food, Joe walked into a gym that had seen better days. Due to the intense heat and humidity, Joe had decided to wear little white tennis shorts, a strappy tee-shirt, and white sneakers with no socks. He looked very "sweet." He sauntered up to the counter where a big brute of a manager was sitting and said, "I wonder if you could help me."

The manager was not a people person and just glowered at him. Joe continued. "I'm looking for a very fit man about sixty, has to be good-looking and well-built with big muscles."

"I'll bet you are," the manager said.

Without realizing where the conversation was going, Joe forged on. "He needs to have big biceps ... nice clear skin with no tattoos ... and preferably no hair on his back."

"Listen, buddy ..." the manager tried to cut Joe off, but to no avail.

"And it's really important that he doesn't sweat too much."

"Listen, pal," the manager exploded. "This ain't the YMCA, and we ain't The Village People! Get your ass out of here!"

Suddenly, it dawned on Joe what was happening. He started backing out the door, but he still wasn't giving up. "I'm staying at the UN Plaza Hotel, room 2115! I'll pay cash!"

"Get the fuck out of here, you pervert!"

By that time, mere mortals might have thrown in the towel. However, two days later, as a bunch of us were sitting around the hotel lobby, Joe walked in with a good-looking, well-built older man by his side—the very embodiment of what we were looking for. "Gentlemen," he said. "I'd like you to meet our grandpa!" Joe Rein had come through.

The director found the perfect gym, and in one marathon day of shooting, the production went off without a hitch. Then, on the flight back to L.A., something magical happened. I had just enjoyed a couple of glasses of chardonnay and was listening to the music in my airline headset. I was about to doze off when I heard a symphony orchestra playing a majestic piece. As I listened to the music, somehow my mind went to the beautiful footage we had just shot, and I imagined how it would feel with this soundtrack.

It was an epiphany. Instead of the cliché sound design that we had originally planned—a stylized percussive treatment to simulate the sounds of the workout—this ethereal music would emphasize the beauty of the physical effort and take our spot to a whole new place. The musical theme was called "Saturday Night Waltz," by the great American composer Aaron Copland. It became the emotional centerpiece of our Bally's spot.

This commercial also marked my official debut as a professional voiceover announcer. We were going to hire someone else, but when I did the scratch track, my voice sounded particularly deep and mellifluous—for good reason. I had a bad case of bronchitis. It got me to thinking, *If I could just get pneumonia, I'd probably have a great second career as a voiceover talent.*

On the big day of the presentation, we screened the spot for the Bally's people. When the last note of music had played and the lights went back on, there was complete silence in the room. Then their president said, "Can we see that again?" The next day, we were awarded the account.

And to think, it never would have happened without the fancy footwork of Joe Rein—prizefighter, producer ... and an honorary member of The Village People.

That's What She Said

To understand just how far we've come in terms of political correctness, let me take you back to a naughty time in the 1980s when the ad business was the Wild, Wild West of sexual innuendo and flagrant flirting. The line that became popularized was, "That's what she said."

This simple four-word phrase became the perfect punchline for almost any innocent remark. For example, you could be sitting in a meeting and a female producer might be speaking about a client's production budget and say, "It's not very big, but it'll do the job!" And a copywriter would say, "That's what she said." Big laugh.

Or an account guy might be talking about a campaign he couldn't sell to the client and say, "It got lost in the big black hole," and a secretary would say, "That's what she said!" More laughs.

If the truth be told, the women in the office used, abused, and adored the line as much as the men did. My personal favorite was uttered by a very bright and attractive blonde account executive named Paula McSpadden. She worked on the Hills Bros. Coffee account at Cohen/Johnson, and we had a big new TV shoot coming up. The client needed to be on the air with two new TV spots. We were actually ahead of schedule and had written four scripts.

This led to a strategic budget discussion. If we shot all four of them, we could gain some efficiencies and save the client some money on production. So the question was: should we shoot all four of them now, finish two of them, and edit the other two at a later date?

Paula pondered this for a minute and said, "I don't know. I'd hate to get it in the can and have it sit there for six months." To which the art director replied, "That's what she said." It got a big laugh—the loudest coming from Paula herself.

While I'm on Paula (that's what she said), I'm reminded of her quick wit. At some point, I was on one of my new miracle diets and had lost fifteen pounds. I came to work wearing my "skinny pants."

Feeling quite proud of my new slimmer look, I said, "Hey, Paula, there used to be an ass in these pants!" Without missing a beat, she said, "Howie, there still is."

The old days were wilder, sexier, and free-er. But there's no doubt that this kind of behavior was misguided and often crossed the line. Thankfully today, the ad business is more enlightened and more politically correct. It's just a little "more stiff." (That's what she said.)

Wells Sells

In 1990, Cohen/Johnson was a bona fide $90 million L.A. ad agency. And Wells, Rich, Greene was so successful that Mary was ready to sell the agency and earn a well-deserved and colossal payday. She was already rich, but now she was about to become *much* richer. As a friend said, "Howie, she's not just going to make F—U money. She's going to make F—Everybody money!"

The agency found a highly attractive suitor in a $1 billion French agency, BDDP. When I heard about the impending acquisition, I was thrilled for Mary, as well as for Ken and Charlie, because they would finally earn their just rewards for all the years of hard work. And they would be able to relax and smell the coffee (although it wouldn't be Hills Bros. or Folgers).

The sale seemed great for both BDDP and Wells, but it didn't turn out that way. Maybe because of the distance or different cultures, there were all kinds of political and logistical problems that turned the dream acquisition into a nightmare. Fortunately for Mary and Charlie, they were long gone when the worst happened. Ken wasn't so lucky since he had stayed to help run the place and suffered through a very bad agency marriage. As Mary chronicled in her book, *A Big Life in Advertising*, "$453 million in billings spiraled out the door between 1995 and 1998, and the agency closed its doors in May 1998."

It was the end of an era. All those years of creative passion and brutally hard work had paid off in building a legendary agency and cementing Mary's legacy as, arguably, the greatest advertising woman who's ever lived. What happened to the agency, in the end, was sad. But that could never take away from what Wells, Rich, Greene accomplished. There have been many great creative agencies over the years, and exciting new ones will always come along. But for humor, originality, showbiz flair, and pure excitement, there will never be another Wells, Rich, Greene.

~

TEN

Family Matters

In the Moment

The advertising business can be glamorous, fun, and highly rewarding. It can also frustrate you, break your heart, and make you fucking nuts. So it's important to have good coping skills. Learn to be centered and sane, so you can perform well at work and live a balanced life at home.

As Cohen/Johnson faced some of its greatest challenges, I realized I needed to get better at living in the moment. My mind was too consumed with thoughts of advertising. I could be at the park with my kids, and they could be talking and laughing and saying, "Daddy, daddy, look ..." and I wouldn't even be conscious that they were there. I could be sitting across the dinner table from a good friend and not hear a word he was saying. I might have been thinking about the campaign I wished I'd done to save an account we lost. Or calculating how much "fuck you money" I needed to retire at the turn of the century—bullshit like that. It finally dawned on me that I was missing out on a lot of the moments that make life special.

So I started making a few changes in my life. I signed up for yoga classes, I dusted off the mantra I had been given in the sixties and started meditating again, and I began reading some self-help books that focused on a simple truth: "Yesterday is gone; tomorrow may never come; all we have is now. Be in the moment."

Soon, I began to enjoy living in the moment. If I looked at a flower, I really looked at it and forced myself to notice and really appreciate the colors, the shape of its delicate petals, and the intoxicating fragrance. If I listened to music, I let the melody flow through my body and absorb the emotion until it lifted my heart—in the moment. It was working for me, and I was proud of myself—until one day when I took a giant step backward. We had taken our family on a ski trip to Vail, Colorado, and I forgot to remember.

On the very first day, Carol and the kids and I were sitting on the chairlift heading up the mountain. It was spring and the sun was shining. The temperature was a perfect fifty degrees, and there was fifteen feet of powder on the ground, but I wasn't enjoying any of it. I couldn't because I wasn't there. My head was back in L.A., thinking about some stupid new business pitch we were going to make. I was gone!

However, when we reached the top of the mountain, something magical happened. As we got off the chairlift, we guided our skis toward the huge ten-foot trail map that was pressed behind glass and standing on stilts in the snow. I looked up at the giant map, trying to see where we were on the mountain to figure out where we wanted to go. The map was a profusion of blue, green, and black lines on a field of white, but my eyes went directly to a big black dot in the middle that represented the exact spot on which we were standing. And on that spot, in big, bold letters it said: "You are here!"

It was like a message from the ski gods. "You are *here!*" Instantly, it snapped me back to the moment. For the next ten days, any time my mind began to wander back to advertising, I would summon up the words, "You are here!" and focus on the joys all around me. I skied with my wife and played with my kids and enjoyed the simple pleasure of being in the moment with the people I love most in the world: my beautiful family.

Let Romance Bubble Up

At this writing, I'm proud to say that Carol and I have been married for forty-six years. People often ask me, "Howie, what's your secret? How do you keep it fresh?" The answer is simple. I use my proven advertising talents in my own personal life to fan the flames of love. I'll give you an example.

A number of years back, on a sexy Saturday evening, Carol and I were alone in the house, and I suddenly got inspired. (Don't turn away ... this is a cute story.)

At the time, we were living in our beautiful home in the canyons of Beverly Hills with a pool and Jacuzzi. There was a full moon that night and steam was rising off the bubbling Jacuzzi that was heated to a hot and throbbing 104 degrees.

Being a child of the sixties, I was occasionally inclined to imbibe in the most delightful ways. Carol, not so much. Except for a glass of wine now and then, her clear-eyed sobriety has kept me from going off the deep end ... most of the time. On this particular night, I started with a dirty martini followed by a couple of glasses of chardonnay. Smart, very smart. All the while, I was using my advertising skills to "sell" an original line. "Carol," I said. "Tonight's the night."

She blushed, as she always does, and that served to fuel my ardor. I went on about how romantic the night would be and hinted at the amorous adventures that lay ahead. "Tonight's the night."

Carol was already relaxing in the Jacuzzi when I lowered myself into the hot, bubbling water. I was still selling my romantic vision to her, "Tonight's the night," when suddenly I started to feel a little queasy. Realizing that I needed to hydrate, I stepped out of the Jacuzzi and made my way through the French doors to the kitchen. All of a sudden, my head started spinning, I saw big white spots in front of my eyes, and I went down. I mean … *I went down!*

I was on my knees on the kitchen floor, and the room was whirling so fast that I put my forehead to the cool limestone floor to try and gather my senses. Carol came running into the house in a panic. "Are you alright?" she asked. "Should I call 9-1-1? Are you having a heart attack?"

Of course, the more she said stuff like that, the more alarmed I became and the worse I felt. "No," I tried to reassure her and myself. "I'll be alright. Just give me a few minutes."

Carol ran into the other room and retrieved a miracle of medical science—a brown paper bag. "What's this?" I groaned.

"Never mind," she said as she put the bag over my mouth and instructed me to breathe into it. Apparently, it was some stupid remedy she had seen in a made-for-TV movie.

So there I was, on my knees on the kitchen floor with my forehead pressed against the limestone, breathing sideways into a crinkled brown paper bag. I stayed down for about five minutes while Carol kept asking, "Is it a heart attack? Should I call an ambulance?"

Finally, my head started to clear. I put my arm over Carol's shoulder, and she used all her strength to lift me up. Then, very slowly, we began to walk toward the stairs, so I could get to the bedroom and crawl safely into bed. As we climbed the stairway, step-by-step-by-step, with me leaning heavily on Carol, I suddenly started to come around again. And what do you know ... my libido was starting to kick in. And being the indomitable adman that I was, I started to get my sales pitch together again.

"Carol," I said. "Tonight's the night." She just groaned and rolled her eyes. When we finally reached the second-floor landing, I felt revived and renewed, and I made my final pitch to Carol. "Tonight's the night!" That's when she lowered the boom. "Yeah," she said, "just you, me, and the paramedics!"

I laughed and sheepishly crawled into bed. Wasn't that just like her? I'd spent the whole night building the narrative. But it was Carol who delivered the perfect punchline.

Steal from the Innocent

A good writer has a knack for hearing great lines and storing them away in his or her memory bank to be used opportunistically at a later date. Lines like:

"Where's the beef?"

"Can you hear me now?"

And my own, "I can't believe I ate the whole thing," were uttered quite innocently in everyday conversation.

But they became famous because when the public picked up on

them they spread virally. Anyone saying the words, "I can't believe I ate the whole thing" got an immediate laugh. Which inspired others to use the line and get a good laugh too. That's the definition of "going viral." And the beauty of it is that every time the words come up in conversation, it reminds people of the commercial and hopefully the product, which adds up to a lot of free advertising.

In a shameless act, I once stole a great line from an unsuspecting young six-year-old child—my daughter Johanna. One night, I came home from work feeling tired and a little cranky. Johanna was always happy to see me, and on this particular night, she was bouncing off the walls with energy. I adore my daughter, but at that moment, all I wanted to do was pour a drink, watch TV, and crash on the couch. Johanna hopped and jumped and laughed, trying to cheer me up, but it just made me irritated.

Finally, I raised my voice, "Johanna, it's time for bed! Go to your room and get into your nightgown … right now!" Her smile quickly turned to a frown, her lips began to quiver, and she raced out of the room. I turned my attention back to the TV and took a sip of vodka. It seemed to me that she had only been gone for a few seconds when she popped back into the room wearing a nightgown.

It happened so fast that I was sure she took a shortcut and was trying to fool me. I raised my voice again. "Johanna, you can't fool me!" I bellowed. "I know you didn't change that fast. Did you just throw your nightgown on over your jeans?"

Without missing a beat, she lifted up her nightgown to reveal her pink panties and said, "Does that answer your question?" She cracked me up and made my day. And the line stuck.

A few months later, we had a TV assignment from our client Hills Bros. Coffee to sell the surprisingly great taste of their decaf coffee. Bob and I created a simple spot with a memorable visual device. A husband and wife are sitting at the kitchen table. He's reading the morning paper, and she's pouring him a cup of Hills Bros. decaf. He takes a long sip, his eyes light up with pleasure, and he says, "This is decaf? How do they make it taste so good?"

Suddenly, the heavens open and a torrent of coffee beans come raining down on their heads, spilling and tumbling all over the table. After a long, slow burn, the wife turns to her husband and says, "Does that answer your question?" The spot was visually arresting, and the line was a winner. Thank you, Johanna.

Now, you might be wondering, did Johanna grow up to be a hopeless creative person like her dad? I'm proud to say that she's a very creative, highly talented casting director in her own growing casting company, Spitfire Casting in L.A. Does that answer your question?

Christmas 1988 – The Cohens living the good life in the house that Jack built

Foster a Little Happiness

Life was good for the Cohens. All the hard work was paying off. We had bought a lovely home with a pool and a Jacuzzi and a jaw-dropping view out to the lush green canyons of Beverly Hills.

Everything was comfortable and nice, and that's something you don't want to mess with ... unless you're my lovely wife, Carol.

One day she came to me and said, "Howie, we have to do something."

"Okay," I responded. "You want to go to a movie? Maybe take a drive to Malibu?"

"No, that's not what I mean. We have to do something to help the Westside Foster Parents Program."

"The Westside who?" I asked.

Bless her heart, Carol is always on a mission to make the world a better place, whether it's saving whales, polar bears, goldfish—or kids.

"But we already have three kids of our own," I told her. "And everything is good. We don't need any problems."

"Howie, they need us!"

That started us on a new journey that was about to add to our lives in a very significant way—although not without our fair share of angst and heartburn. We joined the program and signed the papers, saying we agreed to take children into our home—not to adopt them, but to care for them until their parents were rehabilitated from problems like drugs or jail or mental disorders or spousal abuse. In other words, until their homes were safe to return to.

We began with deep training to learn how to bring a foster child into our home, which included CPR and preparing our home with accident prevention tools like drawer locks and pool covers. The most significant part of the process was emotional training—how to bring a child into your heart and then have to let go. Depending on the circumstances, a child might stay for as little as a day or for a year or more. This was the most challenging part. Care for them and love them, but don't let yourself fall in love with them.

We had many wonderful children pass through our home in the first year, although my kids didn't always find it so wonderful. Our first "placements" were three young African American siblings aged seven, five, and four. While they were innocent and adorable, having three additional children is a house-altering experience. One more child is challenging, two is difficult, and three can be Armageddon.

One day, our son, Jonathan, who was eight years old at the time, came home from school and stormed through the house, out to the backyard, and all the way to the edge of our property, where he started sobbing. I ran over to him and said, "Jonathan, what's the matter. What happened?"

He looked at me with tears streaming down his face and said, "I want my life back!"

To his credit, he sucked it up, and we all got on board with Carol's mission, which was now our family mission. This was a good thing to do, and we were going to see it through. Then something special happened. We met "the one." We got a beautiful two-and-a-half-year-old boy with soulful brown eyes as big as saucers.

His name was Angelo. He stayed in our home for a year, and everything was perfect (except for the time he almost burned down the house, but that's another story). We showered Angelo with love, and we got plenty back in return. We took him with us everywhere we went, including New York and Aspen, where he was the only little Mexican on the slopes doing a snowplow. He belly laughed as he careened down the bunny trail and fell into my arms. It was magical.

But then came the hard part. After one year, it was time. The Foster Parents Program told us they were going to reunite him with his family. His mother had tragically died while he was in our care and nobody knew who his father was. However, he did have three brothers who were living with his aunt. The goal is always to reunite the family, so Angelo went to live with his Aunt Mary and brothers Anthony, Vincent, and Alex.

Fortunately for us, that was not the end of our relationship. It was the beginning. Angelo has been in our lives ever since. He is now a twenty-eight-year-old young man with two beautiful daughters of his own, whom he cherishes and is there for every single day. And, most importantly, he has a very big heart. I like to think he got some of that from us. Thanks to Carol's nagging about getting into the Foster Parents program, our family grew a little bigger—in size and in love.

Mary Wells Lawrence, the Last Goodbye

In February 2000, Charlie Moss called me in L.A. to tell me that Mary was about to receive our industry's highest honor: she was going to be inducted into the Advertising Hall of Fame. What's more, she would consider it an honor if I would fly to New York and attend the festivities. *She* would be honored?

I was thrilled that she thought enough to extend a personal all-expenses-paid invitation to Carol and me. At that point, it had been fifteen years since I had seen her. For weeks leading up to the event, I fantasized about what it would be like, how I would feel, how she would feel, and what I would say.

When the day finally arrived, it was a chilly March afternoon in New York, but the feelings in the Grand Ballroom of the Waldorf Astoria Hotel were radiating warmth. Hundreds of people showed up to pay tribute to Mary, including many I had worked with at Wells in the early seventies.

Since I knew I wouldn't remember most of their names, I made a pact with Carol. I said, "If you see someone walking toward us like they know me, reach out your hand and introduce yourself because I'll never remember who they are." She kindly agreed. And then it happened.

A guy I used to know very well was walking directly toward me with a big smile on his face and his arms outstretched. Who was he ... what was his name? I focused, I concentrated, I went through the alphabet in my head, and—just as he arrived, I remembered. *Dave. His name is Dave.* Victoriously, I said, "Dave, so great to see you. I'd like you to meet my wife ... uh ... uh ... um ..."

"Hi, I'm Carol," she said. I had actually gone blank on my own wife's name. She gave me a forgiving look. (I may be an idiot, but at least I'm her idiot.)

Charlie and Ken were there, of course, and so were Bob Pasqualina and Steve Karmen and lots of friends from the good old days. We all shared laughs and hugs and warm memories. It was great to see everyone again, although many people looked quite a bit older. I'm sure they thought the same thing about me.

When Mary got up to speak, an adoring crowd hung on her every word. Her message was simple, yet poignant. She spoke of the same thing that had driven her and the agency all through her career: it was about the importance of loving your clients (because if you don't, someone else will) and of dedicating yourself, utterly and completely, to their success.

And boy, had she lived up to that, working impossible hours for years on end, sacrificing pleasure to stay focused on the mission of building her agency, working at the office and at home, flying on too many planes, taking too many meetings, and enduring painful account losses and employee defections (I guess I fit into that category).

But here she was—a very rich and successful icon of our industry. She spoke of loyalty and love and courage, and she spoke from the heart. When she finished, there was thunderous applause from all the people whose lives she had impacted in profound ways—particularly mine.

Then came the moment I had been fantasizing about. Mary was standing at the doorway saying goodbye to a long line of people who had come to pay tribute. I watched and waited with my heart in my throat. At long last, she looked up and our eyes met.

It had been thirty-three years since the day I first met Mary when, with trembling hands and a squeaky teenager's voice, I had presented my ten-second Personna TV spot. So much had happened in my life since then—so many opportunities she had given me—so much to be thankful for. It was all welling up inside me, just waiting to come out.

"Howieee," she said. I walked up to Mary and put my arms around her. We looked into each other's eyes, and I held her, maybe a little too tightly and a little too long. And then I began to pour out my feelings.

"Mary, I just want to tell you from my heart what you've meant to me—how you changed my life. If not for you, I never would have had the opportunity to do the famous Alka Seltzer commercials. I never would have met my wife … never would have had the chance to move to California ... never would have had my children ... I never would have become who I am. Mary, you've meant everything in my life."

She leaned back and said, "And you in mine, Howie."

That melted my heart. Then she smiled, turned, and walked away to continue saying her goodbyes. I spotted Carol across the room, walked over, and grabbed her by the hand. "Are you okay?" she asked. That's when I realized there were tears in my eyes. Tears for a time gone by that would never come again—when we were all young and creativity was king and everything was possible. It was a time when Mary Wells Lawrence showed us all that if we were passionate about the work, we could do it all and have it all—and we did.

ELEVEN

Slip Sliding

Stand for Something or Fall

One of the things that helped make Cohen/Johnson successful in attracting big blue chip clients was our singular focus. "Fewer, bigger clients" was our motto.

We were a creative advertising agency that big advertisers could count on for the big idea because we only had relationships with the powerful few. We were laser-focused on doing just one thing for them: coming up with big, creative ideas. We were not a PR company, a promotions company, or a media company. In fact, we didn't even have a media department. We were what is known as a "best of breed" agency.

That's not to say that all the other marketing disciplines weren't important. They were. So important, in fact, that we worked with the best specialists including media giant Western International Media,

headed up by the legendary Dennis Holt, (who I affectionately referred to as Uncle Dennis.) And that was an additional benefit to
us because when their clients were looking for creative help, they
would recommend us. As a result, we got into lots more reviews and
won our fair share of them.

Thanks to our extreme focus, we were able to hire the best people, do some great work, and in the process, make a bunch of money.
Unfortunately, this led to a little personal problem for me. As Robin
Williams famously said, "Cocaine is god's way of telling you you're
making too much money." I should have listened.

Don't Let Success Go to Your Nose

It started quite innocently. I began joining a small group of advertising buddies at Bob Grimaldi's house, another one of my favorite
Italian art directors. There, hunched over a trendy little coffee table,
we would each take out a $20 bill, roll it up, raise it to our nostrils,
and snort a line or two of cocaine from the mirror on the table in
front of us.

As the eighties were in full swing, coke was everywhere. There
was a widespread belief that it was not habit-forming, just good,
clean fun. For a while I was a moocher, taking advantage of "the
kindness of strangers." But then I decided it was time to have my
own stash. At that point, I didn't worry about becoming dependent on cocaine. I just didn't want to be dependent on an Italian art
director.

I decided to take it to the next level and get my very own drug
dealer. If the term "drug dealer" conjures up images of unsavory
people who operate in drug dens on the seedy side of town, don't

be misled. My drug dealer came recommended, like a good proctologist, by friends I admired and respected. My "dealer" turned out to be a nice orthodox Jewish couple that lived in a lovely suburban home on the west side of L.A. I will call them the Klutzmans, Murray and Sheila.

The first time I visited their home, on a Friday after work, I was greeted by Murray, who was wearing a yarmulke, and Sheila, who was adorned in a conservative shawl. I immediately felt at home as the sweet smell of freshly made kugel, a classic Jewish dish made of noodles, raisins, and cinnamon, permeated the air. *How wonderful*, I thought to myself. The Klutzmans weren't just drug dealers. They were nurturers.

"Hi, I'm Howie," I said.

"Hello, I'm Murray, and this is my wife, Sheila. Welcome to our home."

Sheila left the room and Murray closed the door to his office. He handed me a tiny vial, which contained a half-gram of cocaine.

"How much?" I asked.

"Just sixty dollars," he said.

I already knew from my friends that this was the going rate, so I was pleased to see he wasn't trying to screw me. I handed him three twenty dollar bills, stuffed the vial into my pants pocket, and was just about to leave when Sheila came in holding a little plate.

"A little kugel for the road?" she asked.

My eyes lit up. "Yes, thank you!" And so, with coke up my nose and the sweet taste of kugel on my lips, I began my shameless journey of part-time coke abuser in full-time denial.

Coke is a stimulant that revs up your heart, sometimes to a very scary degree. And so, on many Friday nights, that's the condition

I would return home in, feeling guilty and ashamed and nervous. Carol would be fast asleep, and I'd do my best not to wake her up. After washing up and brushing my teeth, I'd quietly slide into bed, but I'd be in no shape to fall asleep. My heart would still be pounding in my chest from the coke. It went on that way for quite a while, until I began feeling very lost.

One morning, I dragged myself out of bed and went to the bathroom to wash up. I looked in the mirror and almost didn't recognize myself. It was the same face, but the eyes were blank. The little twinkle I always seemed to have had disappeared. My face was pale, and my cheeks were sunken. I was on a dangerous path, and I had to do something to stop. I decided to spill my guts to Carol. She was always a stickler for health—eating right, exercising, doing yoga, not drinking or abusing in any way. Given all that, I wondered why she hadn't said anything about the physical changes in me that must have been obvious. My guess is that she was in denial too. Or maybe she just couldn't accept that her nice Jewish husband from The Bronx could develop a stupid coke habit. All I knew was that I was in trouble, and it was time for me to come clean. So one sunny afternoon when all the world seemed right but clearly wasn't, I asked her to join me in the backyard for a little talk. With a lump in my throat and shame in my heart, I said, "Carol, I have a problem." She looked at me with concern.

"What is it?" she asked. "What's wrong, Howie?"

"I feel terrible … out of control … fucked up."

"Howie, what are you talking about? What's going on?"

"I've been abusing drugs, and it's gotten bad. I just feel so washed out. Between the booze, the grass, the cocaine, and the cigarettes …"

Carol's eyes filled with fury. "You're smoking cigarettes!"

She was totally serious, and I couldn't help but laugh. I was going downhill from cocaine, but her biggest worry was Marlboros. I put my arms around her, and she hugged me tightly.

"I'm here for you," she said. It was time to get some real help.

The next day, I got into a twelve-step program: Cocaine Anonymous. It took me awhile. I tried and I slipped and I got back on the wagon and I slipped. Until one day … it was like someone flipped off a switch in my brain. I was done with coke. I didn't want it or need it anymore. And I've never touched the stuff or even wanted to go near it since 1987.

From that day on, I was back to being the Howie I always was— not perfect, but coke-free. I still like a nice, cold, frosty mug of beer, and I enjoy a fine cabernet with my sirloin steak. I thank my lucky stars that cocaine is out of my life for good. But I would kill for one more piece of that kugel.

Bad Meat Kills Relationships

The Jack in the Box account was a big, important part of my career and my life for fifteen years, seven at Wells and another eight at Cohen/Johnson. I will always be grateful for the opportunities they gave us and for the successes we were able to share. I used to affectionately refer to my big house in Beverly Hills as "the house that Jack built." In a business where clients come and go and loyalty is a foreign word, the people at Jack in the Box showed us that hard work and great ideas deserve to be rewarded.

It was such a wonderful relationship that I think Mark and I believed it would last forever. And, in a perfect world, it might have. However, if you've read my book this far you know … advertising is far from a perfect world.

In 1994, the unimaginable happened. I got a call on a Saturday night from Mo Iqbal. "Howie, we need you down here tomorrow." (Sunday? What the hell could be that serious?) "Howie, we have a disaster. People are getting sick from Jack in the Box food. And it's not one store, it's happening everywhere in the Jack in the Box chain. Howie, people may die!"

"Oh my god!" I said. "I'll get on a plane and be there at nine tomorrow."

"Thank you," he said. And he kept on saying, "This is bad. This is bad ..."

The next morning was panic time as the whole executive committee tried to confront a problem they couldn't get their arms around. How many people were sick? Which states and which stores? And the biggest question, "What the fuck was causing this, and what could they do to stop it?"

Then Jack Goodall uttered two words that I had never heard before. "E. coli!" That was the diagnosis. It's a serious infection that can mess you up. It can give you diarrhea, double you up in pain, and (at its worst) shut down your system—and then you die.

But what was causing it? The news there was not good either. We had just introduced a very successful hamburger called The Monster. As the name suggests, it was a huge monster of a product with two huge hamburger patties. Bruce Dundore had come up with a terrific creative commercial that brought the idea to life. It began with a teaser campaign on TV.

In a dark and dank basement, there was a large box wrapped in chains ... something was inside struggling to get out ... it rattled and shook menacingly ... all leading to one line: "The Monster is coming ... from Jack in the Box." That TV spot was followed by an award-winning, full-blown monster commercial. It was intrusive, it was exciting, and it had people rushing to Jack in the Box to experience The Monster. That part was great. But, as we soon learned, that was also a big part of the problem.

With a product that had double the meat, the people at Jack in the Box couldn't make them fast enough. So they took shortcuts—they didn't adhere completely to the fast-food industry's cooking temperature guidelines. Many of the hamburgers were being undercooked and not reaching temperatures that kill bad bacteria. And that can cause E. coli!

In California, Arizona, and five other states, hundreds of people were getting very sick. Even worse, many of them were innocent little children. And a few days later, the tragedy hit its apex. A young child died! It was a human disaster of epic proportions. Everybody who worked at Jack in the Box and at Cohen/Johnson was totally devastated.

Overnight, sales dropped by 70%, and soon there was even talk of selling the company. In the midst of all this, Jack Goodall looked to the agency—and to me in particular—for the big idea that would solve their bad hamburger meat problem and maybe save their business. This time, however, our agency didn't have the answer, and neither did I. I was frozen.

The boldness I had shown in previous years that had led to breakthrough creative ideas like the exploding clown was nowhere to be found. The stakes had become too high. This was a $30 million account that represented a third of our business. I became timid and scared. Jack in the Box was waiting for the big idea, and I didn't know what to do.

So I looked for answers in the wrong places. I listened to the voice of their VP of sales, who said to me, "Whatever you come up with, it has to be gentle. The whole world is pissed off at Jack in the Box right now, and we can't afford to aggravate the situation." In response, we got stupid. We did soft advertising that didn't solve the problem. Even worse, it didn't even get noticed. Fear can make you do dumb things.

Sales continued to slide, and finally, Jack in the Box hired a new marketing director, and he initiated an agency review. It was the beginning of the end. Jack in the Box fired some of its key people, fired its PR firm, and fired us! *Oh, the pain.*

With time, it's easy to look back and second-guess yourself. *Why didn't I do this? Why didn't I think of that?* A month after we lost the Jack in the Box account, I finally came up with the big idea. The problem was bad meat, right? So I came up with a brilliant line that would have turned their business around: "TRY THE CHICKEN."

Okay, it was just a joke, but at least it gave us a smile during some pretty bad days. The agency that won the account from us was Chiat/Day. A talented writer named Dick Sittig came up with the bold idea to bring back the Jack in the Box clown. At that point, we had come full circle. I was the guy who blew up the clown in 1980, blaming all of Jack in the Box's problems on him. Now, Sittig put the blame for E. coli on the board of directors of Jack in the Box and had the clown blow them up.

It was brilliant, and I wish I had thought of it. On the strength of this, Sittig eventually started his own agency with the Jack in the Box account, which he kept for twenty years, making him very rich. His campaign was no "TRY THE CHICKEN," but it seems to have worked.

Stay Silly, My Friends

I'm convinced that the biggest reason we lost Jack in the Box is that we had lost our ability to stay loose and let ourselves be creative. There was just too much at stake and so … we choked.

"Serious" is the enemy of creativity. It strangles free thought and suffocates inspiration. I always try to remember this and stay in touch with my silly self. One of the ways I do this is by hanging out with silly people. Take Steve Platt. (Please!) Steve has been a close friend of mine for over sixty years, ever since we were in high school together. In those days, we acted stupid and silly, and as Carol says, "Nothing has changed."

One day, Steve dropped by my office to say hello. Before his butt hit the chair, he asked, "Howie, did you ever Google yourself?"

I said, "Only when Carol's not home." (Let the silliness begin.)

He said, "Do me a favor: Google Shecky Platt."

Shecky is Steve's "stage name"—a tribute to his talent for telling and retelling old jokes. He got this moniker from the boys in our poker group. We've been playing together every Tuesday night since 1996. Here's an example of the kind of jokes he tells:

> **SHECKY: A man goes to the sperm bank to make a donation. Seeing that the man is quite advanced in age, the nurse says, "Um … sir … may I ask how old you are?"**
>
> **He proudly says, "I'm ninety-two years old!"**
>
> **To which the nurse replies, "That's wonderful, sir, but this is a sperm bank. Are you sure you're up for this?"**
>
> **"Up for this?" the man says. "I'm up for it twice a day, every day; that's how up for it I am!"**
>
> **Looking impressed, the nurse hands the man two**

Playboy magazines and a jar. Then she escorts him to a private room to make his donation. He closes the door, and after several minutes, the nurse hears loud noises coming from inside the room. "Ach ... ooh ... aah ... ohhh ... eeeh ... aaah!" This goes on for so long that she becomes alarmed.

"Sir, is everything alright in there?"

"No!" he replies. "I can't open the damn jar!"

All the poker boys like that joke. Which is a good thing because we'll be hearing it over and over again for the next twenty years.

Our poker group is rich in diversity. We've got three doctors, two lawyers, three ad guys, a financier, and a closet salesman. Most are retired and all are Jewish, except for Ed Liu, who is a Chinese gynecologist but knows more Jewish words than all of us. (It's a *shonda!*)

Dan Pearlman is a great guy who knows everything about everything (just ask him). He's so knowledgeable that, after meeting him, Shecky says he sold all his encyclopedias and gave up Google.

Kenny Spring is a retired lawyer who we call "The Commish," because he keeps us up to speed on whose turn it is to host the game. Kenny earned this role because he's always buttoned up. Well, almost always.

One year, six of us decided to take a group vacation with our wives, so we booked a Crystal Cruise to the Mediterranean. With three months to go, Kenny became "The Commish of the Cruise." He started sending out a torrent of "helpful" emails:

"Don't forget to book your massage. They fill up fast."

"Important! Bring a formal outfit."

"Tell your wives to reserve their facials!"

"Pack extra towels."

Kenny was completely on top of things … until the time arrived and we actually got on the cruise ship. On our very first night, we all got a panic call from Kenny's wife, Cheryl, who asked, "Did you guys bring extra slacks? Kenny forgot his pants!"

And then there's Bob Uhl, the retired lawyer who made a lot of money suing bad stockbrokers. I've known him since he was a skinny little kid in New York back in the seventies. Bob and I used to hang out on Friday nights, drink wine, and maybe take a toke or two. Eventually, we would become very silly and get the munchies. One Friday night I said, "I'm starving. Let's order up some pizza." And Bob said, "Nah, I feel like Chinese."

We debated for a while before Bob came up with a brilliant idea. "Let's order both! And not only that, let's make a $10 bet which order gets here first."

Perfect, I thought. To our sins of booze, grass, and overeating, we were now adding gambling. "Okay, let's go for it." I bet that the pizza would get there first, and Bob put his money on the Chinese.

Twenty-two minutes later, the doorbell rang. When Bob opened the door, there was a Chinese man standing there, and Bob shouted, "I won! I won!"

Not so fast. The Chinese guy was delivering the pizza.

Stay silly, my friends.

It Was a Very Bad Year

In 1994, the earth shook, the winds blew us off our feet, and a financial catastrophe came raining down on Cohen/Johnson. First, we had lost our biggest account, Jack in the Box. *SMACK!* Then, later that same year, we lost our second biggest account, Mervyn's, when they decided to consolidate their advertising back in Minneapolis where their parent company, Dayton Hudson, was headquartered. *SMACK, SMACK!* In that one year, we lost almost half of our business. And then, the worst happened. My father died suddenly, just shy of his eightieth birthday.

I loved my dad, and as he got older, I knew the day would come when I would lose him. I thought I was prepared. I wasn't. The whole process of coming home to New York to hold my mother's hand and lean on my brother, Jerry, as we buried my father, was extremely painful and left me feeling vulnerable at a time when I needed to be strong.

Thank god for Jerry and my sister-in-law, Dorothy, who lived in New York and were able to be there for my parents as they got older. Jerry is a can-do person who immediately took charge of all the details involved with saying an emotional goodbye. He arranged for the funeral services, the announcements, the burial ceremony, and all of the coordination and costs that go with it. He also handled the details of my father's estate, following through on my father's plans to ensure that my mother would be well taken care of for the rest of her life.

For my part, I did what I knew how to do best: I got up at the funeral service and spoke from the heart. I tried to capture the complexity of the man I called my father, using my words to bring to life the person we all remembered as loving, sarcastic, caustic, funny, and generous to a fault.

Although my father had to go to work at an early age and, as a result, never finished high school, he became a successful businessman who used his hard-earned money to provide a nice life for our family and to help everyone around him who might have been down on their luck. Sometimes people took advantage of his kindness, coming back again and again to dip their beak in the well. My father didn't seem to mind. He had a very big heart.

There were lots of tears at the funeral. Afterward, we all went back to my brother's Park Avenue penthouse to sit Shiva. You're supposed to sit on hard boxes, but we sat on soft, expensive chairs from Restoration Hardware. We just weren't that religious ... except when it came to food. True to Jewish and Cohen tradition, we ate very well. My brother filled the dining room table with delicacies from Zabars, and we all ate to our heart's content—something that would have given my father great pride and satisfaction.

The next day, I returned to L.A. to an agency that was sinking fast and a place I no longer wished to be. At that point, I was feeling beaten down and defeated.

If I was acting a little lost and removed, Mark was the opposite. He was becoming more aggressive and brittle. At the very time when I needed someone to commiserate with, I was starting to feel cut off from him. The best description of the difference between Mark and me came from one of our account executives. When a new hire at the agency asked her what Howie and Mark were really like, she said, "Well, Howie is passive-aggressive, and Mark is aggressive-aggressive." It was a funny comment—and quite true.

I liked and respected Mark, and we had a great relationship for many years. If we had any issues, it was easier to gloss over them when things were going well. But when things got bad, we drifted away from each other.

That year, I really wanted to pursue an alternate path—find a global agency to sell to. Maybe merge with another agency. Or

maybe just cash in my chips and walk away. But I didn't. We sucked
it up and actually kept our independence for three more years.

The President Wore Pajamas

With the loss of our two biggest accounts, we had to downsize and
fire a lot of people, and that was demoralizing. We cared about every
one of those people, and it hurt to see them go. I missed them, and
I missed who we used to be. The place was definitely not the same,
but at least we were still alive.

Then one day, opportunity barked. Petco, a fast-growing region-
al pet supply chain, was looking to do its first TV campaign. We met
with their marketing director, and he invited us to pitch the account.
It wasn't a creative shootout. If they liked what they saw, they would
produce it. Then he shared everything he knew about the brand. He
talked about the strengths of Petco in terms of all the retail clichés.
"We have so much going for us," he said. "Great selection, competi-
tive prices, good service, convenient locations ..." *Yawn, yawn.*

A bunch of us huddled at the agency to come up with something that would be fresh and intrusive, something that would appeal
to pet people. Being dog and cat lovers ourselves, we instinctively
knew there was something deeper that we could pin our advertising
on. It was love.

One day, I was discussing this with a terrific writer at our agency, Beverly Chamberlain, the same Beverly who came up with the
winning line for Mervyn's, "For the clothes you love to live in." We
swapped cute pet stories. She spoke of the selfishness of her cats and
how she let them walk all over her, figuratively and literally. "It's
their world. We just live in it," she said. And that became the kernel

of our idea. Petco isn't "our" store. It's "their" store.

And that's when the theme line popped out of my mouth. "Petco, where the pets go!" I said.

And Beverly jumped out of her chair and said, "That's it!"

Really, that's it? I thought to myself. Yeah, that was it.

Now we needed an intrusive TV spot to bring it to life. Beverly was our go-to writer, and she insisted on working with Troy Wilderson, a bright young art director who was still a rookie. Beverly and Troy jammed for several days on this. And when all was said and done, guess who came up with the big idea? Yep, Troy Wilderson, the rookie. Her simple idea was that all the pets in town were on a mission to get down to Petco for all the good food and toys and stuff. In fact, the name of the spot became "Pets on a Mission."

The commercial took place at night. In the opening, a Ford Bronco comes crashing out of a garage, shifts into first gear, and screeches down the street. At the wheel is a big dog that is driving a small menagerie of pet friends—a cat, a cockatoo, a reptile, and a fishbowl full of fish. The image was hysterical, and it completely supported the idea that Petco is "their store." We presented this approach to the marketing director of Petco, who got really excited and said we'd nailed it. Based on that, we made a date to fly down to their headquarters in San Diego to present our idea to the president of Petco, a terrific guy named Brian Devine.

We were all ready to go when we got a bummer of a call. The marketing director told us their president had just had a heart attack. Fortunately, it was a mild one, and he was in recovery, but we would have to wait to present our campaign.

Three weeks later, we were invited down again to make our presentation—only this time at the president's house, where he was still recuperating. Mark and I flew down to San Diego and followed the directions to his house. We arrived at a beautiful, sprawling 10,000-square-foot home, all on one level, with room after room stretched out before us. The marketing director greeted us and guided us into a large den. We set up our storyboards, buttoned our jackets, straightened our ties, and then the president walked in—and our mouths dropped. He was wearing cute animal pajamas and pink fuzzy bunny slippers. Okay, the guy was recovering from a heart attack, so who were we to pass judgment? I took a chance and said, "Brian, you didn't have to get all dressed up for us." He laughed. It broke the ice.

Mark set up our point of view about their business. It wasn't about all that retail jargon—service, convenience, variety, price—it was about the love connection. He nodded approvingly. Then I presented the TV spot ending with our theme line, "Petco, where the pets go."

He seemed to like it, but he wasn't sure. "It's cute. It's catchy, but ... not sure ..."

The marketing director weighed in and said he thought it was good because it clearly said that Petco belonged to the pets, and the simple rhyme would help people remember the name Petco. After all, every competitor had the word pet in their name: PetSmart, Pet Depot, Pet Land, Pet Palace. Still, Brian wasn't ready to bite the bullet.

Then an unexpected guest came along in the form of Brian's lovely wife. She walked down the hall carrying a $50,000 painting she had just bought. It was quite striking, but not exactly my taste. I didn't get it at all. Art is a very personal thing, after all.

The president said, "Honey, would you mind coming in here?"

"Of course, dear," she said. "What is it?"

"Guys, would you mind starting over and presenting the idea to my wife?"

Oh Lord, what have we gotten ourselves into? Clients' wives have killed more great campaigns than all the marketing directors in the world combined. And Brian's wife clearly had different taste than mine.

Well, what can you do? We smiled, took a deep breath, and presented all over again. And when I hit her with the theme line, "Petco, where the pets go!" she lit up.

"I love it!" she said. "It's catchy, and it will help people remember the name."

"Good," the president said. "I feel the same way."

We were in! As Brian's wife started to walk out of the room, she turned to me and said, "By the way, what do you think of my new painting?"

I didn't hesitate. "I love it!"

Pets and Paupers

Now we were ready to shoot Beverly and Troy's TV spot, Pets on a Mission. The spot called for an all-night shoot in downtown L.A. with a multitude of pets and their handlers. To coordinate all of this and maintain control, the production company set up home base in an outdoor parking lot surrounded by a high chain-link fence. There was a big food truck serving meals all night, including burritos, omelets, lasagna, salads—you name it—in addition to several long snack tables that were constantly being replenished with chips and dips and veggies and cheeses. Beside them were big coolers with sodas, waters, and juices. It was a banquet.

But if we thought the people were eating well, you should have seen the pets. Pet trainers make a lot of money from their animals, and they show their appreciation by keeping their pets well-fed and well-stroked.

"Good job, Scooter, here's a treat!"

"Ooh, that's my Bogie ... have a bite ... you're the best!"

Lots of strokes and hugs and gourmet treats that I would describe as the caviar of pet food.

However, while life was good for the pets and us, it was the opposite on the other side of the fence. Poor people, down on their luck, called the other side of the fence their home. At least thirty people were stretched out on dirty blankets and tarps, using cardboard boxes for shelter. It was truly sad to behold. And what made it worse was that they could see all the food activity on our side of the fence. We decided we had to do something about it.

As 4:00 a.m. rolled around and the shoot was nearing its end, we invited everyone on the other side of the fence to cross the line and join us in a feast. It was Thanksgiving in July. They ate and drank heartily and talked and laughed as they experienced the simple joy of eating a good meal. One toothless lady came up to me and said, "Bless you. Bless you." Another elderly gent in a torn, tattered jacket approached our director and said, "Thank you. God watches over."

When their tummies were full, they scooped up the leftovers and tucked them into their threadbare jackets to enjoy at a later time. As I headed home at 5:00 a.m. to enjoy a good day's sleep in the comfort of my own bed, I felt a wave of appreciation come over me for all the blessings I had. It made me feel good to know that, at least for one night, people were eating as well as pets.

Know When to Fold 'Em

By 1997, I felt burned out and just didn't want to do it anymore. We had picked up some accounts and lost some and were basically in a holding pattern. Jack in the Box and Mervyns were history. Our beloved charter account, Hills Bros., had been acquired by Nestle and eventually moved to one of their international agencies. I missed the clients we had lost, and all my fellow Cohen/Johnson people who were no longer there. By then, Mark and I were hardly talking to each other.

One day, I screwed up my courage and asked Mark out to lunch so we could have a heart-to-heart. When the waiter took our drink order, I asked for a chardonnay and Mark ordered an iced tea. To Mark's credit, he had stopped drinking and smoking several years before, and amazingly, he had done it cold turkey. I always admired him for that. When the sandwiches arrived, I told Mark I wanted to sell the agency and move on.

"Let's find someone to merge with, or buy us out, and move on to the next," I said. I don't think Mark was surprised. I believe he wanted to keep trying, but based on where my head was at, he could see there was no point. We paid the check, and as we got back into my car, we agreed to get the word out. Cohen/Johnson was for sale.

TWELVE

A New Lease

When the World Turns, Try a New Spin

By May 1997, the word had gotten around town that our agency was looking for a suitor. There were some inquiries, but nothing seemed right. Then one day, I got a call from a guy named Joe Phelps who ran an agency called The Phelps Group. I had actually never heard of his agency, but he sounded like a nice, smart guy, so we agreed to meet.

When I got to their offices in Brentwood, Joe greeted me with, "Oh, you're the great Howie Cohen." (Flattery will get you everywhere!) Joe was a man in his late forties, who looked older than his years due to a thick mop of white hair and a full white beard. But he exuded a youthful enthusiasm, especially when he was talking about his agency.

After introducing me around, Joe brought me into a small

conference room and launched into a pitch about The Phelps Group with the fervor of an Arkansas preacher. (I later learned that's where he grew up.) He said what made Phelps different is that they'd ripped up the old advertising agency playbook. They'd eliminated departments, top-down authority, bosses in corner offices, power bases, and conflicts of interest—all the things that get in the way of doing a great job for the client.

Then Joe walked up to a whiteboard and started drawing circles—and circles and more circles. Each one represented an independent, self-directed team with the client at the center.

"Howie, we hire the best people we can find and give them wings to fly." He was describing a unique form of empowerment. "They work in independent teams and make their own decisions," he said.

"Sounds great, Joe, but you've got a whole agency here," I said. "How does the left team know what the right team is doing?"

Joe's eyes lit up. "Great question, Howie, and we've got a great answer. It's called feedback."

He described how all of these "self-directed" teams were plugged into the rest of the agency through unique feedback mechanisms, like "The Wall," where all work created by every team was posted for everyone to comment on, and The Brainbangers' Ball, a brainstorming and research session that the whole agency attended every Thursday.

"Everybody in the agency loves it, Howie. And it's how we really get to know what's happening on all the accounts and stay close to each other. Everybody adds ideas, and everybody helps everybody."

I liked that. It's a benefit to clients that Mark Johnson would eventually dub "More Brains on Your Business."

"So, how come I've never heard of Phelps?" I asked.

"We've kept a low profile … probably lower than we'd like," he said. "But here's the thing, Howie. Do you know how many ad agencies have gone out of business in this market in just the last ten years?" I didn't have a clue. "Twelve," he said. "Including hot creative agencies and West Coast offices of big national agencies." That surprised me; I had no idea. "But we're not only still here, we've been growing steadily since 1981," he added. "We must be doing something right."

That "something" had to do with a clear mission and vision and … circles. (You can circle back to it by reading Joe's book, *Pyramids Are Tombs*.)

After our meeting, one thing was crystal clear: What The Phelps Group did and what Cohen/Johnson did were very different things—and yet very complementary. Phelps brought all the services together and truly integrated them, so all the messaging spoke with one voice. And Cohen/Johnson had the creative chops to make the messaging sing. Mark and I agreed that this could be a very good thing for all of us.

In September 1997, Joe Phelps acquired our agency and all of its remaining accounts, including Petco, Blue Shield, Barbeques Galore, and Foundation for the Junior Blind. I agreed to come over as a partner, stockholder, and chief creative officer.

Mark used this agency change as an opportunity to create a life change. He moved his family to Lake Tahoe, where he set up a marketing and advertising consulting business, with The Phelps Group as his first client. In fact, Mark and I continued to work together on the Petco account and new business efforts for Phelps. Ironically, now that we were free of the tensions of running our own agency, our relationship became more enjoyable again.

I was about to celebrate my fifty-fifth birthday, and I figured this would be a great place to be until I retired in five or ten years. I stayed for twenty.

My Client, My Life

As chief creative officer of Phelps, I got to pick my shots and work on the accounts that were most meaningful to me. At the top of the list was City of Hope. They are an amazing organization that has pioneered cancer treatments and cures that have saved tens of thousands of lives.

I loved telling the world their story in several campaigns I wrote for them. Our most memorable campaign was based on a very simple idea. When someone is diagnosed with cancer, suddenly their whole world is turned upside down. They don't know what the future holds for them or if they even have a future. What they want and need more than anything else is answers to their questions. "What are my treatment options? Who are the experts at treating my form of cancer? Who will save my life?"

Knowing this simple truth, a talented art director I was working with, named Mike Cunningham, came up with an iconic word. It perfectly communicated the idea that City of Hope has answers to all your cancer questions. The word was …

CANSWER

It was so simple, yet so magical. It stood out, and you couldn't ignore it. Plus, it said so much. Using this word, we were able to address all kinds of provocative questions in print, outdoor billboards, online, and on TV, such as …

CAN A ROBOT NAMED DA VINCI HELP
YOU RECOVER FASTER?

CANSWER

Of course, the answer was "yes," and we went on to explain why. Each question and corresponding answer proved City of Hope's expertise and leadership in treating and curing cancer. It was an honor to contribute my talents to such a great institution that saves so many lives. Little did I know mine would be one of them.

The Big "C"

In the fall of 2002, I started experiencing shortness of breath and some discomfort in my chest. I also noticed a little bulge on the left side of my stomach. Carol became very concerned and insisted I see the doctor. Being a man, and therefore an idiot, I said it was probably nothing and that I just needed to work out a little more and watch my weight.

Then I started experiencing night sweats and having trouble sleeping. I would wake up in the morning lying in a puddle of my own sweat. Even that didn't get me to see a doctor. In my mind, I was just doing something wrong. *I must be sleeping in the wrong position*, I thought. *Yeah, that's it. I'm straining my neck.* Now Carol was getting really angry with me. "You always do this when it comes to your health!" she said. "You have to listen to your body and take this more seriously. Remember last year when you were having those chest pains?"

Oh yeah, that was a good one—another example of clueless me.

In a visit to the cardiologist, he had asked me, "Have there been any heart issues in your family?"

I thought for a second and said, "No, I don't think so."

Carol bolted out of her chair and said at the top of her lungs, "Howie, your mother had a triple bypass, and your father died of a heart attack!"

"Well, there was that," I said.

Stupid me! It was time to grow up and start taking this health stuff seriously, or I could actually die.

That was my heart issue. Now it was something else, and this time Carol took charge. "I'm making an appointment for you to see the doctor and you are going to see him … tomorrow!"

My appointment was for four o'clock the following day, and I arrived at the doctor's office on time. "So, what's been going on, Howard? How are you feeling? Any problems? Are you experiencing any pain?"

I told him about the bulge in my side and the night sweats and that I didn't think much of it, but my wife insisted I see him for a checkup. "You know how wives are," I added, in an attempt to make light of the situation.

He looked at me as if he were surprised that I wasn't more alarmed. "Okay," he said. "Let's give you some tests."

A short while later, the blood test came back. He suddenly took on a very serious tone as he went over the results with me. The test revealed that my white cell count was ridiculously elevated. "Howard, this is serious. I'm not going to pull any punches. I think you may have cancer."

"What! No way, I've been playing ball, going to work …"

"I want you to see Dr. Beryl (not his real name) at Cedars right away."

"Okay, I'll make an appointment," I said.

"No, I want you to see him *right now!*"

Forty minutes later, Carol met me outside Dr. Beryl's office. He invited us into a small room, where he began to review all the tests I had brought with me from my doctor.

"I can't tell for sure," he told me, "but based on what I see here, there's a strong likelihood you have non-Hodgkin's lymphoma."

"Non-Hodgkin's lymphoma?" I asked. "What's that?"

"It's cancer, Howard." Carol squeezed my hand tightly.

The doctor told us that he was going to do a spinal tap to see what was going on inside my body. Two days later, it was confirmed I had cancer. Stage 4 non-Hodgkin's lymphoma. There is no Stage 5. But, according to the doctor, I had "the good kind" of NHL—a non-aggressive, slow-moving, B-cell, indolent type that was very treatable and had a high survival rate. I don't remember everything else he said, but I seized on that "high survival rate" idea and held onto it for dear life.

We agreed I would begin treatment the following Wednesday. Carol and I left his office, and as we stood waiting for the elevator, I turned to her and said, "Well, that went well."

"What!" she said. "You think that went well? Howie, he just told you that you have cancer!"

"Yes, but he said I was going to make it."

That's always been the difference between Carol and me. She has always been a card-carrying pessimist, while I've always been a hopeless Pollyanna. For that, I have to thank my dear mother.

Lies My Mother Told Me

My mother, Jeanette, didn't just love me. She adored and worshipped me and made me feel like I was the center of the universe. For instance, when I was just seven years old, my parents bought me the best present a little kid could ever have—a shiny red wagon. I was so excited, I wheeled it all the way down Bolton Street, where we lived in The Bronx, to show my prize to the kids who played in the sandlot.

Everyone gathered around me, and I started to show off. I pushed it and pulled it and used the long red handle to turn it this way and that. All of a sudden, a big bully named Jerome grabbed a long stick, scooped up a big pile of dog shit, and plopped it right in the center of my wagon. I burst out crying; he started laughing, and I cried even louder. Then, instead of emptying the wagon, I did what I always did as a child. I ran home to my mother.

I wheeled my soiled red wagon up the street, into our building, up the elevator, and into our little apartment. Most mothers would probably have become irate at the sight of dog shit coming through the front door. Not my mother. She dried my tears, de-pooped the wagon, and scrubbed it until it looked shiny and new again. Then she reminded me that I was the cutest, most adorable child in the world. And she insisted she wasn't the only one who thought so.

She told me that all the women in the neighborhood thought I was just the nicest, cutest, most darling little boy they'd ever seen. "Howie, sweetheart," she said, "do you know what Mrs. Klinghoffer said about you just yesterday?"

"No, Mom. What?"

"She said that you have the most sparkly blue eyes and adorable face and she wished she had a little boy like you." Then my mother smiled and added, "But she better get her own little Howie because I'm never letting you go."

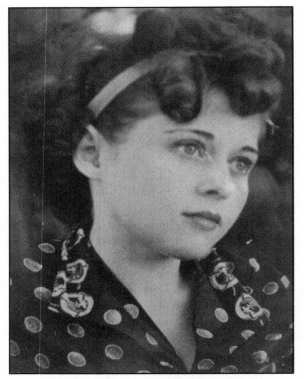

My mom loved music and poetry and me

Apparently, Mrs. Klinghoffer was just one of the many friends and relatives who thought I was god's little Jewish gift to humanity and The Bronx. Of course, I believed my mother completely, and it was her deep adoration that helped shape my self-image. I grew up feeling I was the golden child who could do no wrong.

I don't believe my mother thought she was telling me lies, or even exaggerating. Everything she said she truly felt in her heart.

Her love and praise were invaluable to me as I got older. She made me believe I could conquer worlds—be wild and creative without shame or fear of failure—succeed in a tough profession, not just because I had talent, but because everybody loved me. If not for my mother, I wouldn't be what I am today—blissfully delusional.

The Good Fight

One week after my diagnosis, I returned to Cedars, unafraid and ready to kick cancer's ass. After all, you don't die from cancer if you're a golden child. Dr. Beryl helped to reinforce my point of view. He told me that a miracle drug called Rituxan would be the cure for my disease, and it would save my life. Ironically, Rituxan was one of four new miracle drugs that came from research conducted on the campus of my client, City of Hope.

I showed up for my first treatment, but it didn't go well. In fact, it was terrible to the point of being life-threatening. I was reclining on a hospital bed in a small private room as they slowly dripped Rituxan into my vein. After only about ten minutes, I began to feel strange and very weak, like I was fading away. With each drip and each passing minute, I felt like I was slowly dying. Finally, I called out with a weakened voice, "Help ... help ..."

The nurses came rushing into the room and immediately started working on me. They took out the IV and put an oxygen mask on my face and began to take my blood pressure. It had dropped precipitously, and I had truly been in trouble.

About an hour later, when I was feeling a little better, I called Dr. Beryl. I told him what had happened and that I thought I almost died. He listened but seemed very distracted. He said, "Well, if the Rituxan doesn't work for you, we can switch to chemotherapy."

The fast, easy answer didn't feel right to me. I wanted to understand what had gone wrong. I wanted to know that he had carefully diagnosed the situation so he could make the best recommendation. "Doctor," I told him, "I think we need to talk. Can I come in tomorrow for a half hour?"

His answer astounded me. "Well, I don't know if I have a half hour."

I couldn't believe it. My life was on the line, and he was basically saying he couldn't give me the time of day. *What an idiot I am*, I thought to myself. What was I doing with the fancy shmancy Beverly Hills oncologist anyway?

I was a firm believer in City of Hope. Carol made an appointment for me there with Dr. Nademanee, and all of a sudden, everything changed. As we sat in her office, she took her time studying my tests, examining my body, and analyzing the results. She showed me the x-ray from my CAT-scan and pointed to various parts of my chest and abdomen. "Those are the tumors," she said. There were many of them. "And you see this ... it's your spleen ... it's about ten times the normal size." *Oh, so that's why my stomach has a bulge in it.* Well, at least I wasn't getting fat.

Her approach was so thorough and thoughtful that I immediately felt a sense of confidence. I told her about my experience with Rituxan and asked if she knew why my body had reacted that way. "Probably because you're Stage 4 ... too many tumors for the Rituxan to overcome." Dr. Nadee (her nickname) prescribed a much more fine-tuned treatment regimen. It would be a combination of three drugs.

The main one would be a form of chemotherapy called Fludarabine. The secondary one would be another chemo treatment called Cytoxan. This was a blue-colored chemo that the doctor said would make me lose my hair. (Thankfully, it never did.) She explained that I would be treated with these two drugs for six months, after which, hopefully, the lymphoma would be gone. Then they would treat me for one more month with Rituxan to seek out and destroy any cancer cells that the chemo might have missed.

My chemotherapy treatments began at City of Hope in November 2002. I would lie in bed for six hours at a time while they dripped the lifesaving drugs into my vein. On most treatment days, Carol was with me, sitting in the corner of the room reading a magazine or a book.

The chemo was preceded by Benadryl, which relaxed me and made me sleepy. But every time I woke up and looked across the room, Carol was there for me, as always. Sometimes, my kids took turns staying with me, and instead of waking up and seeing Carol, I would see the loving face of my daughter Johanna or my son, Jonathan. It's in those moments that you truly appreciate the wonders of life and family.

With each passing month, my tests showed dramatic progress. The tumors steadily shrank until they disappeared completely. And my spleen returned to its normal size. And when the tests showed that the cancer was gone, I received one more month of treatment with Rituxan, just as Dr. Nadee had outlined.

In June 2003, I was pronounced cancer-free. A big *Yippee!* goes here. I've remained free of non-Hodgkin's lymphoma ever since, and I'm grateful to be alive. I continued to do the advertising for City of Hope, committed to spreading the word about this amazing scientific institution that is treating—and beating—cancer.

And here's the fun part. My experience gave me a unique

perspective on the disease and on City of Hope—one that even the doctors who work there don't have. I'm referring to what it's really like to be a patient and a survivor. With every meeting, I was able to say to my client, "I don't just write your ads, I'm a satisfied customer."

Open Apology to a Child

The word "CANSWER" was becoming famous. It was on billboards and bus shelters and in print ads for several years all over Los Angeles. The campaign was a big success in attracting new patients and saving lives, and that was good news for everybody—except for one little girl.

As it turned out, she was cute and smart and a champion speller. And when her school held its annual spelling bee, she made it to the finals, beating out hundreds of young boys and girls her age. It was down to just her and one little boy. And when she was given the word she needed to spell, her face lit up because she knew it backwards and forwards. The word was cancer. She took her time, composed herself, and then delivered her answer very deliberately, one letter at a time. "Cancer ... C-A-N-S-W-E-R ... cancer!"

She waited confidently for validation, but instead of applause, a hush came over the crowd. "I'm sorry," the judge said. "That's incorrect." The little girl was crushed and walked off the stage in tears.

How can I ever express how sorry I am? Little girl, if you're reading this, I owe you a beer. Um, make that a milkshake.

Bob and Howie's Excellent Google Adventure

In late 2011, I started getting mysterious voicemails that I didn't answer because I thought it was just somebody trying to sell me something. "Hello, Mr. Cohen, my name is Aaron and I have something top secret I need to talk to you about. Please call me at …" Yeah, right. *Click!* What does he think … I just fell off the turnip truck?

Then I started getting emails from this same guy that told me a little more. "You and your partner, Bob Pasqualina, created the advertising that inspired the world and changed the game." *Okay, flattery will get you everywhere.* I continued to read.

Aaron said he needed to talk to me about a secret project—for Google. *Hmm, I think I've heard of them.* He asked me to please make a secret call to a secret telephone number. Now the secrets were starting to sound exciting.

I dialed the number, and Aaron picked up the phone in New York. He told me that he was the project director on a top-secret assignment for Google called "Project Re-brief." He said that Google wanted to reunite me with my former partner, Bob Pasqualina, to take on an amazing creative challenge.

"Here's the deal, Howie," he said. "Google has some breakthrough technology they want to promote to everyone in the advertising industry. They're so excited about the potential to change how we advertise on the internet that they want to get the word out in a big way."

To this end, Google had hired a hot creative New York ad agency named Johannes Leonardo. Their breakthrough idea was to take classic campaigns from the golden age of advertising and re-imagine them for the internet using this advanced Google technology.

This is where Bob Pasqualina and I came in. They decided that

"I can't believe I ate the whole thing" would be the perfect candidate for reimagining. The commercial was honored in the Clio Hall of Fame, and the line was listed as one of the top ten most remembered ad slogans of all time.

We soon found out that our work would be in good company. Another classic commercial they had zeroed in on was the famous Coca-Cola spot with the emotional song, "I'd like to teach the world to sing …" In that famous TV spot created by Bill Backer and Harvey Gabor, hundreds of young people from all over the world stood arm in arm on a hilltop in Italy, holding their Cokes and singing of a world in perfect harmony.

Then there was the disarming Avis campaign, "We're number two, we try harder," written by Paula Green, and a highly awarded classic campaign for Volvo, "Drive it like you hate it," by Amil Gargano.

Aaron described the plan to me. Google would fly me to New York (*Yay!*) where I would be reunited with Bob Pasqualina. (*Yippee!*) They would put us up at the trendy Gansevoort Hotel in the meatpacking district, just a block from Google's New York headquarters. Once there, we would spend an entire week tackling our reimagining project. We would start by attending briefings at Google, where they would share their breakthrough technology with us. This would be followed by intense creative sessions in which Bob and I would collaborate with a group of hot young copywriters and art directors from Johannes Leonardo, the agency that had come up with the idea.

But wait, there was more. To capture this event for posterity, Google hired a terrific documentarian named Doug Pray, the same guy who directed the Emmy award-winning documentary *Art &*

Howie Cohen and Bob Pasqualina

A secret Google project reunited us after thirty years

Copy, featuring interviews with many of the famous creative people who had changed the advertising business—George Lois, Hal Riney, Lee Clow, and our very own Mary Wells Lawrence, to name a few.

In this new effort, Doug Pray's mission was to capture this whole creative adventure—the meeting of classic and new, the combining of wisdom and wizardry—and put the viewer in the rooms and hallways and streets from start to finish as this grand collaboration unfolded. I was over the moon with excitement. This was going to happen!

Three weeks later, Doug Pray was aiming his video cam at my private car as we pulled up to the Gansevoort Hotel, where Bob was waiting to greet me. As I got out of the car, I rushed into his arms like a long-lost lover, and we hugged each other tightly.

For the next week, we collaborated creatively, just like we used to do. We walked the streets of the meatpacking district and talked, bouncing ideas off each other, Bob picking up on my thoughts and me picking up on his. And just like the old days, we played different parts and built script ideas and found ourselves laughing at our own dialogue. We walked the Highline together, looking for inspiration, and we holed up in hotel rooms with the Johannes Leonardo people.

It was great to have Bob as a creative partner again after all those years. We were still enthusiastic and creative and alive, and we were having fun again. By the end of the week, we and our team had come up with an Alka Seltzer campaign idea, as did the other teams working on Coke, Avis, and Volvo.

After that, honor of honors, we were invited to present our campaigns to our original client companies. In other words, after forty years, Bob and I got to present our big idea to Alka Seltzer. What a thrill! We even got a personal note from the current Alka Seltzer people that said, "Welcome home, Bob and Howie." When I read it, a tear actually came to my eye.

The night before the presentation, Bob and I went out to dinner at a little out-of-the-way Italian restaurant right there in the out-of-the-way meatpacking district. As we were about to dive into our pasta, Bob looked across the room, and guess who he saw? Stan Dragoti. Stan was deep in conversation with two friends and didn't see us, so we decided to surprise him. We walked across the room to his table and stood right next to him without saying a word. Finally, he looked up, squinted, and his face lit up with a smile.

But before I could say, "Stan, how are you?" he looked me directly in the eye and said, "Five more inches and it would be all over, pal!" Great lines never die!

The next day at Google, all of us veterans presented to all of the client companies. It was nerve-wracking, it was exciting, it was emotional, and … there was applause! To our delight, Google got the green light from all four clients to produce the campaigns and put them on the internet. That kicked off a lengthy production schedule that spanned six months in both New York and L.A.

One day on location in L.A., Bob and I were treated to a heart-lifting surprise. Google had flown in Milt Moss, the original funny character in our "whole thing" commercial. Milt was the guy who sat on the bed and personified all of the heartburn and pain of over-eating in the most hilarious way. Milt was now ninety-one years old, but totally spry. We greeted each other with hugs and shared great memories. And then Milt thanked us for what he said was a life-changing event for him.

Milt told us that the commercial made him famous in ways no one could have imagined. Suddenly, he was the featured speaker at major conventions all over America, but not in the traditional sense—in the funny sense. Milt would be introduced to these vast audiences of corporate execs as a very special and important guest—the ambassador from France. He would walk onto stage wearing a beret and French military garb with ten pounds of medals on it. He would quietly walk to the mike, acknowledging applause from the enthusiastic audience. Then he would launch into a speech in pigeon French. "Mes amis, je m'appelle Henri de Bulllsheet, ze French am-bassadeur, et joie de poopy …"

He'd go on like this for five minutes until everyone was scratch-ing their heads, and then, in a dramatic reveal, he would whip off the beret and say, "I can't believe I ate the whole thing!" The audi-ence would go crazy with laughter. Milt did different versions of this *shtick* for years, having great fun and making a good living out of it.

Of course, we would have been remiss if we didn't thank Milt too. His amazing performance was the reason America connected with the commercial, why it was hilarious to watch, and why the words are still remembered almost fifty years later. Thank you, thank you, Milt Moss.

Bob and I loved our time together—casting, shooting, and editing alongside our brothers and sisters from Johannes Leonardo and the tech geniuses from Grow Interactive. Then came the pièce de résistance. When all four productions were done and the documentary was in the can, Google flew us all to France to attend the Cannes Lions Awards ceremonies, where the finished productions and one-hour documentary were on display. We were also invited to teach a master class to hundreds of bright, young, creative people from all over the world.

It was an amazing honor in an extraordinary year that I will never forget. And to think, I almost didn't pick up the phone.

THIRTEEN

Ambition Turns to Appreciation

A mbition can be a valuable thing. It can drive you forward when your body is tired and your mind is turning to mush. It can inspire you to work harder and be the smartest person in the room. And when the odds are against you, it can push you across the goal line for the big victory dance.

I was pretty ambitious in my career, and it served me well. But I also paid a price, in that there were important things I would occasionally miss: one of my kids' birthday parties, a significant wedding anniversary with Carol, cutting a family vacation short to race home and be in a dumb, new business pitch.

Carol, in her infinite wisdom, always told me to give myself a break. Relax, smell the coffee. Enjoy my family, my friends. Work a little less, play a little more. And as I got older, I slowly came to understand. In Carol's words, "Ambition turns to appreciation." I started to look around me and see how much we had. Amazing kids, a beautiful home, incredible friends and family, a winner dog. It was all there. I just needed to relax and enjoy it.

As appreciation began to sink in, I started to loosen up. Carol and I packed our bags and flew to Aspen, where we had a nice little condo just a few blocks from the gondola on Ajax Mountain. It's an easy flight from L.A., just two hours directly into the Aspen Airport. And the beauty of having a condo there is that you can leave all your stuff behind. No schlepping skis and ski boots, hats, goggles, gloves, sweaters, and ski outfits. It's all there, neatly put away in a storage closet, just waiting for you to wake it up and take it out into the fresh fallen snow.

Aspen is a far cry from Vermont, with its twenty-six-below-zero temperatures and treacherous icy slopes. While that first ski weekend with Carol in Sugarbush had been a wonderful, romantic starting point in our relationship, it had also marked the end of any skiing ambitions I might have had at the time. I just didn't get it. Why would anybody want to subject himself to such torture?

That all changed shortly after we moved to L.A. One of the important accounts that Wells, Rich, Greene/L.A. had was Ralston Purina, with products like Bran Chex and soft-moist cat food—not exactly sexy. But then the Ralston people acquired an entire ski resort called Keystone, Colorado, and awarded us the account. That's when the whole, magical, white powder, blue sky world of western skiing revealed itself to me.

Keystone was a virtual ski paradise. And shortly after we were awarded the account, they invited a group of us from Wells to fly out and experience it for ourselves. What a revelation! This wasn't a cold eastern winter in Vermont; this was spring skiing in the magnificent

Rockies. The skies were a piercing blue, the snow was an alabaster white, and the temperature was a balmy fifty degrees.

Since we were the honored guests of Ralston Purina, we got first-class treatment all the way. It started with our very own personal ski instructors who tended to our every need. When we got hungry, we were ushered into Keystone's exclusive private club for a gourmet meal. And when it was time to get back on the ski lift, we were escorted right to the front of the line—no waiting with the plebeians for us big-time ad executives. We were pampered and spoiled silly, and we loved every minute of it. Keystone, Colorado, was the turning point for me. I was now a bona fide skier.

After a frigid start in Sugarbush, we found ski heaven in Aspen

Carol and I bought our first ski condo in Aspen in 1990, eventually trading up to a house on the east side of town, and then moving to a beautiful condo near the base of Ajax Mountain. It was there that we found ourselves one magical night in January 2004.

A light snow was falling outside our window, gently piling up on the railing of our balcony that faces the gondola. Carol and I had enjoyed a simple dinner of pasta and salad and were halfway through a bottle of fine cabernet. Now we were beginning to feel that pleasant glow that follows a long hard day well skied.

Carol turned to me and said, "I'm a little chilly. Are you?" I was. I got up and lit a fire in the fireplace and turned on some classical music. That's when inspiration hit. I let go of Carol's hand and headed toward the bedroom. "Where are you going?" she asked. I smiled a cunning Jewish smile and said, "Trust me."

When I came back into the room, Carol looked up, wrinkled her nose, and said, "Oh no." And I responded, "Come on. They were made for nights like this." I was proudly holding two bright blue Snuggies. I handed her one, slipped into the other, and we Snuggied up together by the fire. (I knew they would come in handy someday.)

It was getting late now, and as we sat with our arms around each other, I reflected on the wonder of this moment and all the life events that had conspired to get us here. From that shaky start in Sugarbush, we had now shared more than twenty-five years of blissful *shussing* together.

Across the room from where we were sitting, there was a multitude of framed family photos on an antique pine hutch, visual reminders of the many mountains we and the kids had skied together, from Aspen to Vail to Deer Valley and Park City. Some of the photos were of just the two of us wearing the outdated ski fashions of years gone by. Others showed our whole family posed at the tops of mountains when our kids barely came up to our hips and we had put them on their first skis and taught them their first snowplows.

The years had come and gone so quickly and the kids had grown into beautiful adults. How did it all go so fast?

Cristina was now happily married and living with her doting husband, Hans, in Wisconsin. Our daughter Johanna and her husband, Charlie, in appreciation of their magical wedding at the Beverly Hills Hotel, went on to give us a glorious gift in the form of our beautiful granddaughter, Zoe. (Just one "I love you, Grandpa" is worth a hundred Clios.) Our son, Jonathan, has grown up to be a tall, good-looking, and very smart young man who is a successful VP of digital marketing for an exclusive skincare brand and is living comfortably in Beverly Hills. And little Angelo is now big Angelo with two adorable daughters of his own. How lucky we are to have a healthy, loving family all living within driving and hugging distance.

To think, it all started so innocently that night at the MGM movie screening. What if I hadn't walked over and talked to Carol? What if I hadn't gone to Gary and Julie's after-screening party and asked for her number? What if Carol had liked the big dumb guy who drooled on her shoulder better than me?

I felt myself getting a lump in my throat as I realized how lucky we were to have found each other in this vast universe, not to mention the crowded hustle and bustle of New York City—how fortunate we were that our relationship had flourished through all of the stresses of life and the craziness of the advertising business. Yet, here we were, still sharing our lives and creating more wonderful memories together.

The snow was coming down heavily now outside the window. I put another log on the fire, and it cast a warm golden glow across the room. I walked back to the couch where Carol was cuddled up in her bright blue Snuggie that was a perfect match for mine. I put my arms around her, and we gazed into each other's eyes for several seconds. Then she said, "I know." Just two words, but they said it all. "I know." When you've been together for so many years, when you've shared a family, a life, and a love, you don't have to say more than that. "I know."

I pulled her close to me, and we locked in a warm embrace by the light of the fire—hand-in-hand, cheek-to-cheek, Snuggie-to-Snuggie. And then Carol put her lips right up to my ear and softly whispered …

"Don't you just love skiing?"

Epilogue

Gratitude to the Business

I'm a very lucky guy. I was fortunate enough to find a creative profession that was always fun and rarely felt like work—one that kept my mind buzzing and my heart thumping, that fueled my curiosity, nourished my creativity, and made me happy to be alive.

For sure, it wasn't all roses. This is a very challenging business, and I had to face my share of adversity and insanity. I lost accounts, lost new business pitches, lost my New York ad agency, and occasionally lost faith in people when someone betrayed my trust. But the good far outweighed the bad, and I never lost my love of creativity. For most of my career, I couldn't wait to get up in the morning and rush to the office. I always looked forward to the next big creative challenge. And when an idea made it from the storyboard onto the screen, I couldn't wait to show it off—first to the agency, then to the client, and finally to the whole world! (You can't do that if you're an ironworker in The Bronx.)

Doyle Dane Bernbach and Wells, Rich, Greene were my advertising universities. For anyone who wants to get into this crazy amazing business—or get ahead in it—I strongly recommend that you pursue a job at a truly great creative agency, preferably a completely integrated one, where you can get a 360-degree education from mentors who are passionate about the work. Abandon a bigger job if you have to. Give up a higher salary or a fancy title. Put in the time and learn the difference between good and great. If you love being creative, this business can provide you with a lifetime of creative satisfaction, great friendships, and rich memories. You might even go on to write a book about it.

Gratitude for the People

Nobody makes it in this challenging business on their own. Advertising is a creative business, and creativity is (by nature) a collaborative effort. My work, reputation, and very identity are the sum total of all the amazing relationships I've been fortunate to have, both inside and outside the business. So this is a shout-out to all of you who have blessed me with your smarts, passion, humor, friendship, and most of all, your love.

To my beautiful wife, Carol: Thank you for showing up at Gary and Julie's movie screening that night. The film sucked, but life with you has been a gift that I treasure. As I've often said, you dragged me kicking and screaming to my own happiness. Every important decision we've made in our relationship was an idea that you pushed, including escalating our relationship by moving in together, taking up skiing, getting married, having kids, moving to California, getting a dog, and eating more fiber ... did I miss anything? With every one of those important decisions, I was, "No, no, no." But you were always, "Yes, yes, yes!" And our lives have been so much richer for it. Without you, there would be no Howie Cohen.

To my amazing kids, Johanna, Jonathan, Cristina, and Angelo: My life became more meaningful and infinitely more beautiful when each of you came into it. In watching you grow and become amazing adults, you have helped me to grow—with appreciation and boundless love.

To my stunning granddaughter, Zoe: You are living proof that this is a beautiful world and that life is worth living. You're as pure on the inside as you are perfect on the outside. And you kick a mean soccer ball.

To my advertising family, all of you who were there through all the years as we collaborated and made magic together:

Doyle Dane Bernbach '65–'67: For putting up with a wise-ass twenty-two-year-old snot-nosed kid. Thank you for your mentoring and your incredible patience. I was a Bronx kid who knew nothing, nothing, nothing. You helped me develop my taste in everything from ads to art to architecture. And you helped me begin to grow as an advertising person—and as a person-person.

Gilbert Advertising '67–'68: It was a hot creative boutique, and I was in way over my head. Thanks for the tough love and the easy friendships that improved my work and bolstered my confidence and actually prepared me for "the whole thing."

Wells, Rich, Greene '68–'73; '78–'85: To all my creative co-conspirators in New York and L.A., thank you for making me jealous of your brilliant work. It made me work harder, reach higher, and stretch my creative abilities beyond what I thought was possible.

Cohen, Pasqualina & Lowe (Timberman) '73–'78: To our hearty band of creative warriors who helped a little upstart agency achieve short-lived but unexpected greatness during five tumultuous years. Thank you for your belief, your bravery, and your balls.

Cohen/Johnson '85–'97: To my Cohen/Johnson family who helped propel us to incredible size, stature, and creative greatness as we became the largest producer of broadcast advertising in the West. We shared account victories, industry awards, and we shared the wealth. You guys were unbelievable—and did we have an amazing ride or what?

Phelps '97–2017: To my dear friends and collaborators at Phelps who got me out of my big corner office and up onto the stage to speak and share and teach and mentor. You broadened my horizons at a time when I could have closed down—and you helped extend my career by at least ten years.

After fifty years in the advertising business, it's safe to say I knew how to write ads. But when it came to writing a book and getting it published, I was a babe in the woods.

So I would like to express my gratitude to a handful of experts who held my hand the whole way and helped make this book a reality.

To Polly Letofsky, book publishing expert extraordinaire, for guiding me every step of the way, for always being there with advice and an honest opinion, and for introducing me to an amazing band of talented specialists:

To Donna Mazzitelli, world's best book editor. You fell in love with a pretty good book and worked with a passion to shape it, fine tune it, and make it much better.

To Victoria Wolf, my artistic book cover designer. Your talent and patience for trying different looks and ideas resulted in a cover that's brilliant in its simplicity.

To Andrea Costantine, visionary book designer. When all was said and done, you created the look and layout that brought it all together with simple style and grace.

To Roxana Keikavousi, public relations, and Alexis Antoniadis, social media, for your brilliance in helping to spread the word throughout the media and across the internet.

Thanks to you all! It was great to work with such a dedicated bunch of talented experts who also happen to be very nice people.

Where Are They Now?

I've always found it interesting to know where people's lives have taken them after a career in advertising. Did they go on to bigger and better things? Did they find new spirituality? Are they still taking Alka Seltzer?

Mary Wells Lawrence. She lives on her luxury yacht somewhere in the Mediterranean, surrounded by an attentive and admiring staff. Her new life is a million miles away from the pressures of advertising. She enjoys yoga, meditation, and visits from her loving family.

Charlie Moss. He lives in a ritzy apartment on New York's Fifth Avenue with his lovely wife, Susan. He has returned to his first love, acting, and can be seen in off-Broadway plays as well as performing interesting character roles on hit TV series.

Ken Olshan. He enjoys a nice, relaxing, quiet life with his wife, Patsy, in a retirement community in Connecticut. Rumor has it that his daughter is an excellent chef, and Ken has used some of his financial rewards to help her launch her own trendy restaurant.

Stan Dragoti. Sadly, he died this year at the age of eighty-five. I will always remember Stan for his intimidating good looks, his great sense of humor, and his outsized directing talents that made our TV spots sparkle. And the world will always remember him for the very funny movies he directed, including *Love at First Bite* and *Mr. Mom*. Rest in peace, my friend, and always remember: five more inches and it would be all over.

Bob Pasqualina. He lives in a quaint country house in Connecticut with Trish, his significant other. He loves to work with his hands and, as a hobby, builds full-size boats in his workshop. When I asked Bob how he gets all the proportions right, he gave me the answer I should have expected. "By eye."

Mark Johnson. He lives in Lake Tahoe with his wife, Sue, where he stays busy consulting for advertising and marketing companies around the country. For fun, he skis at breakneck speed down the slopes of Squaw Valley and spends many a night singing and playing lead guitar in his own rock band. Mark also creates original songs, which can be downloaded at www.bluedynomusic.com.

Joe Phelps. He splits his time between L.A. and the ranch he built for his family on a river in Montana. Joe enjoys planting trees, doing ranch work, and fishing in a river that runs through his property. He is also on a mission to make the world a better place through his Getting Better Foundation.

Alan Kupchick. He is an accomplished photographer whose iconic work is featured at various exhibitions and shows in L.A. He and I meet up once a month for lunch at the beach, where we get lost in laughter and deep conversation. Alan is a true "artisto," and his number one "patroni" is a guy named Howie Cohen.

Mo Iqbal. He continues to be a successful restaurateur who owns high-quality restaurants in Orange County and Manhattan Beach. He lives quite comfortably with his wife and two grown children in a house (with two huge kitchens, no less) high on a hill overlooking the Pacific Ocean.

Barry Reis. He is living a nice, relaxed life in Northern California with his wife, Margo. He works as an executive coach, helping professional executives find a "better way." In addition, Barry is an avid oil painter and travels the world seeking out the perfect landscape to paint.

Steve Karmen. He still lives in the same sprawling home in Bedford, New York, where he created unforgettable jingles for Budweiser ("When you say Bud"), Hershey's ("The great American chocolate bar"), the City of New York ("I love New York"), and hundreds of others. Creativity is still in the air, as Steve is working diligently on the book, music, and lyrics for an exciting new Broadway show.

Bruce Dundore. He lives with the same beautiful woman, Maria, who inspired him to move to Los Angeles in 1986. He runs his own creative ad agency, and his talents have grown to include writing screenplays and fiction novels—*The Seduction Diet* and the well-reviewed *The Calamities*.

Dick Tarlow. My cousin made a small (make that very big) fortune opening, growing, and selling three of his own ad agencies. He also went on to write a wonderfully original off-Broadway play about the trial of George W. Bush for treason. Now retired and happily married to his beautiful wife, Kristin, they split their time between showcase homes on Manhattan's Fifth Avenue, Shelter Island, and Boca Raton. Just as I did when I was starting out in advertising, I asked Dick for his opinion of my work—this time on my manuscript. Except for pointing out that I overused the word "cute" (mostly in reference to myself), Dick loved the book. Which is fortunate ... or the world might never know the whole thing.

Made in the USA
Coppell, TX
08 December 2019